MW00709844

Janet's Plan-its™
CELESTIAL PLANNER
2015 Astrology Calendar

by Janet Booth

ISBN 978-0-9846499-3-8

Cover image courtesy of NASA.

Design and layout by Bryan R. Bonina, Always Amazing Results, LLC

Ilene J. Wolf, Editor

Portrait by Ray Pioggia
Back cover talisman by Israel Regardie ©1972.

Special thanks to Numerologist Sally Faubion for her insights on the year 2015
and to Walter Booth and Delia Marshall for proofreading help.

Ephemeris pages reproduced by permission of the publisher:
Starcrafts LLC, 334-A Calef Hwy., Epping, NH 03042.

Moon Family table reprinted by permission from Dietrech Pessin from her book,
Lunar Shadows III The Predictive Power of Moon Phases and Eclipses.

While every effort to ensure the accuracy of information in this calendar has been made,
we cannot be held liable for errors, omissions or inconsistencies.

Published by:
Astrology Booth, LLC
P.O. Box 271133
West Hartford, CT 06127
AstrologyBooth.com

Printed in the USA

CONTENTS

ABOUT THE COVER

Front: Our sun is also a star, our spark of the Big Bang. Without it, we would not just be in the dark, we wouldn't exist! The heart of our solar system, astrologers refer to it as a planet, but only for conversational convenience. As we know from the efficacy of Sun-sign astrology, its importance in a chart cannot be underestimated. The front cover is a collage of images of the sun from NASA's Solar Dynamics Observatory (SDO). (Credit: NASA/SDO/GSFC) It features various wavelengths and aspects of the sun's surface and atmosphere (including magnetic and Doppler information) that have been colorized. White and ultraviolet light, photosphere and chromosphere, corona and coronal loops, solar flares—all are part of the sun's magnificent power and beauty. Twinkle, twinkle, our favorite star!

Back: An image of a talisman (magical symbol) depicting the "seal of the planet" for the sun is included in honor of our cover celebrity, Sol.

**Visit JanetsPlan-its.com to learn about astrology
or to arrange a personal consultation.**

Janet's Plan-its™ Celestial Planner

For more about major influences in 2015, read the Star Pages (p. 72).

Introduction

In ancient times, everyone knew the constellations, planets and moon's phases. These were the basis of stories, myths and songs, a teaching device before books or computers. At night, there wasn't much to do except enjoy the sky and learn from it. Nowadays, few people look up, night or day. But the stars and planets are still there, telling their stories to those who understand them and like a giant cosmic clock, showing us the time.

Astrology helps explain life in general and individuals' lives in particular. My goal is to put the power of astrology into the hands of everyone, rather than only those who study it in depth. Use this tool to whatever level of detail you wish to be able to take advantage of the best moments the planets offer and dodge their difficult times. It's easy—just tap the knowledge of your celestial guide.

Overview of 2015

After years of tumult, more hurdles and curveballs are in store. Fear not: forewarned is forearmed! We've been in a key transitional period since 2011, driven by a battle between two major forces for evolution. One, Uranus, strikes like lightning. It's the planet of revolution, invention and shock. It's also related to the masses and rules Aquarius, the sign of the New Age. The other actor in our drama, Pluto, is more like the slow drip of erosion or Chinese water torture. Associated with big business and economics, Pluto also correlates with resources everyone shares, such as air and water. These two slow planets are positioned at cross purposes, about ninety degrees apart. They're precisely in this angle seven times from 2012 to 2015 (the last is March 16) and roughly in this formation another year. Quicker planets frequently enter their web, directing their influence into various arenas of experience, from personal and international relations to finances, laws, science and technology, the media, education, health care, the environment—you name it. Everything and everyone is going through changes.

Two medium-speed planets, Jupiter and Saturn, also come into a harsh 90-degree link from the second half of 2015 into 2016. Growth will not be smooth nor steady. Besides harassing one another, these two also manage to fight with all the outer planets, further impeding progress. Their initial jolt comes in early August, just as Venus (a planet related to love and money) passes Jupiter. September and November are bumpy, as well.

Another difficult connection, a 45-degree separation, is in place for much of 2015 between Eris, the dwarf planet of disorder, and Neptune, a dissolving influence associated with entropy (the tendency in nature for systems and organisms to break down over time). A lot will be falling apart in 2015!

This giant dose of change is part of our journey into the New Age. We'll get a preview of it in the four weeks beginning at the New Moon February 18. It occurs at the dividing line between Pisces, the sign of the Age that's ending, and Aquarius. During that cycle, we should have evidence of developments and issues that will color the transition, which is already underway. Readers of Janet's Plan-its may recall the 2013 celestial planner featured an article by astro-historian, Don Cerow. His research pinpointed the end of the Age of Pisces as February of 2013.

Another important lunation is on March 20. This New Moon is an eclipse (always a more potent variation) coming at the final degree of the zodiac, a position thought to signify suffering and karmic come-uppance. The Full Moon of that cycle, another eclipse, is similar to the Lunar Eclipse of October 8, 2014 and likewise in jarring connections to Uranus and Pluto.

Not everything is topsy-turvy in 2015. There are several fortuitous formations called Quintile Triangles sprinkled throughout spring, summer and fall, and a handful of Finger of God triangles to steer us on divine detours. Uranus, the Awakener, is involved in many of these and is also part of one of the easiest links this year, an angle of 120 degrees with Jupiter in March and June. They are, respectively, the planet of surprises and of luck, offering opportunities for heavenly blessings. The year draws to a close with a Full Moon on Christmas, the same day Uranus appears to stop in its tracks, thus exerting extra power.

The "world" number (per the Gregorian calendar) for 2015 is eight: $2 + 0 + 1 + 5 = 8$. Its number position in this decade is 5, which generally indicates change for the positive. Numerologist Sally Faubion anticipates it will be better monetarily for most people. She breaks it down as follows: $20 + 1 + 5 = 26$ ($2 + 6 = 8$): in a 26 year, you work harder than you want to. It's also $20 + 15 = a 35$ ($3 + 5 = 8$), pointing to a time of honor and reward. Eight is a number of abundance. However, that depends on what you've done in the past seven years. "If you put yourself in a position to make money, it should happen in an eight year." It's a number that keeps you on a straight and narrow path, the number of rules. Feedback from the Universe comes around fast! In the seven year just past, you wondered where you were going. In the eight year, you know what you'd like to be and do. Fruits will be borne for your expansion of consciousness in 2014, a year when people were slated to wake up. For some, that happened through tragedy and loss. "We can't stay where we've been; we've got to go up a level in evolution." An eight year can help us do that.

May you navigate the churning waters of 2015 well!

Yours in the stars,
Janet Booth

Times of highest stress and greatest ease are identified and explained throughout Janet's Plan-its.

USING THIS PLANNER

Interpretations in this planner are based on solid astrological theories, but how a day affects your chart and your life can be different than its general nature suggests. For your most important activities (business start-ups, major purchases, marriage, surgery, etc.), it's always recommended you consult with your astrologer.

Like a "cosmic weather report," this planner applies to everyone, regardless of zodiac sign. Whatever your level of astrological knowledge, there's guidance here for you. Just by reading the weekly pages, you're using astrology to your advantage. There are tools galore to explore further, as well, but don't feel as if you must tap them all. Read through these instructions to see what's available to you.

Astrology helps us make better-informed selections. It offers an educated guess about the future based on similar conditions in the past. This isn't easy since planetary patterns never repeat exactly and each astrological indication can express in a multitude of ways. All planets and signs have positive and negative potentials. Rather than letting the planets have their way with you, put their energies to work and keep them busy in a manner of your preference. Get in the driver's seat and steer!

Janet's Plan-its™ Celestial Planner lists the generic nature of astrological occurrences and possibilities the planets present. As the planets and signs are mentioned, you can use the Keywords on pp. 98-99 (or from other sources) to arrive at your own speculations. Some days, the influences apply to your life noticeably. Other times, you may see the described situations happening around you but not to you. When a day

doesn't sound so nice, it doesn't mean you're doomed to have a bad experience. The message is a warning to watch out for difficult behavior in others and to monitor your own. This is just information to help you on your journey through life.

To determine your individual impact, consult your natal chart, determined by your exact date, time and place of birth. It's more accurate than any astrology calendar can be, though Janet's Plan-its™ is the next best thing. You could order a report that shows the links to your chart from the moving planets ("transits") and interprets these for you. To look for connections to your chart on your own, see Making It Personal (p. 4) and the All Star List (p. 70). You might also want to learn to read an ephemeris (you'll find instructions on p. 62).

If you want to understand astrological conditions, learn about "aspects" (see p. 98). They are spatial relationships connecting planets for varying periods of time. Making It Personal and How to Read an Ephemeris describe how aspects are determined. Aspects are most potent when exact and still effectual when close to precise in a range of influence called "orb." They may be described as "tight" (close to exact) or as "loose" or "wide" (almost out of orb). Aspects lie at the heart of astrological forecasting.

 MOON CYCLES

The Moon orbits the earth (and thus circles the zodiac from our viewpoint) in about 27 days. A New Moon happens as it passes the Sun, beginning a new cycle that takes on the flavor of the factors present at that moment, extending their sway over the next four weeks. Since the Sun is also in motion, it takes the Moon 29-30 days to pass the Sun again. Their cycle crests at the halfway point, which is the Full Moon. It marks a peak of awareness and often the culmination of a process or trend. Like a New Moon, the effects of a Full Moon are modified by conditions occurring then. The Full Moon's influence starts two or three days before and extends two or three days beyond the date it's exact (or much longer in the case of an eclipse). Weekly Highlights outline how to optimize the influences of New and Full Moons, including eclipses (a stronger version of New and Full Moons), which are also discussed in the Star Pages. Energy shifts at Quarter Moons, which are times to turn a corner. Both types require decisions: at a First Quarter Moon, rely on instincts; at the Third Quarter, let experience and information guide you.

Every two to three days, the Moon changes the sign through which it travels, which gives a general indication of moods, behavior and circumstances (see p. 72). The planner's weekly pages tell you the Moon's position each day and exactly when it changes signs.

The amount of the Sun's light that the Moon reflects back to earth increases from New Moon to Full Moon, then decreases until the next New Moon. Every day, Janet's Plan-its™ shows you what the Moon looks like in its current phase. If you want growth in an activity, begin it during the waxing phase between a New Moon and a Full Moon (see illustration). Continue ongoing activities any time. A natural use of the Moon's cycle is to complete projects after a Full Moon and before the next New Moon (waning phase). If there's something you want to decrease, begin it during the waning phase. For example, hair shouldn't grow as quickly after a haircut then, and surgery to remove a tumor or reduce tissue is better during the waning phase.

The lunar cycle consists of eight lunar phases, which relate to stages of your life and can be used for timing rituals. Guest writer, Maria Kay Simms, a Wicca High Priestess and professional astrologer, details these on pp. 90-91. Groups of four related moon phases across 2-1/4 year periods describe developments in the stories of our lives, according to astrologer Dietrech Pessin, who noticed these patterns and named the phenomenon "moon families." Check her table of lunar phases for 2015 on p. 69. Degrees where New and Full Moons occur repeat from sign to sign for five to six months in "Moon Grooves," Janet's discovery and term (see p. 60).

Don't be caught unaware – read ahead at least a couple weeks in advance.

Adjust for Your Time Zone: Eastern (E) and Pacific (P) zones are listed, adjusted for Daylight Saving Time. For Atlantic, add one hour to Eastern. For Central, subtract one hour from Eastern. For Mountain, add one hour to Pacific.

Moon Void of Course: Every two or three days, there is a period lasting from minutes to hours (sometimes more than a day) when the Moon nears the end of a sign and its motivating energy ebbs. Continue ongoing endeavors or complete projects but avoid major purchases or new initiatives after the time listed for the Moon becoming Void until after the Moon enters the next sign.

Day Ratings: Each day is rated as to the stress or ease that the planets present us. A **1** is most difficult; a **5** is smoothest. There aren't many **5**s. It's much more likely for a day to be challenging than stress-free! The rating is the small number next to the designation for the day of the week (**SA** = Saturday, **SU** = Sunday, etc.). A **C** denotes a calm day with little or no astrological activity. Powerful days (marked **P**) are potent but not necessarily easy, just a stronger version of that day's rating.

Weekly Highlights: These are a must read each week! In fact, read ahead to be prepared for challenging periods.

2015 On a Page: See important information (pp. 60-61) about periods when planets appear to move backward, called Retrograde. There's also a list of the year's New and Full Moon dates and their zodiac degrees. When degrees are close to positions of planets in your birth chart (+ or - 2°), the cycle will affect you strongly. 2016 data is on p. 89.

Retrogrades: Try not to start anything new during Mercury Retrograde (days marked **MR**). If you must take action, be careful with all information exchanges, allow extra time to arrive for appointments and read contracts carefully before signing. When Venus is Retrograde (days marked **VR**), challenges arise in relationships or finances. We may have to repeat lessons or re-do activities in these areas. Recommendations for other planets' Retrograde periods are included in the Star Pages.

Star Pages: A ★ on a daily line guides you to the **Star Pages** (pp. 72-88) for interpretations and details about timing.

Planning with the Planets: When scheduling important activities, aim for days rated **4** or **5** and avoid **1** or **2** ratings. Stay clear of days when a planet changes direction (shown on p. 61). See **Best and Worst Days** for various activities (p. 95). Check daily messages and weekly Highlights for times that sound good for your plans. Avoid the Moon Void of Course. For a complete picture of a given day, read earlier to find what's in effect then. (You may need to go back several months or see **As We Begin 2015**, p. 73.) Realize that even a **4** or **5** day may not be great if it's during Mercury or Venus Retrograde.

Activities Associated With the Planets:

- **Moon:** spend time with family, do something for your home or décor, enjoy cooking or eating
- **Mercury:** make a decision, initiate an important communication, teach, learn
- **Venus:** handle relationship or monetary matters, be with loved ones, treat yourself to something special, make a purchase
- **Sun:** shine, enjoy the spotlight, lead, create, entertain, play, bring out your "inner child," be with children
- **Mars:** do something physical, be assertive, compete, watch out for anger or pushiness
- **Ceres:** nurture yourself or others, garden, commune with nature, enjoy the fruits of your labors
- **Jupiter:** travel, share your ideas, contact those at a distance, handle legal matters
- **Saturn:** get organized, write goals, act with authority, attend to your career
- **Uranus:** bring out your uniqueness, do something different or inventive, help people
- **Neptune:** rest, pray, meditate, spend time in the water (including hot tubs, pools), volunteer
- **Pluto:** release something, clean out closets, attend to investments, enjoy sensuality
- **Eris:** stand up for yourself, confront the competition, make waves, deal with discord or disorder

Janet's "cheat sheet" has symbols and keywords for planets and signs. Download it free at JanetsPlan-its.com.

If you're working with your chart:
- **Ascendant:** (1st House cusp) blow your own horn, seek attention, get a new outfit or hairdo
- **Midheaven:** (MC) (10th House cusp) meet with your boss, go on an interview, enhance your reputation

Your Birthday Influences: Conditions present at your birthday affect you from three months before until nine months after, when your next birthday's factors kick in. Read the Highlights and Star Pages for the week of your birthday. Check the closest prior New Moon. Look at the daily message for your birthday and the day before and after. A **4** or **5** rating signals an upbeat year; a **1** or **2** shows an uphill battle. See if your birthday is on the Best and Worst list.

For Your Health: Guest writer, Medical Astrologer Diane Cramer, contributes an examination (p. 93) of astrological associations with anatomy and affiliated conditions, along with ideas regarding good health for each sign.

Use the following tools and tips to delve more deeply into Janet's Plan-its:

Following the Highlights, **Astro-Overviews** are summaries provided for astrologically inclined readers, as are the **Details** of the week's planetary activities. Daily messages take these into account and some are explained in the Highlights or the Star Pages. You can infer their meanings from Keywords (see p. 98).

If you have your birth chart: Read Making It Personal (p. 4). Also look for your chart's degrees on the **2015 All Star List** (p. 70), which sorts the year's astrological happenings in zodiac order. Read the Star Pages about the phenomena that apply to you.

Ephemeris: This table (p. 63) shows the planets' daily zodiac positions and other astrological data useful for seeing when planets connect to your chart. It might look intimidating, but the instructions on p. 62 will guide you.

MAKING IT PERSONAL

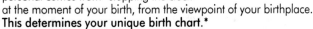

The planets appear to spin around us, their positions ever-changing, a bit like intricate clockworks. The difference is they never repeat the same configuration.

A planner like this tells you the energies at a given time in a generic way that anyone can utilize. What makes astrology personal comes from "stopping the clock" at the moment of your birth, from the viewpoint of your birthplace. **This determines your unique birth chart.***

In a chart, life's circumstances are described in twelve sectors, called the houses (see next page). Think of them as parts of a stage for the drama of your life. The planets are like actors, showing what's happening as they move around on the stage. Just as actors interact, planets also interact, sometimes harmoniously, sometimes discordantly. Their relationships are affected if their positions are separated by certain fractions of the sky, known as aspects. Planets close together join their powers. Across from each other (six signs away), they conflict or complement one another. When perpendicular (three signs apart), they're at cross purposes. Planets a third or a sixth of the sky apart (four signs or two signs away) blend harmoniously. The concept of aspects applies to planets in a birth chart, planets in motion (called transits), or those in motion making connections to the positions of birth planets.

Aspects are a rather complicated to figure out. The easiest method is to count the number of signs between planets. (The signs are always in the same order, counterclockwise, Aries, Taurus, Gemini, etc., through Pisces.) The effect of an aspect is strongest if the degrees of the signs of both planets are within 2° of each other. For example, a planet at 14° Aries is opposite another at 16° Libra, but is not considered opposite a planet at 28° Libra. The leeway allowed from the exact fraction is called the orb. Astrologers debate how big of an orb has an effect. A pretty safe allowance is 5°. If you'd rather not try to figure out aspects, order a transit list and let a computer do it for you.

Everyone has the same houses in the same order. However, your birth time and place determine your personal alignment of signs relative to houses. The sign positions of the planets are based on their movement through the zodiac (transits). Their house positions in your chart are specific to your birth time and place, too.

Some keywords for the planets, signs and aspects are at the back of the planner. You can read more about them in the Study Booth at my website, and I offer conference call classes on various topics, as well.

Your chart's houses won't align perfectly with signs. Signs are exactly 30° while house size varies. If you don't have a transit report with exact dates, estimate when a planet enters or leaves your houses, judging by the time the planet spends in the sign and how far into the sign your house begins. The Star Pages tell when planets enter signs and how long they'll be there. (For the Moon, see the daily boxes on the Weekly Calendar Pages.) Find the house(s) where you have that sign, showing the department(s) of your life affected during the planet's visit. For instance, if your 1st House begins in the middle of Scorpio, then the Sun enters your 1st House halfway through its time in Scorpio, staying there about a month. If you want to be more precise, check the Ephemeris (p. 63). You'll find instructions there on p. 62.

Check the degrees and signs of New and Full Moons on 2015 On a Page (p. 60). Locate their positions in your chart. A New Moon emphasizes a house (or a planet to which it makes an aspect) for the next four weeks. Do something new in the applicable part of your life. A Full Moon influence lasts a few days before and after the Full Moon. Eclipses are extra powerful New and Full Moons, with effects lasting several months. Take major action in the area of your life indicated by the house where the Eclipse occurs or by any aspect it makes. Also see if any of your planets are at "Moon Groove" degrees and will receive repeated attention.

To find your best time for an activity, locate that activity in the Houses table. See what sign you have at the beginning of that house (looking counterclockwise). Note when quick planets (Moon, Sun, Mercury, Venus or Mars) are in that sign and in that house. Check for aspects between slower planets in the Star Pages (p. 72) and on the All Star List (p. 70). Your planets and your life will be strongly affected if their degrees are within 2° of planets you have in the same sign or in a sign 2, 3, 4 or 6 signs away. Other good options are when New or Full Moons are in the applicable houses. There should be a New Moon once a year in each house and the same is true for Full Moons. The weekly Highlights and daily messages contain clues for dealing with people or what behavior to maximize or avoid.

EXAMPLE: Say you want to have elective surgery or a procedure to improve your appearance, something like a cosmetic dental treatment or laser reduction of varicose veins. The First House rules one's body. Specific body parts have other rulers, such as Capricorn for teeth and Sagittarius for legs. In the Keywords (p. 98), find the planet that rules the sign at the beginning of your First House. Also determine the sign ruler of the particular body part affected (see p. 93). Note any planets in your First House. Scan the 2014 All Star List (p. 70) for positive aspects (see Keywords again) at degrees of signs that make positive aspects to your First House ruler or occupants. (How to Read an Ephemeris on p. 62 explains determining aspects.) Such influences improve chances for a successful treatment on the days around that time. Weekly Highlights, Astro-Overviews and Details can also help identify positive applicable aspects. Look at the Best/Worst List to see if any Best days for your First House ruler or occupants, or for health in general, fit with the other criteria listed below. Certainly, avoid the Worst days! Also keep in mind that people tend to bleed more if surgery is close to a Full Moon.

Criteria for a good appointment time would be:

- the ruler or an occupant of your First House receives a positive aspect
- the day rating is **3** or better and the Moon is not Void (see p. 3)
- the ruler of your First House or the applicable body part is not Retrograde
- the Moon is in the portion of its cycle appropriate for the procedure

If you're removing a growth (wart, mole, etc.), choose a date in the waning lunar phase (the two weeks after a Full Moon). If you're plumping up your lips or adding a wrinkle filler, you want the growth potential of a waxing moon (the two weeks after a New Moon).

A Best health day or a Best day for a planet that occupies or rules your First House is good as long as it qualifies in the other ways noted above. If none of the Best health days has a desirable aspect to your First House ruler or occupant, seek a qualifying day that does have such an aspect even though it's not a Best health day. You want what's good for you personally. Check for any negative aspect or other disqualifier occurring within two days (other than an adjacent Void Moon period).

For instance, a Best day for health is December 8. It's rated 3, the Moon is waning and is not Void. That's a very good day for a procedure to reduce or remove something, especially if you don't want it to grow back, at all or at least not in a hurry. The Moon in Scorpio is ideal for elimination. In the Astro-Overview, the only difficulty that Tuesday involves the Moon early in the morning. The Moon moves a degree in about two hours, so see if you can arrange your appointment for mid-afternoon or later. Got the idea?

*A precise chart requires an exact birth time. The records department in your birthplace should have that. If you can't get yours, a chart using sunrise on your birthday is an adequate substitute. To find out sunrise on a given day, see the Naval Observatory's free calculator: http://aa.usno.navy.mil/data/docs/RS_OneYear.html. I can calculate your chart. (It's free with a consultation or class.)

AREAS OF LIFE ASSOCIATED WITH THE TWELVE HOUSES

NATURAL RULERS

 1st House
Aries/Mars

 2nd House
Taurus/Venus

 3rd House
Gemini/Mercury

 4th House
Cancer/Moon

 5th House
Leo/Sun

 6th House
Virgo/Mercury

 7th House
Libra/Venus

 8th House
Scorpio/Pluto

 9th House
Sagittarius/Jupiter

 10th House
Capricorn/Saturn

 11th House
Aquarius/Uranus

 12th House
Pisces/Neptune

1 House of the Self, personality, outlook on life, outward behavior, self-awareness, self concern, mask ("persona"), build, health, appearance, vitality, individuality

2 Possessions, values, resources, personal financial security, how you make money or meet obligations, material and non-material resources, self-worth

3 Conscious mind, communications, near environment, short journeys, early education, how you learn, self-expression, siblings, neighbors, ground transportation

4 Roots, home, parents (particularly mother), heredity, traditions, subconscious, places of residence, real estate, property, conditions in early and late life

5 Creativity, personal self-expression, pleasures, objects of affection (children, pets, lovers), vacations, hobbies, games, speculation, talents, need for attention

6 Work, employment, co-workers or subordinates, working conditions, health, the work you do on your body, diet, hygiene, service, duties, daily tasks

7 Partnerships, relationships, marriage, close associates, concern for others, peers, agents, open enemies, contracts, close associates, negotiations, lower courts

8 Birth, death, reproduction, transformation, your money mixing with other people's money (credit, tax, insurance, joint finances, investment, inheritance), big business, sex, spirituality

9 Foreign environments and languages, long journeys, the Higher Mind, philosophy, religion, higher education, ethics, higher courts, publishing, in-laws, media, the internet

10 Public standing, reputation, status, worldly attainment, ambition, sense of mission, profession, career, responsibilities, authority, father, guardian, boss

11 Hopes and wishes, goals, ideals, humanitarianism, associates, acquaintances, groups, friends, business contacts, money made from career

12 Spirituality, subconscious, sleep, unseen or hidden causes, limitations, secrets, fears, need for withdrawal or privacy, hidden enemies, confinement, House of Self-Undoing

To have grown wise and kind is real success.
Unknown

Moon in Aries • Void 4:46 pm (P), 7:46 pm (E)

29 MO 2

We begin the day with confidence. Second-guessing could eat into that, though some people will manage to be cocky while others feel put down.

Moon Void in Aries
Moon enters Taurus 2:56 am (P), 5:56 am (E)

30 TU 3

Tenacity, commitment and vision combine to enhance productivity. However, it takes good management and boundaries to keep disorder at bay.

Moon in Taurus

31 WE 3

Practical solutions and improvements arise early. Jump on them before resistance to change quashes them or moves the focus to all talk, no action.

New Year's Eve

Moon in Taurus • Void 4:19 am (P), 7:19 am (E)
Moon enters Gemini 9:09 am (P), 12:09 pm (E)

01 TH 1 ★

A shift in direction requires self-control and some kind of completion or release. Even with these, we may fail by doing too much or too little.

New Year's Day

Moon in Gemini

02 FR 2

Despite donning a thick skin, our feelings can get hurt. The pain is short-lived. Talking about it helps IF all involved can tell their story.

Moon in Gemini • Void 3:55 am (P), 6:55 am (E)
Moon enters Cancer 5:07 pm (P), 8:07 pm (E)

03 SA 3 ★

By being nimble and quick, you can sidestep a collision with someone bossy or self-righteous. Still, beliefs clash and cutting words may fly.

Mawlid al-Nabi (Muhammad's Birthday)

Moon in Cancer • Full Moon (Wolf Moon)
Void 8:53 pm (P), 11:53 pm (E)

04 SU 3 P ★

Kindness and an obliging, helpful attitude start the day smoothly. Later people can be selfish or pushy, and it isn't easy to find sympathy.

DEC. 29, '14-JAN. 04, '15 HIGHLIGHTS

As 2014 turns into 2015, uncertainties set us on edge, provoking irritability. Monday we're anxious and in a fog. Tuesday we find some patience and surer footing. Wednesday and Thursday the jitters return. Exercise or something using muscles provides an outlet for nervous energy. Many people react to pressures with "every man for himself." This shuts down cooperation and interferes with relationships, both of which take a hit Monday night and Friday. Sunday brings a measure of recovery but it's limited by poor or strange communication. Intensity comes with any Full Moon and the one Sunday [8:53 pm (P), 11:53 pm (E)] is a doozy! It's a key turning point in the current multi-year trend of major changes, one that requires decisions and action. Expect big news in the U.S. since the Full Moon's degree connects to the nation's "birthday" and affects the President as the leader of the country. On a personal level, developments impact real estate, homes, family life and food or nutrition. This is not a time to sit on the sidelines. Each of us will be challenged to examine and adjust our heading, and tested as to the influence we can wield and how we go about being effective.

Astro-Overview: *Mars and the sign it rules, Aries, are featured every day this week one way or another. Monday the Aries Moon sextiles Mars and conjuncts Eris. Tuesday Mercury squares Eris. Wednesday the Moon is in a T-square with Mars and Jupiter, which are opposite Thursday. Overnight Thursday, Mars is sextile Eris. Friday the Moon sextiles Uranus and Eris. The Moon is trine Mars Saturday and sesquiquadrate Mars Sunday. The few unrelated aspects include Mercury semisquare Neptune Monday and Chiron Sunday, Venus semisquare Chiron Friday and sextile Saturn Sunday. Both Venus and Mercury enter Aquarius on the weekend. The Sun is sextile Chiron Sunday, providing a little relief from the intense Full Moon then, halfway between the 10/8/14 and 4/4/15 Lunar Eclipses. All of these ignite the Uranus-Pluto square. The Moon and Sun now are midway between the North and South Nodes (said to be "at the bendings" – a turning point). Their Grand Cross with Pluto and Uranus is in the Cardinal mode, presenting the most strain and demanding a response.*

Details: *Monday Mercury semisquare Neptune; Tuesday Mercury square Eris; Thursday Mars opposite Jupiter; Thursday (P)/Friday (E) Mars sextile Eris; Friday Venus semisquare Chiron; Saturday Sun square Uranus, Venus enters Aquarius, Sun conjunct Pluto; Saturday (P)/Sunday (E) Mercury semisquare Chiron; Sunday Venus sextile Saturn, Sun sextile Chiron, Mercury enters Aquarius*

FEBRUARY

SU	M	TU	W	T	F	S
1	2	3	4	5	6	7
8	9	10	11	12	13	14
15	16	17	18	19	20	21
22	23	24	25	26	27	28

December-January
2014-2015

Sharp minds clearly outline the difficult choices we face, pointing out how unclear we are about the right answer. A change of direction is needed.

Twelfth Night, Mahayana New Year

Moon Void in Cancer

2 MO 05

A busy, productive morning is uplifted by a touch of creativity and the aid of friends or acquaintances. Later stoic discipline is the theme.

Epiphany

Moon Void in Cancer • Moon enters Leo 3:03 am (P), 6:03 am (E)

2 TU 06

An adjustment early yields a positive course correction, opening a wider range of possibilities. Tonight is great for fun, entertainment or art.

Orthodox Christmas

Moon in Leo

3 WE 07

The stress of being pulled in multiple directions is no fun and makes us irritable. It seems all we get for our efforts is more work on our plate.

Moon in Leo • Void 9:05 am (P), 12:05 pm (E)
Moon enters Virgo 2:58 pm (P), 5:58 pm (E)

★ 1 TH 08

Be cautious: chaos has the upper hand and klutziness or haste may cause mishaps. This evening is good for cleaning, organizing and discarding.

Moon in Virgo

★ 1 FR 09

Take action to vent aggravation or transmute anger. Try an exhausting workout or addressing a problem directly, registering your complaints.

Moon in Virgo • Void 7:46 am (P), 10:46 am (E)

1 SA 10

Rather than face tribulations on your own, find supportive company to lend an ear or a shoulder, maybe someone older and wiser who has seen it all.

Moon Void in Virgo • Moon enters Libra 3:57 am (P), 6:57 am (E)

1 SU 11

There's high energy to begin the week, supplied by last Sunday night's Full Moon. It's jarring and uncomfortable, though, and might be setting us up for a crash. If you stumble, use the experience as inspiration to make alterations and try new tactics. The planet of action is under duress all week (with a climax Thursday). We have no choice but to make a hard decision and do something, even though we are unsure of what route to go. As long as nothing is set in stone, adjustments can (and likely must) be made later. We can only do our best under circumstances that are bigger than we are, with a generous dollop of disorder thrown in the mix. We aren't likely to be able to accomplish all our ambitious objectives. Continually confronted with surprises and interruptions, after a while we realize we need to build extra time into our already jam-packed schedules. Something has to be sacrificed or delegated. Simplifying and streamlining may provide relief, and a condition that begins Thursday could help in that regard, thanks to a love of order. Yet you can see from the string of 1-rated days that there are plenty of tribulations and enough strain to go around. Adopt a philosophical attitude to weather the week's whitecaps.

JANUARY 05-11, 2015 HIGHLIGHTS

Astro-Overview: *This month offers us a chance to re-orient ourselves relative to the ongoing Uranus-Pluto square. The Nodes square Pluto Jan. 20-21 and the South Node joins Uranus Jan. 31. This week foreshadows these events as Mars moves through the midpoint of the Uranus-Pluto square, semisquare each and grating against the Nodes. The Moon scrapes all of them Thursday, the roughest day of this tough week. Like last week, Mars is in the hot seat. The Sun is in difficult straits, too: square the Nodes Monday, semisquare Saturn Tuesday and semisquare Neptune Saturday night. Mercury begins the shadow of its first Retrograde of 2015 Monday, making a sextile to Saturn that recurs twice in the coming two months. Next week, it makes the first of three sextiles to Uranus and the South Node, its other repeating connections. With only smooth aspects for this zigzag cycle (including a link to the ruler of Aquarius, where the backtrack occurs), it's likely to be a tame Mercury Retrograde for once.*

Details: *Monday Sun square North & South Nodes, Mercury sextile Saturn; Tuesday Sun semisquare Saturn; Thursday Ceres enters Capricorn; Friday Mars semisquare Uranus, Eris turns Direct; Saturday Mars semisquare Pluto; Saturday (P)/Sunday (E) Sun semisquare Neptune; Sunday Mars sesquiquadrate North Node & semisquare South Node*

*People who matter are most aware that
everyone else does, too.*
Malcolm S. Forbes

DECEMBER							JANUARY						
SU	M	TU	W	T	F	S	SU	M	TU	W	T	F	S
	1	2	3	4	5	6					1	2	3
7	8	9	10	11	12	13	4	5	6	7	8	9	10
14	15	16	17	18	19	20	11	12	13	14	15	16	17
21	22	23	24	25	26	27	18	19	20	21	22	23	24
28	29	30	31				25	26	27	28	29	30	31

Moon in Libra

12 MO 1 ★

Despite diplomatic efforts, consensus is elusive. People are at odds and at least one person is especially difficult. Tonight may improve slightly.

Moon in Libra • Third Quarter Moon • Void 1:46 am (P),
4:46 am (E) • Moon enters Scorpio 3:44 pm (P), 6:44 pm (E)

13 TU 3

Experience has taught you to draw a line when necessary, with manners and respect, of course. Find ways for teamwork to lighten your load.

Moon in Scorpio

14 WE 3

Today communication is smart, laced with cooperation and sympathy. Later, highly charged emotions hamper addressing hurts or seeking solutions.

Moon in Scorpio • Void 3:52 pm (P), 6:52 pm (E)

15 TH 2

The going is slow, especially early, and we're sluggish; allow extra time for your tasks. This afternoon improves, thanks to friendly aid and inspiration.

Moon Void in Scorpio • Moon enters Sagittarius 12:01 am (P), 3:01 am (E)

16 FR 2

Effort and ambition yield futility instead of the desired results. Maybe we stray off course too much. Still, we salvage some optimism or elicit sympathy.

Moon in Sagittarius • Void 11:25 am (P), 2:25 pm (E)

17 SA 4

An upbeat outlook and stimulating interactions lift spirits. Competitive or educational activities (especially involving technology) blend well with socializing.

Moon Void in Sagittarius
Moon enters Capricorn 4:04 am (P), 7:04 am (E)

18 SU 2

Impulsive urges in spending or relationships conflict with frugality or practical concerns. We want to relent but austerity likely prevails.

World Religion Day

JANUARY 12-18 HIGHLIGHTS

With room to spread out, water flows smoothly. It churns when confined in a tight space. Likewise, we may feel agitated when our energy is reined in. That's the intent of a planetary scrape exact overnight Wednesday but felt more on Monday afternoon and Friday morning. It involves a mellowing influence that starts a five-week stint early Monday. This supposedly softens assertiveness and quells anger but you may not notice that right away. Instead the week gets off to a contradictory start. Some people find it hard to keep selfish inclinations at bay. (Using manners would help!) We're well aware of others' needs but it's tricky to balance those against our own or to know where to draw lines. A friendly, humanitarian tone emerges Tuesday, continuing through Thursday afternoon and re-surfacing Saturday (which is easily the best day of the week, great for sports or competitions). Some stubbornness intrudes Wednesday evening and Thursday morning, though not enough to sour the sweetness. It fact, it could counteract vacillation: without an anchor, we might drift. Wavering is a problem Friday unless there's a gentle nudge from good judgment. Sunday, we keep goals clearly in sight and pursue personal desires, trying not to step on others' toes.

Astro-Overview: *The week gets off to a scratchy start with a Sun-Eris square Monday (continuing at Tuesday's Third Quarter Moon) and a T-square between the Moon, Uranus, the Nodes and Pluto. Rivalries abound and respect is lacking, despite Mars entering Pisces. Its square to Saturn Wednesday night, amplified by the Moon Friday morning, means extra work and the burden of rules (though they're flexible). Efforts should be rewarded, thanks to the Mars-Ceres sextile (exact early Friday). Friends come to our aid, courtesy of sextiles from Venus and then Mercury to Uranus and the South Node across the week. The Moon squares Venus and Mercury Wednesday night, interrupting the assistance briefly. A quick Grand Trine Saturday afternoon from the Moon to Jupiter and Eris (which were trine late last year and will be again 7/10) boosts energy and ups a spirit of rivalry, expressed well through athletics. Sunday afternoon is more somber, with the Moon in Capricorn passing Ceres and triggering its semisquare with Venus.*

Details: *Monday Mars enters Pisces, Sun square Eris; Tuesday Venus sextile Uranus; Wednesday Mercury sextile Uranus, Venus trine North Node & sextile South Node; Wednesday (P)/Thursday (E) Mars square Saturn; Thursday Mercury trine North Node & sextile South Node; Friday Mars sextile Ceres; Sunday Venus semisquare Ceres*

Retrograde motion (see p. 60) is an optical illusion when a planet appears to go opposite its normal direction. It's closest to the earth then, signaling a time to embrace and embody its qualities.

You may need to reinforce your boundaries if someone plays the victim and preys on your sympathies. Assess the motives. A big heart has its limits.

Martin Luther King Jr. Day (US)

Moon in Capricorn • Void 2:51 am (P), 5:51 am (E)

P 1 MO 19

Heartfelt humanitarian overtures abound. If someone's offer or request is imbalanced or designed for personal gain, it's easy to determine the truth.

Sun enters Aquarius

Moon Void in Capricorn • Moon enters Aquarius 4:59 am (P), 7:59 am (E) • New Moon

★ 2 TU 20

There's a tug o' war (or maybe a balancing act) between self-interest and loving kindness. Check the big picture to see which is gaining the upper hand.

Moon in Aquarius • Void 5:45 pm (P), 8:45 pm (E)

★ MR 3 WE 21

People are very sympathetic and quite emotional, especially tonight. This morning, they may turn a bit of a cold shoulder but that won't last long.

Moon Void in Aquarius • Moon enters Pisces 4:48 am (P), 7:48 am (E)

MR 3 TH 22

This is a great day for continuing projects that are already in motion (but not for starting new ones). Support surrounds us and solutions surface.

Moon in Pisces • Void 3:13 am (P), 6:13 am (E)

MR 4 FR 23

There's an argumentative (and stubborn) edge in the air but we manage to state differences of opinion politely, while not conceding our point.

Moon Void in Pisces • Moon enters Aries 5:31 am (P), 8:31 am (E)

MR 3 SA 24

Early-risers grumble and tonight, many people will be tense and prefer their own company. But midday may offer some pleasant moments.

Robert Burns' Birthday

Moon in Aries

MR 2 SU 25

We're moved to straighten out a range of matters in the four weeks following the New Moon Tuesday [5:14 am (P), 8:14 am (E)]. (Some conditions may stem back to last fall.) It could take until this weekend to get a clearer idea of how to go about the tasks. Other issues of this cycle involve meeting financial and emotional needs and seeking an appropriate level of nurturing. The tendency is to have too much or too little, and for work or other commitments to interfere with time for friends and pleasurable pursuits.

Between this week and next, we're pushed to get over a hurdle in making changes and releasing what's outworn or doesn't work for us any longer. This could apply to possessions, finances, values and relationships. If a situation has gone too far, reparations or corrections are in order. As soon as Monday, we feel the urge but we're unsure just what to do, and that's not a good day for choices or action. In fact, now is a better time for reflection and research with the planet of thinking at a standstill all week. (Mercury heads backwards from our viewpoint Wednesday.) Next week, the impetus for newness continues and either Tuesday (Jan. 27) or Saturday (Jan. 31) are better days for decisions and forward progress.

JANUARY 19-25 HIGHLIGHTS

Astro-Overview: *Venus was semisquare Ceres this past Sunday. Monday, it opposes Jupiter, which is sesquiquadrate Ceres Tuesday, in a nasty little knot in place at Tuesday's New Moon, which propels the influence through the coming lunar cycle. Mars joins Neptune Monday evening, after the Moon semisquares them hours earlier. Their union is still strong as the Moon passes them Thursday evening. Overnight Tuesday, the Nodes square Pluto. When the Moon aggravates them Monday and Thursday and assuages them Wednesday, it's early enough in the morning to go unnoticed. Venus jostles them next Monday, scratched by the Moon next Wednesday, the toughest point in their crossroads. Mercury has been at Venus's heels for two weeks but never catches up because it turns Retrograde Wednesday. (Going in opposite directions, they'll be semisquare Feb. 9.) Venus steps in the way of the Uranus-Pluto square from Sunday to next Monday, but Mercury doesn't until March 12-13.*

Details: *Monday Venus opposite Jupiter, Sun semisquare Chiron, Mars conjunct Neptune; Tuesday Sun enters Aquarius, Ceres sesquiquadrate Jupiter; Tuesday (P)/Wednesday (E) North & South Nodes square Pluto, Venus sextile Eris; Wednesday Mars semisquare Eris, Mercury turns Retrograde; Thursday (P)/Friday (E) Sun sextile Saturn; Friday Ceres sextile Neptune; Sunday Venus semisquare Uranus*

Revolutions never go backward.
Wendell Phillips

| JANUARY | | | | | | | | FEBRUARY | | | | | | |
SU	M	TU	W	T	F	S		SU	M	TU	W	T	F	S
				1	2	3		1	2	3	4	5	6	7
4	5	6	7	8	9	10		8	9	10	11	12	13	14
11	12	13	14	15	16	17		15	16	17	18	19	20	21
18	19	20	21	22	23	24		22	23	24	25	26	27	28
25	26	27	28	29	30	31								

Moon in Aries • Void 6:23 am (P), 9:23 am (E) • Moon enters
Taurus 8:37 am (P), 11:37 am (E) • First Quarter Moon

26 MO 2 MR

Reach out to friends for encouragement or a sympathetic ear. There's pain that needs to be processed and that's easier with support and even a hug.

Moon in Taurus • Void 6:18 pm (P), 9:18 pm (E)

27 TU 3 MR ★

People who stick to their opinions early may relent when challenged about fairness. But their adaptability is temporary; obstinacy returns later.

Moon Void in Taurus
Moon enters Gemini 2:36 pm (P), 5:36 pm (E)

28 WE 1 MR

An experiment or inventive idea fizzles in the face of resistance to change or disagreements over values or funds. Tonight disappointment looms.

Moon in Gemini

29 TH 3 MR

Communication flows and cooperation greases the wheels of progress until we drift off course this evening and a foot may end up in a mouth.

Moon in Gemini • Void 1:24 am (P), 4:24 am (E)
Moon enters Cancer 11: 09 pm (P)

30 FR 3 MR

It's a better day for reflection than assertion. Finding agreement is iffy and attempts to throw weight around lack the muscle to back it up.

Moon in Cancer (P), Void in Gemini (E)
Moon enters Cancer 2:09 am (E)

31 SA 3 MR ★

Sensitivity is high. Psychic connections are strong. It's a good day for charitable acts or health repairs. Tonight relationship imbalances are awkward.

Moon in Cancer • Void 5:37 am (P), 8:37 am (E)

01 SU 2 MR

This morning, hurts are assuaged with tenderness and creativity (possibly in the kitchen) is amusing. By evening, we're emotionally waterlogged.

Black History Month begins

JANUARY 26-FEB. 01 HIGHLIGHTS

The challenging trend in matters of the heart and wallet continues this week (see last week's Highlights). Karma is afoot. (This means good deeds and right action will be rewarded, and the price must be paid for negative intentions or deeds.) Monday and Wednesday, observe the signals you get about what needs to be set aside or put to rest. Things cannot remain as they have been, at least not without some hard decisions. Possibly by Wednesday night and certainly by Friday, the picture should be crystal clear and the obstacles or needed work will be identified. A softer, less judgmental viewpoint begins creeping in Tuesday, subtly at first but very noticeable over the weekend. Be careful how much leeway you give someone, or at least assess if it's deserved and if you're comfortable with any resulting vulnerability to which you would be exposed. We're in the thorny time of Mercury Retrograde (halfway over Friday), when you're more apt to do something that later you'll lament, "What was I thinking?" Say what's on your mind rather than letting it roll around your head repeatedly until you think you've discussed it. And, while you want to be helpful, don't put yourself last on the list. You count! Make time for yourself as well as for others.

Astro-Overview: *It could be a bad week for the markets: Venus ended last week semisquare Uranus and starts this one semisquare Pluto, at the midpoint of their square. The Moon slaps all of them Wednesday, finishing the night in a T-square with Venus and Saturn (square Friday). Tuesday Venus enters Pisces, where it's "exalted" (supposed to operate well), for 3-1/2 weeks. We should be aiming for unconditional love and unselfish charity. The down side is fear or a sense of suffering. We'll see which attitude is stronger when Venus joins Pisces' ruler, Neptune, Sunday. Mercury has a better week, connecting harmoniously with the Nodes and Uranus Tuesday and the Sun Friday. Mars' sextile to Pluto Friday and conjunction with Chiron Saturday incline us to be helpful and counteract the self-interest of Saturday's South Node-Uranus conjunction.*

Details: *Monday Venus sesquiquadrate North Node & semisquare South Node, Venus semisquare Pluto; Tuesday Venus enters Pisces, Mercury trine North Node & sextile South Node; Tuesday (P)/Wednesday (E) Mercury sextile Uranus; Friday Venus square Saturn, Mars sextile Pluto, Mercury conjunct Sun; Saturday Mars conjunct Chiron, Uranus opposite North Node & conjunct South Node; Sunday Venus conjunct Neptune*

MARCH

SU	M	TU	W	T	F	S
1	2	3	4	5	6	7
8	9	10	11	12	13	14
15	16	17	18	19	20	21
22	23	24	25	26	27	28
29	30	31				

January-February

Emotional detachment aids interacting, especially if competition gets ugly. Even being jolly can't gloss over hurts. Choose words carefully.

Groundhog Day, Candlemas, Imbolc

Moon Void in Cancer • Moon enters Leo 9:41 am (P), 12:41 pm (E)

★ MR 3 MO 02 〇

An upbeat mood adds to creativity and cooperation, making this a great day for team activities. Confidence helps solo efforts go smoothly, too.

Moon in Leo • Full Moon (Storm Moon) • Void 9:31 pm (P)

MR 4 TU 03 〇

Too bad we couldn't save some of yesterday's support to sprinkle around today. Walls are up and people would rather be alone than compromise.

Moon in Leo, Void (P) • Void 12:31am (E)
Moon enters Virgo 9:46 pm (P)

MR 1 WE 04 〇

A combination of imagination, optimism and practicality struggles to outweigh skepticism and/or belligerence. In the end, kindness prevails.

Moon in Virgo (P), Void in Leo (E) • Moon enters Virgo 12:46 am (E)

MR 3 TH 05

Helpfulness begins the day but soon is replaced by a misunderstanding or opposing views. Stubbornness fuels a fight but flexibility disarms it.

Moon in Virgo • Void 2:09 pm (P), 5:09 pm (E)

MR 1 FR 06

Most people are even-tempered and polite, and good boundaries enable easy communication. But there may be someone too self-interested to get along.

Moon Void in Virgo • Moon enters Libra 10:44 am (P), 1:44 pm (E)

MR 3 SA 07

Kicking around ideas with someone who thinks differently provides an assessment that might be surprising and head you in another direction.

Moon in Libra

MR 2 SU 08

Finally a less turbulent week! Of course, we're still in the midst of a back-up of the communication planet (though this is a good time to give something a second try). We can make some progress or more easily straighten out situations that have become off-kilter. We are at the end of a stretch since 2012 when two heavenly bodies align fortuitously to promote helpful, transformative healing and improvements. ("Really?" you rightfully ask. Things have not been all that good. Well, this factor has been operating during one of the most difficult planetary clashes for decades, working to counterbalance intense changes. Things could have been worse!) Tuesday's Full Moon [3:09 pm (P), 6:09 pm (E)] accentuates their mixture and adds a dollop of good fortune and positive opportunities. These items blend in a formation that operates like this: one weird event leads to another bizarre circumstance, which in turns leads to something quite good and we couldn't have arrived there without going through the strange sequence. Add your own inspired action to the mix and you have a formula for success. The cornucopia planet is involved and by the end of the week, the planet of relationships and finances joins in. See what you can heal in your life.

FEBRUARY 02-08 HIGHLIGHTS

Astro-Overview: *The long-term Chiron-Pluto sextile moves out of the one-degree orb range on 2/2 (see Star Pages) but is strong at the Full Moon Tuesday. The Sun is at their midpoint then with the Moon forming the apex of a Finger of God triangle with them. Jupiter creates a Finger of God with Chiron and Pluto three times: Sept. of 2014, Feb. of 2015 and May-June of 2015. This is the time when the aspects are most exact and the only time a Full Moon participates in the triangle. There are two other players in the mix, as well: Mars (still close to Chiron after passing it 1/31) and Ceres (approaching Pluto, reaching it 2/15). By Sunday night, Venus passes Chiron and keeps the beat of the Finger of God thumping. Venus is sextile Ceres Thursday, highlighted by the Moon that night. Then Venus is sextile Pluto Saturday night. The Sun-Jupiter opposition (exact Friday) acts in a positive fashion at the Full Moon but the Moon scratches against them Saturday night.*

Details: *Monday Venus semisquare Eris, Sun trine North Node & sextile South Node, Sun sextile Uranus; Thursday Venus sextile Ceres, Mercury sextile Saturn, Mercury semisquare Mars; Friday Sun opposite Jupiter; Saturday (P)/Sunday (E) Venus sextile Pluto; Sunday (P) Venus conjunct Chiron*

▶ See p. 3 for meaning of symbols ★, **MR, VR, P.**

Do not think you will necessarily be aware of your own enlightenment.

Dogen

JANUARY							FEBRUARY						
SU	M	TU	W	T	F	S	SU	M	TU	W	T	F	S
				1	2	3	1	2	3	4	5	6	7
4	5	6	7	8	9	10	8	9	10	11	12	13	14
11	12	13	14	15	16	17	15	16	17	18	19	20	21
18	19	20	21	22	23	24	22	23	24	25	26	27	28
25	26	27	28	29	30	31							

Moon in Libra • Void 3:58 am (P), 6:58 am (E)
Moon enters Scorpio 11:05 pm (P)

09 MO 1 MR

Sensitivity to each other's agenda is high. Before you speak, consider carefully the impact your words will have on the receiving end.

Moon in Scorpio (P), Void in Libra (E)
Moon enters Scorpio 2:05 am (E)

10 TU 2 MR

The right blend of being firm and tender as you show support to someone dear to you will ensure you honor yourself and won't feel used in the process.

Moon in Scorpio • Third Quarter Moon • Void 9:32 pm (P)

11 WE 3 ★

Research or probing below the surface reveals the worth of investments of time or energy. To achieve the desired effect, ego may need to be set aside.

Moon in Scorpio, Void (P) • Void 12:32 am (E)
Moon enters Sagittarius 8:46 am (P), 11:46 am (E)

12 TH 1

In the midst of serious circumstances that need a smart response, some people are aloof and brush things off lightly, leaving the duty to others.

Lincoln's Birthday

Moon in Sagittarius

13 FR 3 ★

Brainstorming yields inventiveness and hopes for striking it rich. Check for a flaw in thinking or the pay-off may not live up to the good idea.

Moon in Sagittarius • Void 7:15 am (P), 10:15 am (E)
Moon enters Capricorn 2:24 pm (P), 5:24 pm (E)

14 SA 2

Distractions (perhaps pleasant ones) draw us off course this morning. We fritter away our time until evening, when a serious mood puts a damper on fun.

Valentine's Day

Moon in Capricorn

15 SU 2 ★

Relationships surf some wild waves today and manage to survive, stronger for the effort and friendly respect that go into keeping them afloat.

Susan B. Anthony Day, Nirvana Day

FEBRUARY 09-15 HIGHLIGHTS

A Monday doesn't get much blue-er than this week's, with the planet of the mind nearly motionless (Mercury ends its Retrograde Wednesday morning) and the Moon on auto-pilot (Void of Course) all day. (If you are not familiar with these terms, see p. 60 and p. 3. Such conditions affect your chances at success, whatever you're doing.) It doesn't have to be totally unproductive, but it is better suited for reviewing or revamping something already in progress than for starting anything new. Many people will be attempting to improve or repair conditions involving money matters or relationships as the week begins, but communication about these gets stymied or all mixed up. Don't expect to iron things out right away. The situation is exacerbated Tuesday (when deep feelings emerge) and likely to be re-visited Friday. Maybe you can achieve clarity or closure then. If not, try again in a week. Efforts to grow something or bring about a blossoming take a surprising turn this week, especially Thursday morning. By the weekend, we may feel like going back to the drawing board and starting over. Take a big picture view on Friday afternoon to see what wisdom arises. Competition is on the docket Saturday and you'll get a chance to see how you stack up.

Astro-Overview: *Though we'll probably pay more attention to Mercury's return to Direct motion Wednesday, the key player this week is Ceres, which gets mired in the Uranus-Pluto square. Ceres is square the Nodes Tuesday and square Uranus Thursday (harking back to the South Node-Uranus conjunction Jan. 31). Then it joins Pluto in the wee hours Sunday morning. The Moon messes with them Thursday morning, the low-point of the week. Venus passes Chiron just after midnight (E) Monday and by that afternoon is tangled in a semisquare with Mercury. The Moon aggravates these two Friday afternoon, offsetting what would otherwise be a pretty good time as the Moon forms a Grand Trine then with Uranus and Jupiter. Such a triangle can bring luck but in this case, it doesn't look like it will benefit communications, finances or relationships. The Sun's lone aspect of the week is a sextile to Eris overnight Tuesday, unlikely to be of much help since Eris seems to prefer harsh aspects.*

Details: *Monday (E) Venus conjunct Chiron; Monday Mercury semisquare Venus; Tuesday Ceres square North & South Nodes; Tuesday (P)/ Wednesday (E) Sun sextile Eris; Wednesday Mercury turns Direct; Thursday Ceres square Uranus; Sunday Ceres conjunct Pluto*

MARCH

SU	M	TU	W	T	F	S
1	2	3	4	5	6	7
8	9	10	11	12	13	14
15	16	17	18	19	20	21
22	23	24	25	26	27	28
29	30	31				

Superstitions flare on Friday the 13th, but it is not inherently unlucky. In fact, it has some fortuitous associations. Read about them in the Star Pages.

February

Moon in Capricorn • Void 12:17 pm (P), 3:17 pm (E)
Moon enters Aquarius 4:13 pm (P), 7:13 pm (E)

2 MO 16

A course correction is needed, aided by the right contacts. Morning into midday, there's a chance for cooperation. Later, assumptions get in the way.

Presidents Day (U.S.), Family Day (Canada)

Moon in Aquarius

★ 2 TU 17

"No man is an island" but some will wish they were on one instead of diverted from their agenda by others' needs. Reciprocity reduces resentment.

Mardi Gras

Moon in Aquarius • New Moon • Void 3:47 pm (P), 6:47 pm (E)
Moon immediately enters Pisces 3:47 pm (P), 6:47 pm (E)

★ 1 WE 18

Let go of what needs to fall away or it might be ripped out of your hands. It's time for old notions to yield to a new vision, one that supports growth.

Ash Wednesday, Chinese New Year - Year of the Sheep (Wood Element) • Sun enters Pisces

---

Moon in Pisces • Void 3:02 pm (P), 6:02 pm (E)

★ 4 TH 19

Innovation and planning join forces to spark improvements. Sympathy is strong for those who suffer but don't let it stand in the way of progress.

Moon Void in Pisces • Moon enters Aries 3:13 pm (P), 6:13 pm (E)

★ P 2 FR 20

A big day for news, with international conflicts at the center. For individuals, self-interest trumps compassion and competition brings out one's best.

Moon in Aries • Void 4:36 pm (P), 7:36 pm (E)

★ 1 SA 21

Make your own luck; nobody is going to tap you with a magic wand. Ingenuity and old-fashioned hard work combine for your best shot at success.

Moon Void in Aries • Moon enters Taurus 4:28 pm (P), 7:28 pm (E)

★ 1 SU 22

Disturbing dreams this morning may show a way out of misery. Love is a healing force and many will act on amorous inclinations today or tonight.

Washington's Birthday

FEBRUARY 16-22 HIGHLIGHTS

Astro-Overview: Three weeks ago, Venus was semisquare Uranus and Pluto at the midpoint of their square. This week, the Sun follows suit but with the added power of a New Moon, just as the Sun is about to enter Pisces. The Moon and Sun at the New Moon are semisquare Ceres (since Ceres passed Pluto last Sunday) and semisextile Mars at 29 Pisces, the degree of the next New Moon. Mars and Venus join overnight Saturday after each enters Aries (Mars Thursday, Venus Friday). Friday to Saturday, first Mars and then Venus is sesquiquadrate Jupiter (at the potent center of a Fixed sign). The bright spot of the week is Thursday with two sextiles (Mercury-Saturn and Ceres-Chiron) and only one harsh aspect (a pre-dawn Moon-Eris semisquare). A Jupiter-Chiron quincunx (exact Tuesday) forms a Finger of God with Pluto.

Details: Monday Sun sesquiquadrate North Node & semisquare South Node; Tuesday Sun semisquare Uranus, Jupiter quincunx Chiron; Wednesday Sun semisquare Pluto, Sun enters Pisces, Ceres quincunx Jupiter; Thursday Mercury sextile Saturn, Ceres sextile Chiron, Mars enters Aries; Friday Sun semisquare Ceres, Venus enters Aries, Mars sesquiquadrate Jupiter; Saturday Venus sesquiquadrate Jupiter; Saturday (P)/Sunday (E) Venus conjunct Mars

The New Moon Wednesday [3:47 pm (P), 6:47 pm (E)] comes just minutes ahead of the Sun moving from Aquarius to Pisces. (Due to "rounding up," you'll see this listed some places as 0 degrees Pisces, but it's really at the very last inches of Aquarius.) The last degree of a sign brings an intense dose of the sign's energy, as if we're trying to pack in all it has to offer ahead of the deadline. In the case of Aquarius, knowledge and intelligence are magnified, but so too are opinions and obstinacy. The humanitarian urge should be strong, as well. There may be conflicts about how to treat people because this New Moon stands right in the middle of two planetary titans engaged in a monumental 6- to 7-year tug-of-war that pits the rich and powerful against the masses. (Remember "Occupy Wall Street" in 2011?) There are other manifestations possible, of course, including the possibility of big, positive changes that occur quickly. (See March 16 in the Star Pages for more potential impacts.) Fortunately, a nurturing and supportive influence is closely involved in the New Moon pattern in a realistic sign. This inclines us to help those in need even if only for the practical outcome that benefits us as well: self-concern parading as altruism.

A candle loses nothing of its light by lighting another candle.

James Keller

FEBRUARY								MARCH						
SU	M	TU	W	T	F	S		SU	M	TU	W	T	F	S
1	2	3	4	5	6	7		1	2	3	4	5	6	7
8	9	10	11	12	13	14		8	9	10	11	12	13	14
15	16	17	18	19	20	21		15	16	17	18	19	20	21
22	23	24	25	26	27	28		22	23	24	25	26	27	28
								29	30	31				

Moon in Taurus • Void 6:57 pm (P), 9:57 pm (E)

23 MO 2

Multiple obstacles present many opportunities for improvement. Persistence and flexibility help turn a weird situation around by tonight.

Moon Void in Taurus • Moon enters Gemini 8:54 pm (P), 11:54 pm (E)

24 TU 2

Morning may bring a reward or accomplishment, and is a good time to assess value or consolidate a relationship. This evening is fraught with snags.

Moon in Gemini • First Quarter Moon

25 WE 3 P

Early on, harmony reigns. Midday, chaos ensues, arguments erupt. Later, we're congenial and enjoy entertainment, competition or physical activities.

Moon in Gemini • Void 12:43 am (P), 3:43 am (E)

26 TH 1 ★

Speak up on your own behalf; others aren't apt to. They're consumed with their own misery, mishaps or mischief. But be careful not to miscommunicate.

Moon Void in Gemini • Moon enters Cancer 4:50 am (P), 7:50 am (E)

27 FR 2 ★

The question is how much to do for someone else or should you concentrate on yourself. It's tricky to strike a balance. Listen to your divine guides.

Moon in Cancer • Void 9:53 am (P), 12:53 pm (E)

28 SA 1

We're pulled in a myriad of directions this morning and can't possibly satisfy all the demands. Let compassion help you make the decision.

Moon Void in Cancer
Moon enters Leo 3:34 pm (PDT), 6:34 pm (EDT)

01 SU 2

Don't jump at your first thought or instinct. Check the big picture to ascertain the most practical result in the long run, even if it means more work now.

Women's History Month begins

FEBRUARY 23-MARCH 01 HIGHLIGHTS

Normally the time of year when the Sun's in Pisces is oriented toward hibernation, rest, dreams, retreat and reflection. It promotes using one's imagination and engaging in sympathetic, charitable activities. While these inclinations are not necessarily negated, this time around in Pisces there's a harder edge that comes into play. Defending oneself against abuse or fighting for beliefs (à la a crusade) are key themes, particularly Wednesday (at the First Quarter Moon) and Thursday. Boundaries may be part of the issue: affection, self-interest or a familial connection can dilute enforcement of rules. Walls are up, though, at the beginning and end of the week. If you want someone's agreement, ask early Wednesday morning. More so than usual, people want admiration and respect now. But these don't just happen on demand or as a result of position; they must be earned. To navigate the week's precarious, emotion-packed waters, you'll need rational and cool-headed communication, along with perspective and humor. These are easiest to achieve Wednesday afternoon and Sunday morning to afternoon, and more difficult to summons the rest of the week, especially Saturday morning. Though tumultuous, there may be a turning point in feelings then.

Astro-Overview: *Saturn won't be precisely square Neptune until November. They're within three degrees of the aspect now, accented by the Sun square Saturn Monday and conjunct Neptune Wednesday night, the important item now. Neptune and Eris reach an exact semisquare Thursday, hours after the Sun passes Neptune. We'll feel the effects most at the First Quarter Moon midday Wednesday, when Eris is in the middle of the Moon's square to the Sun and Neptune. Meanwhile Saturn has a trine with Venus Tuesday and with Mars Wednesday, caressed by the Moon Wednesday morning. Then Saturn has a semisquare with Ceres Sunday, provoked by the Moon Saturday night. Mercury has a good week, trine the North Node Friday and on Sunday sextile Uranus and opposite Jupiter, highlighting their trine March 3. Jupiter is quincunx Pluto Friday, which was part of last week's Finger of God. Who's left out? Chiron.*

Details: *Monday Sun square Saturn; Tuesday Venus trine Saturn; Wednesday Mars trine Saturn, Sun conjunct Neptune; Wednesday (P)/ Thursday (E) Sun semisquare Eris; Thursday Neptune semisquare Eris; Friday Mercury trine North Node & sextile South Node, Jupiter quincunx Pluto; Sunday Mercury sextile Uranus, Ceres semisquare Saturn, Mercury opposite Jupiter*

APRIL

SU	M	TU	W	T	F	S
			1	2	3	4
5	6	7	8	9	10	11
12	13	14	15	16	17	18
19	20	21	22	23	24	25
26	27	28	29	30		

Daylight Saving Time begins March 8.

February-March

Fun and freedom pervade the atmosphere on this playful, creative day - one of the year's best! Enthusiasm soars. Risks pay off. Amor may be in the air, as well.

Moon in Leo

5 MO 02

We awake with optimism after yesterday's excitement but it's unsustainable. Frustration sets in by evening, provoked by someone's selfishness.

Moon in Leo • Void 12:47 am (P), 3:47 am (E)

★ 3 TU 03

You'll need all the pluck and ingenuity you can muster to endure or surmount the flood of trials today and tonight. Be grounded to stay on task.

Moon Void in Leo • Moon enters Virgo 3:58 am (P), 6:58 am (E)

P 1 WE 04

Simplicity is beautiful and the more uncomplicated you can keep things, the happier you'll be. Get into a good groove and flow; you'll reach your goal.

Purim

Moon in Virgo • Full Moon (Chaste Moon) Void 10:36 am (P), 1:36 pm (E)

4 TH 05

An overload of details mars most of the day. This evening is delightful, perfect for socializing and enjoying team or solo sports or competitions.

Moon Void in Virgo • Moon enters Libra 4:52 pm (P), 7:52 pm (E)

3 FR 06

We like a good debate and rise to challenges presented by adversaries, seeking to find common ground. Understanding and problem-solving pave the way.

Moon in Libra

3 SA 07

Everyone seems to be off-balance and cantankerous, feeling unappreciated. Use tact and friendly diplomacy to avoid a skirmish or mend a fence.

International Women's Day, Daylight Saving Time begins at 2:00 am

Moon in Libra • Void 6:24 pm (PDT), 9:24 pm (EDT)

★ 1 SU 08

MARCH 02-08 HIGHLIGHTS

The German phrase "glück im unglück" means luck in the midst of unluckiness. The reverse doesn't have a catch phrase but undoubtedly also occurs: unluckiness in the midst of luck. Whichever way you want to look at it, that's what we seem to have this week, peaking the day before the Full Moon Thursday [10:05 am (P), 1:05 pm (E)]. The blessings come from happy surprises or a sudden liberation. Monday (especially that night) holds the most promise. The misfortune stems from pushing too hard against resistance and forcing issues, probably for selfish reasons. The planet of relationships and finances is in the thick of things. The importance of contacts, colleagues and camaraderie is emphasized. If there's a change in any of these, it's likely to be for the best even if it's precipitated in a difficult way. The Sun in Pisces inclines us to be nonjudgmental but the Full Moon in the opposite sign, Virgo, implores us to pick and choose, discerning who and what hurts us or helps us, or whom we want to assist or reject . Like it or not, we need to draw a line. Some tough fiscal choices may be required by the end of the week, as well. Happily, there's a potent force for healing also in effect, bolstered by the Full Moon, to provide some relief.

Astro-Overview: *One of 2015's top aspects, Jupiter trine Uranus, occurs early Tuesday. As if putting a pretty ribbon on the gift, Venus joins Uranus and trines Jupiter Wednesday. But there's a down side: Venus is also square Pluto that night. (Wednesday evening is spoiled further by the Moon scratching the impending Ceres-Neptune semisquare and Ceres-Eris square, exact early next week.) Venus, now outpacing Mars, makes the aspects first that they each form. Both join the South Node this week (Venus Monday, Mars Friday) and Mars replicates the other links next week. Fortunately, when the Moon pricks the difficult aspects, it does so at hours when the impact is less odious (early morning on Wednesday and Sunday). The Sun tries to bandage the wounds with its sextile to Pluto Thursday (exact at the Full Moon) and its conjunction with Chiron Saturday. Venus ends the week in a sour sesquiquadrate to Saturn.*

Details: *Monday Venus opposite North Node & conjunct South Node; Tuesday Jupiter trine Uranus; Wednesday Venus trine Jupiter, Venus conjunct Uranus, Venus square Pluto; Thursday Sun sextile Pluto; Friday Mars opposite North Node & conjunct South Node; Saturday Mercury sextile Eris, Sun conjunct Chiron; Sunday Venus sesquiquadrate Saturn*

The true sign of intelligence is not knowledge but imagination.
Albert Einstein

FEBRUARY							MARCH						
SU	M	TU	W	T	F	S	SU	M	TU	W	T	F	S
1	2	3	4	5	6	7	1	2	3	4	5	6	7
8	9	10	11	12	13	14	8	9	10	11	12	13	14
15	16	17	18	19	20	21	15	16	17	18	19	20	21
22	23	24	25	26	27	28	22	23	24	25	26	27	28
							29	30	31				

Moon Void in Libra • Moon enters Scorpio 6:10 am (P), 9:10 am (E)

09 MO 2

Cold insensitivity may be displayed early in the day but by afternoon, deep feelings are evident. This evening, sympathy and warm encouragement arise.

Moon in Scorpio

10 TU 2

Logic counteracts emotions, keeping them from going over the top. Yet that energy has to go somewhere, either for the betterment of another or oneself.

Moon in Scorpio • Void 12:46 pm (P), 3:46 pm (E)
Moon enters Sagittarius 4:30 pm (P), 7:30 pm (E)

11 WE 1 P

Anxiety has us on alert. Mixed with unpredictability and doubt, they block effective action until tonight, when something's gotta give.

Moon in Sagittarius

12 TH 3 ★

If someone tries to feed you fear or guilt, seek a bigger, brighter outlook. Luck and laughter are in the air this evening, amidst strange observations.

Moon in Sagittarius • Third Quarter Moon • Void 4:11 pm (P),
7:11 pm (E) • Moon enters Capricorn 11:40 pm (P)

13 FR 2

It's easy to drift off course unless you have a passion for your objectives; obligations are not enough incentive. But maybe you need time to wander.

Moon in Capricorn (P), Void in Sagittarius (E)
Moon enters Capricorn 2:40 am (E)

14 SA 2 ★

A checklist could keep your mind on goals; still, there's an obstacle. An afternoon nap or diversion is tempting, but you have other considerations.

Moon in Capricorn

15 SU 2

The nurturing instinct is strong. With so many needs, priorities must be set. Those who feel overlooked or underserved are apt to register complaints.

MARCH 09-15 HIGHLIGHTS

Some people have strange ways of showing they care, like being pushy (nearly manipulative) or foisting examples from their lives on others. Throughout the week, if someone seems to promote your good, examine the motivation; self-interest is likely in play. Not that we shouldn't all watch out for ourselves but there's a healthy means of achieving that and then there are dysfunctional doses. More during the work week than on the weekend, we face the need to determine limits, particularly in close personal relationships or where finances are involved. Rivalry or some kind of chaos intrudes into these areas. A high level of energy Tuesday is dampened by misgivings or second thoughts, probably sparked by a conversation that turns one's thinking. Wednesday, patience runs thin and explosions are possible, especially that evening (the low-point of the week). Miscommunication is a problem Friday and Saturday; even what you tell yourself might be muddied or deluded, colored by anger or ambition. Seek to differentiate reality from imagination and stick to what is verifiable. That's the best way to take care of yourself now. And find something enjoyable to do Thursday afternoon; it's the best part of this trying week.

Astro-Overview: *Mercury gets caught in the Uranus-Pluto-Mars web. After it is sesquiquadrate North Node and semisquare South Node Tuesday, Mercury is semisquare Uranus overnight Thursday, semisquare Pluto Friday and semisquare Mars Saturday. The Moon pinches them Wednesday afternoon to evening (the week's low point) and early Sunday. Mars is trine Jupiter Tuesday, then conjunct Uranus and square Pluto Wednesday. Venus steps into the Ceres-Neptune-Eris mess, concurrently with Ceres' square to Eris Monday and semisquare to Neptune Tuesday. Tuesday night, Venus is conjunct Eris and Wednesday, Venus is semisquare Neptune and square Ceres. Saturn turns Retrograde Saturday (with no close aspects) and that night, the Sun and Ceres are sextile.*

Details: *Monday Ceres square Eris; Monday (P)/Tuesday (E) Mars trine Jupiter; Tuesday Ceres semisquare Neptune, Mercury sesquiquadrate North Node & semisquare South Node, Venus conjunct Eris; Wednesday Venus semisquare Neptune, Mars conjunct Uranus, Venus square Ceres, Mars square Pluto; Thursday Mercury enters Pisces; Thursday (P)/Friday (E) Mercury semisquare Uranus; Friday Mercury semisquare Pluto; Saturday Saturn turns Retrograde, Mercury semisquare Mars; Saturday (P)/Sunday (E) Sun sextile Ceres*

March

APRIL

SU	M	TU	W	T	F	S
				1	2	3	4
5	6	7	8	9	10	11
12	13	14	15	16	17	18
19	20	21	22	23	24	25
26	27	28	29	30		

On March 16, the finale of a momentous force for change is upon us. A long-term clash between slow, powerful outer planets reaches its seventh and last peak in a series that began in 2012.

Here is how to keep calm, though it won't be easy! Breathe. Look for solutions instead of seeing just the problems. Be willing to let go and move on.

Moon in Capricorn • Void 1:02 am (P), 4:02 am (E)
Moon enters Aquarius 3:14 am (P), 6:14 am (E)

★ **1 MO 16**

Excitement and ingenuity make for a lively day, good for friendly competition as long as no one gets whiny or tries to cheat. Then the gloves come off.

St Patrick's Day, Maha Shivaratri

Moon in Aquarius • Void 11:18 am (P), 2:18 pm (E)

★ **2 TU 17**

We may feel like we're trying to drive with one foot on the accelerator and the other on the brake. Emotions cloud thinking and muddy communication.

Moon Void in Aquarius
Moon enters Pisces 3:58 am (P), 6:58 am (E)

2 WE 18

See if you can use your imagination to break out of your usual mold (if you can get over the inertia to do so) and still remain practical in the process.

Moon in Pisces

2 TH 19

Someone has to lead the way into a new day, a new paradigm. If you have chutzpah, a plan and a way to engage others in teamwork, it could be you!

Spring Equinox, Ostara, Sun enters Aries

Moon in Pisces • Solar Eclipse New Moon • Void 2:36 am (P),
5:36 am (E) • Moon enters Aries 3:28 am (P), 6:28 am (E)

★ **3 FR 20**

Going solo, even with feats of individual strength, may feel hollow if one is disconnected from the whole, stepping on or over others to advance.

Zoroastrian New Year, Ramayana (Hindu New Year) begins

Moon in Aries • Void 3:51 pm (P), 6:51 pm (E)

2 SA 21

Composure and faith make the difference between succumbing to weakness or worry and seeing a way out of the woods. Morning is shaky; evening is serene.

Moon Void in Aries • Moon enters Taurus 3:40 am (P), 6:40 am (E)

3 SU 22

Water puts out fire, but fire can heat water up. Dirt also extinguishes flames and that's the analogy for the calming force coming this week, just in the nick of time for the spring equinox [Friday 3:45 pm (P), 6:45 pm (E)] and the Aries part of the year. We've been having a steamy spell and people have been hot under the collar. A factor that brings grounded patience commences Tuesday morning. Ahead of that, though (Monday night), is the last of seven occurrences of the most difficult planetary stand-off of the decade. The impact is greater when other planets interact with it. We've had multiple instances of that on an ongoing basis, including the past few weeks, but not this week. The gentle salve won't work its magic immediately; there are hurts to address right off the bat Thursday, and it isn't easy to find supportive words then. Wait for Sunday afternoon to evening for that. They may include an apology for an outburst on Saturday. Tongues held in check Monday succumb to frustration and a flood of feelings Wednesday night, letting loose in what might be a tirade. Be on the lookout for projection then. In the midst of all this, a powerful Solar Eclipse New Moon Friday [2:36 am (P), 5:36 am (E)] sets us up for major hurts or healing.

MARCH 16-22 HIGHLIGHTS

Astro-Overview: *The last Uranus-Pluto square is Monday, with no other planets aspecting it. When the Moon aggravates them, it's very early in the mornings of Wednesday and Saturday. After an early morning square to Saturn Monday, Mercury tangoes with the Ceres-Neptune-Eris tangle of the past few weeks, from Tuesday to Thursday, with the Moon bumping into them Wednesday night. Mars also starts wading in that muck Saturday and Sunday (continuing until next Sunday). Venus enters Taurus Tuesday and promptly semisquares Chiron Thursday evening, rubbed by the Moon that morning. The Sun is sesquiquadrate Jupiter overnight Wednesday-Thursday but the honor of its last act in Pisces goes to the pre-dawn Solar Eclipse Friday in the last degree of the zodiac, just ahead of the spring equinox before sunset.*

Details: *Monday Mercury square Saturn, Uranus square Pluto; Tuesday Venus enters Taurus, Mercury semisquare Eris; Tuesday (P)/Wednesday (E) Mars sesquiquadrate Saturn; Wednesday Mercury conjunct Neptune; Wednesday (P)/Thursday (E) Sun sesquiquadrate Jupiter; Thursday Venus semisquare Chiron, Mercury semisquare Ceres; Friday Solar Eclipse New Moon, Sun enters Aries; Saturday Mars conjunct Eris; Sunday Mars semisquare Neptune, Mercury sextile Pluto*

  ▶ See p. 3 for meaning of Moon Void.

Don't compromise yourself.
You are all you've got.

Janis Joplin

Moon in Taurus • Void 7:25 am (P), 10:25 am (E)

23 MO 3

Persistence keeps you on task. You can accomplish a lot if you tackle work in series of short bursts. Stick to ongoing projects, though.

Moon Void in Taurus
Moon enters Gemini 6:22 am (P), 9:22 am (E)

24 TU 3 ★

Any tenderness and understanding present early fades quickly. Later, affection must be based on respect. Avoid difficult people tonight.

Moon in Gemini

25 WE 3

Inspiring talk and smart decisions this morning add force to the day's drive and ambition. This evening, superficial support fails to satisfy deeper yearnings.

Moon in Gemini • Void 5:35 am (P), 8:35 am (E)
Moon enters Cancer 12:45 pm (P), 3:45 pm (E)

26 TH 3

You're forward-leaning and able to hustle but need to leap a hurdle of conflicting values (whether within yourself or between you and someone else).

Moon in Cancer • First Quarter Moon

27 FR 2

A mood or impulse tonight could spoil what you achieved this afternoon with patience and practicality. Stick to your guns about what's important.

Moon in Cancer • Void 6:58 pm (P), 9:58 pm (E)
Moon enters Leo 10:48 pm (P)

28 SA 2

Mix-ups are likely this morning. Clarity is possible later, provided you slow down and try to keep feelings from dominating the conversation.

Moon in Leo (P), Void in Cancer (E)
Moon enters Leo 1:48 am (E)

29 SU 3

Be conscious of boundaries and rules to keep from overstepping lines, possibly due to enthusiasm or impatience. Lead by upright example.

Palm Sunday

MARCH 23-29 HIGHLIGHTS

We need a quiet break after last week's thundering crescendo! Take advantage of the calm to regroup and lick any wounds or press forward on projects that experienced a slow-down or setback. We're in the growth part of the lunar cycle and with several fairly good days in a row, you may be able to move your agenda along. If there is something you want to launch, midday Wednesday holds the most promise and even offers a little luck to go with creativity and resolve. If you owe someone an apology, Tuesday afternoon and Wednesday evening are good for that or for forgiving someone else. These times are also suitable for brainstorming solutions to problems. Although we're in a practical period about finances and relationships (see March 17 in the Star Pages), there can still be moments with problems in these areas. Monday evening, we might be too trusting or unrealistic. Thursday morning and Friday night, we could go overboard, expect too much or experience an imbalance. People in long-range liaisons will feel the downside of that distance. Those in relationships that are too close will long for more freedom. On the weekend, nurturing may feel like smothering. Watch what you say about it; the potential for misunderstandings is increased.

Astro-Overview: *Not much can compete astrologically with the intensity of last week's final Uranus-Pluto square and eclipse at the equinox! This week doesn't come close at all. Even the Moon's quick abrasive brushes with the Uranus-Pluto square (Tuesday morning and Friday night) are not complicated by interactions with other planets. The Sun has just one aspect, a trine to Saturn Wednesday, amplified by the Moon Tuesday afternoon. Mercury and Venus have a couple connections each: Mercury is conjunct Chiron Tuesday (squared by the Moon Wednesday evening) and sesquiquadrate Jupiter Sunday; Venus is sextile Neptune Tuesday and square Jupiter Friday (magnified by the Moon semisquare both Venus and Jupiter from their midpoint Thursday morning). A square between Mars and Ceres exact Sunday is in a brief T-square with the Moon Saturday night. With only a few aspects (see the short list below) and not all of them difficult, the week's day ratings show a lot of 3s, though no 4s or 5s. At least, it's an easier week than the past couple.*

Details: *Tuesday Venus sextile Neptune, Mercury conjunct Chiron; Wednesday Sun trine Saturn; Friday Venus square Jupiter; Sunday Mercury sesquiquadrate Jupiter, Mars square Ceres*

MAY

SU	M	TU	W	T	F	S
					1	2
3	4	5	6	7	8	9
10	11	12	13	14	15	16
17	18	19	20	21	22	23
24	25	26	27	28	29	30
31						

In spring, our fancy turns to love. The afternoon of March 24 is one of the best times this year for a marriage ceremony.

People are busy with their own affairs and focused on practical matters. Creative imagination might foster worries but is better used constructively.

Moon in Leo • Void 6:57 am (P), 9:57 am (E)

★ 3 MO 30

This morning, a fortunate turn of events brings a healing or improvement. Midday we're hopping and productive. Tonight everyone seems to be critical.

Moon Void in Leo • Moon enters Virgo 11:12 am (P), 2:12 pm (E)

★ 2 TU 31

Be selective with whom you vent complaints. Someone may be willing to help but others don't have the time or find it in their interest to bother.

April Fool's Day

Moon in Virgo

2 WE 01

Early in the day, progress is achieved through honesty, candor and wisdom. Empathy blends with kindness. Later, minds clamp shut and humor wilts.

Moon in Virgo • Void 2:01 am (P), 5:01 am (E)

3 TH 02

Even if you and someone else don't see eye-to-eye on values, you can still strive politely for a win-win compromise and maintain a friendly alliance.

Good Friday

Moon Void in Virgo • Moon enters Libra 12:07 am (P), 3:07 am (E)

★ 3 FR 03

Some may vacillate, but circumstances now require action (probably quickly) and force a decision. Check in with your gut instincts.

Passover begins

Moon in Libra • Lunar Eclipse Full Moon (Seed Moon) Void 8:58 am (P), 11:58 am (E)

★ 1 SA 04

If your personal creed clashes with society's conventions, assess which hurts more: to dig in your heels and stick to your principles or to yield.

Easter, Orthodox Palm Sunday

Moon Void in Libra • Moon enters Scorpio 12:04 pm (P), 3:04 pm (E)

P 1 SU 05

Change is in the air! Spring began with an eclipse New Moon just ahead of the equinox (see two weeks ago). Now we have the Full Moon of that cycle, which is also an eclipse [Saturday 5:06 am (P), 8:06 am (E)], coming in a week with three planets going into new signs. Just as the planet of thinking and communicating accelerates Monday, entering a quick and impatient sign, the planet of action downshifts Tuesday from its brisk-paced home sign to a mellow stroll through territory where we take our sweet time. Each of these influences lasts only two or three weeks and they balance one another out fairly well. The other sign change will last for more than four months, beginning Friday when the dwarf planet that shows how we nurture and support one another moves from a strict sign with high standards to an area that encourages developing uniqueness and individuality. Meanwhile, the planet of relationships and finances indicates improvements in those areas this week, especially Wednesday night (as long as there is no pressure for a speedy decision then) and Saturday morning, when a special lucky triangle sparks psychic ability. This can draw partners closer together and help anyone handle money matters using visualization and intention to advantage.

MARCH 30-APRIL 05 HIGHLIGHTS

Astro-Overview: *Three planets change signs this week: Mercury enters Aries Monday (after finishing Pisces sextile Ceres that morning), Mars enters Taurus Tuesday and Ceres enters Aquarius Friday. Mercury is semisquare Venus Wednesday and trine Saturn Thursday. Venus is trine Pluto Monday and sextile Chiron Wednesday, then Mars is semisquare Chiron Sunday. The Nodes are in the spotlight. The Sun (Monday) and Mercury (Saturday) join the South Node. The Moon passes the North Node Friday. With the Full Moon Saturday on the Node axis, it's an eclipse AND in a T-square with the Uranus-Pluto square (still in orb another month). The Sun squares Pluto Sunday and joins Uranus the next day. A bonus is Tuesday's Jupiter-Chiron biquintile.*

Details: *Monday Venus trine Pluto, Mercury sextile Ceres, Mercury enters Aries; Monday (P)/Tuesday (E) Sun opposite North Node & conjunct South Node; Tuesday Mars enters Taurus, Jupiter biquintile Chiron; Wednesday Mercury semisquare Venus, Venus sextile Chiron; Thursday Mercury trine Saturn, Sun trine Jupiter; Friday Ceres enters Aquarius, Venus quintile Neptune; Saturday Lunar Eclipse Full Moon; Saturday (P)/Sunday (E) Mercury opposite North Node & conjunct South Node; Sunday Sun square Pluto, Mars semisquare Chiron*

Find out who you are and do it on purpose.
Dolly Parton

MARCH								APRIL					
SU	M	TU	W	T	F	S		SU	M	TU	W	T	F	S
1	2	3	4	5	6	7					1	2	3	4
8	9	10	11	12	13	14		5	6	7	8	9	10	11
15	16	17	18	19	20	21		12	13	14	15	16	17	18
22	23	24	25	26	27	28		19	20	21	22	23	24	25
29	30	31						26	27	28	29	30		

Moon in Scorpio

06 MO 4

Bright minds and high energy are great for meetings, generating ideas and allocating resources. Don't push too far too fast or get ahead of yourself.

Moon in Scorpio • Void 1:42 pm (P), 4:42 pm (E)
Moon enters Sagittarius 10:08 pm (P)

07 TU 1

Sharing and fairness are issues, ruffling feathers between even close mates and sparking disagreements. Know the facts before you state a case.

Moon in Sagittarius (P), Void in Scorpio (E)
Moon enters Sagittarius 1:08 am (E)

08 WE 2 ★

When all of us want to assert our individuality and get our way, it won't work. It's possible to be good-natured in figuring out an orderly plan.

Moon in Sagittarius • Void 10:42 am (P), 1:42 pm (E)

09 TH 2

Respect isn't automatically offered due to position or rank. Talking through differences and listening to all viewpoints bring solutions closer.

Moon Void in Sagittarius • Moon enters Capricorn 5:47 am (P), 8:47 am (E)

10 FR 4

We are well-grounded, practical, trusting and extraordinarily patient today and tonight. It's a good time to use vision for long-range planning.

Orthodox Good Friday

Moon in Capricorn • Third Quarter Moon

11 SA 2 ★

A confrontation is needed to straighten out a situation. It's a chance to stand up for yourself. Handle it with humor and empathy. Discuss what matters.

Moon in Capricorn • Void 1:15 am (P), 4:15 am (E)
Moon enters Aquarius 10:44 am (P), 1:44 pm (E)

12 SU 3 ★

Heads and hearts are in sync this morning and it's easy to act on beliefs. Later, benefits come via friends or groups, especially with a good leader.

Orthodox Easter

APRIL 06-12 HIGHLIGHTS

The ancient Greek maxim, "Know thyself" (inscribed above the gate to the Temple of Delphi) is perennially sage advice and an appropriate theme for this week. It has sometimes been interpreted as an admonition to know your place, but more often as advocating the benefits of assessing one's strengths (the better to leverage them) and weaknesses (to mitigate those). Whether such self-awareness is achieved through introspection or interaction, surprising revelations are in store if we have open ears and minds. Monday through Wednesday, situations demonstrate what we need to alter in our lives in order to be more authentic and bring out our uniqueness (even if that clashes with others' standards or traditional values). Thursday and Friday, expressing our true thoughts and feelings can facilitate greater responsibility for them and to others, and make evident where boundaries need firming up. A tense turning point comes Saturday with the Third Quarter Moon showing us "shoulds" and "should nots" as we round a bend to try a different heading. Also on the weekend, a fabulous triangle of beneficial factors is good for strategies to improve finances or relationships, as well as offering grand ideas about travel, education or legal matters.

Astro-Overview: *Mercury and the Sun dominate the week. Mercury is trine Jupiter Monday (as the Sun was April 2). They join the Uranus-Pluto square, boosted Saturday as the Moon passes Pluto. The Sun squared Pluto last Sunday and conjuncts Uranus Monday. Mercury follows suit on Tuesday and Wednesday. They're both sesquiquadrate Saturn Thursday, ahead of their conjunction that night, halfway between two Mercury Retrogrades. On the weekend, first Mercury (Saturday) and then the Sun (Sunday) conjunct Eris. Venus enters Gemini Saturday and quickly forms a Quintile Triangle with Chiron and Jupiter (which turns Direct Wednesday), and is sesquiquadrate Pluto. Mars has a lone sextile to Neptune Sunday.*

Details: *Monday Mercury trine Jupiter, Sun conjunct Uranus; Monday (P)/ Tuesday (E) Venus sesquiquadrate North Node & semisquare South Node; Tuesday Mercury square Pluto; Wednesday Mercury conjunct Uranus, Jupiter turns Direct; Thursday Sun & Mercury sesquiquadrate Saturn; Thursday (P)/ Friday (E) Mercury conjunct Sun; Saturday Mercury conjunct Eris, Venus enters Gemini, Mercury semisquare Neptune, Venus sesquiquadrate Pluto, Venus quintile Jupiter; Sunday Mars sextile Neptune, Venus quintile Chiron, Sun conjunct Eris; Sunday (P) Venus semisquare Uranus*

MAY

SU	M	TU	W	T	F	S
					1	2
3	4	5	6	7	8	9
10	11	12	13	14	15	16
17	18	19	20	21	22	23
24	25	26	27	28	29	30
31						

At most New Moons, the Moon and Sun interact strongly with one or more planets. Failing that, there is usually some kind of major planetary pattern present. The April 18 New Moon is a bland exception.

Surrounded by surprises (not all bad), you can try to assert your will but forces beyond your control are at work. Turn to comrades for comfort or aid.

Moon in Aquarius

3 MO 13

You may think you have the answers but don't rush into anything. More solid information will emerge soon. Meanwhile, focus on faith, not fear.

Moon in Aquarius • Void 12:45 pm (P), 3:45 pm (E)
Moon enters Pisces 1:12 pm (P), 4:12 pm (E)

★ 2 TU 14

Who can you trust? Yourself? "Informed sources?" A direct inquiry yields an answer, though it might not be to your liking. Knowledge is power.

Moon in Pisces • Void 2:37 pm (P), 5:37 pm (E)

3 WE 15

Actions speak louder than words in the help or healing we give or receive. We feel a push for change even if we can't make it happen just yet.

Holocaust Remembrance Day

Moon Void in Pisces • Moon enters Aries 2:00 pm (P), 5:00 pm (E)

★ 2 TH 16

Too much, too little – there's some of each today. We try to take the easy way out this morning, but a turn of events by tonight requires more effort.

Moon in Aries

2 FR 17

Good thing we feel quite self-reliant; we can't be sure what we'll get if we turn to others. Most people are entrenched in their own struggles.

Moon in Aries • New Moon • Void 11:57 am (P), 2:57 pm (E)
Moon enters Taurus 2:31 pm (P), 5:31 pm (E)

2 SA 18

Something goes over the top today. Don't try to handle it all on your own. Assistance is there but you have to ask for it. You could offer to reciprocate.

Moon in Taurus • Void 4:07 pm (P), 7:07 pm (E)

★ P 3 SU 19

APRIL 13-19 HIGHLIGHTS

Astro-Overview: *The Neptune-Eris semisquare is still in place, with the Sun and Venus (heading toward a semisquare May 27) scraping against them. The Sun, conjunct Eris last Sunday, semisquares Neptune Monday night. Venus is semisquare Eris Saturday and square Neptune Sunday. Venus opens the week semisquare Uranus. Ahead of the Ceres-Saturn sextile Sunday, Venus is trine Ceres Monday and opposite Saturn Tuesday night (right after the Moon forms a T-square with them). Venus ends the week saluting the Nodes Sunday. Meanwhile Mercury enters Taurus Tuesday, is square Ceres and semisquare Chiron Thursday and sextile Neptune Sunday. Mars has only one aspect this week: square Jupiter Friday. Pluto quietly turns Retrograde Thursday with no tight aspects.*

Details: *Monday (E) Venus semisquare Uranus; Monday Venus trine Ceres; Monday (P)/Tuesday (E) Sun semisquare Neptune; Tuesday Mercury enters Taurus; Tuesday (P)/Wednesday (E) Venus opposite Saturn; Thursday Mercury square Ceres, Mercury semisquare Chiron, Pluto turns Retrograde; Friday Mars square Jupiter; Saturday Venus semisquare Eris, Mercury semisextile Venus; Sunday Mercury sextile Neptune, Ceres sextile Saturn, Venus square Neptune, Venus trine North Node & sextile South Node*

The New Moon Saturday [11:57 am (P), 2:57 pm (E)] is noteworthy only for its insignificance. We could be in for a quieter month in the four-week cycle that follows, when most of the planetary interactions are gentle ones. But first, there are issues to handle on financial and/ or relationship fronts. These areas are subject to craziness as the week begins and chaos and confusion as the week ends. In between, we try to achieve some clarity but that doesn't go too well (especially Tuesday night). It can help to look at the big picture and take a long-term approach, seeing where we can simplify rather than complicate. We also need to enlist support from friends or a group and pump each other up. Confidence is not at a peak. In fact, we may have fearful dreams that expose insecurity Monday night or Wednesday morning. An open chat about what worries us Wednesday evening may be very healing. On the weekend, there's a strong inclination to try to do too much. Optimism argues that we can manage it all; practicality asks, "Really?!" We're not thinking or moving as quickly as we do ordinarily. The planet of the mind and the planet of action are both in slow signs now and we'll perform best by doing just one thing at a time. Forget multi-tasking.

▶ See p. 3 for meaning of Moon Void.

I'm extraordinarily patient provided I get my own way in the end.
Margaret Thatcher

	APRIL							MAY					
SU	M	TU	W	T	F	S	SU	M	TU	W	T	F	S
				1	2	3	4						1	2
5	6	7	8	9	10	11	3	4	5	6	7	8	9
12	13	14	15	16	17	18	10	11	12	13	14	15	16
19	20	21	22	23	24	25	17	18	19	20	21	22	23
26	27	28	29	30			24	25	26	27	28	29	30
							31						

Moon Void in Taurus • Moon enters Gemini 4:28 pm (P), 7:28 pm (E)

20 MO 2 ★

The week has a languid start. Most of today, we'd rather amble than scamper, until evening, when the unexpected requires a nimble response.

Patriots' Day (MA & ME), Sun enters Taurus

Moon in Gemini • Void 10:38 pm (P)

21 TU 3

A little mayhem mars the morning but by afternoon, we're happily engaged interpersonally, tackling tasks and making tracks with aplomb and gusto.

Moon in Gemini, Void (P) • Void 1:38 am (E)
Moon enters Cancer 9:25 pm (P)

22 WE 4 P

Act from the heart decisively and you'll make a positive difference. However, with the Moon Void all day, it's not the time to begin something new.

Earth Day, Administrative Professionals Day

Moon in Cancer (P), Void in Gemini (E)
Moon enters Cancer 12:25 am (E)

23 TH 3

Adjustments are needed to better balance care of yourself and attention to a partner. Trust your inner voice or guidance from a higher power.

Moon in Cancer • Void 10:04 am (P), 1:04 pm (E)

24 FR 3

Strive to stay calm early amidst bumps and surprise. Smart solutions arise this afternoon. Tonight, we're back to jarring uncertainty.

Arbor Day

Moon Void in Cancer • Moon enters Leo 6:13 am (P),
9:13 am (E) • First Quarter Moon

25 SA 1

Stubbornness stands in the way of advancement and an overblown ego spoils fun. Flexibility, though not easy to achieve, is the saving grace.

Moon in Leo

26 SU 3

Warm hearts, camaraderie and joviality blend into a delightful mix, perfect for a party or artsy activity. Watch out for impulsive spending, though.

APRIL 20-26 HIGHLIGHTS

Taurus time starts with the Sun's entrance into the mid-spring sector of the zodiac early Monday. In keeping with Earth Day Wednesday, this earth sign is concerned with the material realm, values, objects and money, all of which have extra sparkle Tuesday afternoon and all day Wednesday. That's a good day for shopping and investments, too (especially since the Moon is now in the growth portion of its cycle). Projects requiring a lot of mental energy, organization, backing and stamina will see progress this week, particularly on Tuesday and Wednesday. However, the scope of work may need to be trimmed as the week begins; we tend to take on more than is practical. Innovation and out-of-the-box thinking come into play Friday, when they might enhance an enterprise, as well as Saturday, but they may not produce desired outcomes. There is some difficulty finding either the assistance or resources to bring ideas to fruition and possibly a problem with leadership (such as a lack thereof or an intrusion of a personal conflict of interest). Thursday evening is a fine time to enjoy entertainment, the arts or something spiritual, perhaps with family members. Sunday is wonderful for socializing, fun and creativity, despite minor communication mix-ups.

Astro-Overview: *Venus has a lovely week. The Sun enters Taurus, the sign Venus rules, Monday, increasing a Venusian influence. Venus is sextile Jupiter Wednesday and sextile Uranus Sunday, with the Moon boosting them that evening as well as Tuesday late day into evening. (Jupiter is still within 5 degrees of a trine to Uranus, exact 3/3 and 6/22.) Mars is trine Pluto Tuesday, just ahead of Mercury's trine to Pluto and conjunction to Mars Wednesday. Friday afternoon, Mercury is sextile Chiron, magnified hours earlier by the Moon sextile Mercury and trine Chiron. Mercury begins the week with a square to Jupiter Monday night and ends it in a tangle with the Nodes. A Ceres-Chiron semisquare (exact Friday morning) is amplified by the Sun square Ceres and semisquare Chiron Saturday, all of which the Moon aggravates that night.*

Details: *Monday Sun enters Taurus; Monday (P)/Tuesday (E) Mercury square Jupiter, North Node quincunx Neptune; Tuesday Mars trine Pluto; Wednesday Mercury trine Pluto, Venus sextile Jupiter, Mercury conjunct Mars; Friday Ceres semisquare Chiron, Mercury sextile Chiron; Saturday Sun semisquare Chiron, Sun sesquiquadrate Ceres; Sunday Venus sextile Uranus, Mercury sesquiquadrate North Node & semisquare South Node*

JUNE

SU	M	TU	W	T	F	S
	1	2	3	4	5	6
7	8	9	10	11	12	13
14	15	16	17	18	19	20
21	22	23	24	25	26	27
28	29	30				

Appropriately in the fecund spring season, the dwarf planet of fertility, Ceres, is very busy the second half of April (see the Star Pages).

April-May

Friendly congeniality might trump strong-willed and obstinate egotism. If not, progress is impeded. This evening, humility finally creeps in.

Moon in Leo • Void 7:12 am (P), 10:12 am (E)
Moon enters Virgo 6:07 pm (P), 9:07 pm (E)

★ **1 MO 27**

Early in the day, personal concerns dominate. Soon empathy and a helpful attitude draw us into selfless service. It's a good day to attend to health.

International Astronomy Day

Moon in Virgo

3 TU 28

Adaptability facilitates making changes, yet values must play a key role in decisions. Our feet are on the ground, tamping down over-optimism, keeping us real.

Moon in Virgo

2 WE 29

We encourage one another and with cooperation, we find ways for everyone to benefit from teamwork. This evening is great for socializing.

Moon in Virgo • Void 5:23 am (P), 8:23 am (E)
Moon enters Libra 7:03 am (P), 10:03 am (E)

★ **4 TH 30**

We walk a tightrope balancing self-interest versus others' requirements. We might bring humor to the process early but that evaporates under stress.

May Day, Beltane

Moon in Libra

1 FR 01

This morning, we're convivial but the mood may not last all day. We could feel put upon by needy requests or perhaps just prefer our own company.

Moon in Libra • Void 7:03 am (P), 10:03 am (E)
Moon enters Scorpio 6:47 pm (P), 9:47 pm (E)

2 SA 02

Feelings go to extremes and repressed emotions may erupt before the night is over. Gentleness and consideration smooth the way, but only a little.

Buddha's birthday observed

Moon in Scorpio • Full Moon (Hare Moon)

★ **2 SU 03**

Affection and caring at times seem to require a reality check or revelation. As Hamlet said, "I must be cruel, only to be kind." That's a theme this week, particularly Tuesday evening and Wednesday, with the potential for a follow-up or add-on Sunday, when a Full Moon [8:42 pm (P), 11:42 pm (E)] brings a culmination. Such action may be seen as necessary to bring about a healing or improvement, and can successfully alter someone's heading, as evidenced Saturday. Affirmation of a person's individuality, if done as nicely as possible Monday or Tuesday, will likely pay off in loving dividends Thursday to Sunday next week (May 7-10). Compassion is strong Wednesday (with another dose Sunday) and combines with patience to point us in the direction of better relationships. A nine-week focus on communication begins Thursday and immediately we're thrust into situations that must be approached delicately. Issues center on confidential information, boundaries and respect. People want to follow their unique path but need to see where doing so could step on others. Knowing the lines not to cross takes a frank discussion. Friday is the most difficult day in this regard, but at least people will feel what it's like in another person's shoes then.

APRIL 27-MAY 03 HIGHLIGHTS

Astro-Overview: *Last week, Ceres was semisquare Chiron. This week, Venus steps into their fray Tuesday night into Wednesday, aggravated by the Moon Wednesday afternoon and Sunday. Mars is nicer to Chiron, with a sextile early Tuesday (boosted by the Moon Wednesday afternoon), but not so nice to the Nodes (sesquiquadrate/ semisquare) Saturday. After entering Gemini Thursday, Mercury is sesquiquadrate Pluto Friday, and semisquare Uranus and opposite Saturn in Sunday's wee hours, activating the Saturn-Uranus sesquiquadrate (exact overnight Sunday). The Moon irritates all four Friday afternoon and evening. The other aspects this week are Ceres quintile Uranus Monday, Sun sextile Neptune and quincunx North Node Wednesday (forming a Finger of God) and Venus sextile Eris Friday.*

Details: *Monday Ceres quintile Uranus; Tuesday Mars sextile Chiron; Tuesday (P)/Wednesday (E) Venus square Chiron; Wednesday Sun quincunx North Node, Venus sesquiquadrate Ceres, Sun sextile Neptune; Thursday Mercury enters Gemini; Friday Mercury sesquiquadrate Pluto, Venus sextile Eris; Saturday Mars sesquiquadrate North Node & semisquare South Node; Saturday (P)/Sunday (E) Mercury semisquare Uranus; Sunday Mercury opposite Saturn; Sunday (P) Saturn sesquiquadrate Uranus*

You must first have a lot of patience to learn to have patience.

Stanislaw Lec

Moon in Scorpio • Void 6:49 pm (P), 9:49 pm (E)

04 MO 2 ★

Floodgates open and feelings pour out. What was private is revealed, yet the result could be healing. Still, anger festers long after dark.

Moon Void in Scorpio • Moon enters Sagittarius
4:13 am (P), 7:13 am (E)

05 TU 2

Boundaries are breached amidst chaotic miscommunication. A sweet apology is a glossy frosting that can't make a cake of discontent taste good.

National Teacher Day, Cinco de Mayo

Moon in Sagittarius

06 WE 3

Optimism and a pleasant surprise work to dissipate dissatisfaction. Friends or neighbors add cheer. Still, there may be a discouraging word.

Moon in Sagittarius • Void 10:51 am (P), 1:51 pm (E)
Moon enters Capricorn 11:16 am (P), 2:16 pm (E)

07 TH 2 ★

This morning, too much is too much! This afternoon, self-concern is disconcerting. Tonight, heads turn in a different direction and hearts open.

National Day of Prayer (U.S.)

Moon in Capricorn

08 FR 3 ★

Manners may constrain irritation simmering sub-surface. Nobility or pride helps some rise above volatile emotions; others are aided by a loved one.

Moon in Capricorn • Void 1:35 pm (P), 4:35 pm (E)
Moon enters Aquarius 4:22 pm (P), 7:22 pm (E)

09 SA 2 ★

Clarity seems nearly impossible this morning; maybe fear stands in the way. Later, people become better grounded and are more resilient.

Moon in Aquarius

10 SU 4

Everyone is gregarious and open to ideas. Communication and fondness flow easily, with well-balanced give and take. Laughter and smiles abound.

Mother's Day

MAY 04-10 HIGHLIGHTS

This week, reverberations rattle from the Full Moon last Sunday. People are riled up, the likely issues being values and principles or situations that have gone too far and need to be dialed back. Power trips may be in play and there could be legal or international implications. The ugliest time is Tuesday morning, when exaggeration may make things seem worse than they are. Friday evening, there's a discordant refrain. Discussions will help, especially if they involve how needs are (or are not) being met. Communication is mixed throughout the week (and particularly jumbled Saturday morning). Though Wednesday sees some improvement, an inequity still stings. Thursday afternoon, a warmer touch arrives on the scene as the planet of affection enters the sign of caring and maternal love, increasing everyone's urge to nurture over the next four weeks. Immediately, it creates a special harmonious triangle Thursday through Saturday with the planet of uniqueness and surprises and the dwarf planet related to support and growth. This is the perfect formula for random acts of kindness. The Moon joins the triangle briefly Sunday morning for a grand finale on the best day of the week. Everyone gets along. You couldn't ask for a nicer Mother's Day.

Astro-Overview: *Two titans clash overnight Sunday to Monday in a sesquiquadrate between Saturn and Uranus (see last week and the Star Pages). Their intensity spikes as the Moon passes Saturn Tuesday morning and opposes Mercury that afternoon. Extremes emerge with the Sun square Jupiter Monday and trine Pluto in the wee hours Wednesday (magnified by the Moon joining Pluto Friday afternoon) and Venus semisquare Jupiter Wednesday afternoon. Mercury has friendly aspects with Ceres Wednesday evening and the Nodes Thursday night, but a harsh semisquare with Eris Thursday afternoon and a square with Neptune Saturday morning, scraped by the Moon. After Venus enters Cancer Thursday afternoon, it forms a Quintile Triangle through Saturday with Uranus and Ceres (which were quintile 4/27). The Moon passes Ceres Sunday morning, boosting the QT and making a Grand Trine/Kite with the Nodes and Mercury.*

Details: *Monday (E) Saturn sesquiquadrate Uranus; Monday Sun square Jupiter; Wednesday Sun trine Pluto, Venus semisquare Jupiter, Mercury trine Ceres; Thursday Mercury semisquare Eris, Venus enters Cancer, Mercury trine North Node & sextile South Node, Venus quintile Uranus; Friday (P)/ Saturday (E) Venus biquintile Ceres; Saturday Mercury square Neptune*

JUNE

SU	M	TU	W	T	F	S
		1	2	3	4	5	6
7	8	9	10	11	12	13
14	15	16	17	18	19	20
21	22	23	24	25	26	27
28	29	30				

Echoing four weeks ago, Venus steps into a new sign and promptly forms a fortunate configuration. Other planets form the same type of pattern days later. (See the Star Pages for May 7-9 & May 15-18.)

There's some uncertainty and a lack of confidence to start the day, but we get our mojo back quickly. Tonight, stress and anxiety breed friction.

Moon in Aquarius • Third Quarter Moon • Void 3:36 am (P),
6:36 am (E) • Moon enters Pisces 7:53 pm (P), 10:53 pm (E)

★ 2 MO 11

Staying on track is difficult due to tangents and distractions. It's easier if you forego going solo and focus on something or someone other than yourself.

Moon in Pisces

3 TU 12

Catch the wave of positive imagination early. Then, try to stay upbeat or at least steady on your feet as minor interpersonal mishaps rock your boat.

Moon in Pisces • Void 9:55 am (P), 12:55 pm (E)
Moon enters Aries 10:13 pm (P)

2 WE 13

Get in the driver's seat and floor it. Today is all about going after what you want. Until tonight, when you remember you're not the only one around.

Moon in Aries (P), Moon Void in Pisces (E)
Moon enters Aries 1:13 am (E)

2 TH 14

The day starts erratically, with disruptions into afternoon. This evening, wishful thinking may be misdirected. If aimed correctly, it works like magic.

Moon in Aries • Void 5:03 am (P), 8:03 am (E)

★ 2 FR 15

A hug helps hurt feelings this morning and a friend may need a warm pat this afternoon. Tonight is delightful, until very late, when tempers flare.

Armed Forces Day

Moon Void in Aries • Moon enters Taurus 12:02 am (P), 3:02 am (E)

★ 3 SA 16

Patience and kindness are the way out if stubborn selfishness blocks cooperation. This evening, we seek self-indulgent creature comforts.

Moon in Taurus • New Moon (P) • Void 9:13 pm (P)

2 SU 17

MAY 11-17 HIGHLIGHTS

The busiest planet this week is the one associated with action, aggression and self-assertion. Monday, it enters a new sign, initiating a six-week spell of quick thinking, fast talking and agile movement. By Tuesday, it brings pressure for change and/or power struggles. Thursday to Friday, this planet signals a stand-off with someone in an authority position or a frustrating obstacle to long-range goals. Friday to Saturday, it opens doors and offers luck, healing, improvement or solutions in travel, education, legal matters or marital affairs. Friday morning, late Saturday and next Monday, it increases klutziness and accident potential. Slow down and pay extra attention when engaged in any form of on-the-ground motion: walking, running, biking, skating, jogging, driving, even dancing! Another emphasized astrological factor is the axis that indicates where we're coming from and heading to. You might experience several shifts across the course of the week in your idea of a desirable or wise direction. The most potent or important time for a course correction is midday Thursday, with the runner-up late Sunday night just ahead of the New Moon. Saturday night is sweet for romance, fruitful for creativity, enjoyable for entertainment.

Astro-Overview: *For the second week in a row, we have a Quintile Triangle, this time Mars with Jupiter and Chiron, Friday to Saturday. And Saturday, the marriage asteroid joins Jupiter. Like Venus last week, the quickest planet (Mars) forms the pattern shortly after entering a new sign (Gemini, Monday). But Mars has difficulties this week: it's sesquiquadrate Pluto Tuesday, opposite Saturn overnight Thursday and semisquare Uranus early Sunday. The Nodes see a lot of action: linking to Ceres Tuesday and the Sun Wednesday, then in a T-square with Venus Thursday. The Moon passes the South Node that afternoon, activating these aspects. The Sun has a nice sextile with Chiron Monday and Venus has a lovely trine with Neptune Saturday. The New Moon ends the week - in Pacific Time (see next week).*

Details: *Monday Sun sextile Chiron, Mars enters Gemini; Tuesday Mars sesquiquadrate Pluto, North Node trine Ceres & South Node sextile Ceres; Wednesday Sun sesquiquadrate North Node & semisquare South Node; Thursday Venus square North & South Node; Thursday (P)/Friday (E) Mars opposite Saturn; Friday Mars quintile Jupiter; Friday (P)/Saturday (E) Mars quintile Chiron; Saturday Venus trine Neptune, Juno conjunct Jupiter; Sunday Mars semisquare Uranus*

 ▶ See p. 3 for meaning of Moon Void.

The senses deceive from time to time, and it is prudent never to trust wholly those who have deceived us even once.

Rene Descartes

Moon in Taurus, Void (P) • New Moon (E) • Void 12:13 am (E)
Moon enters Gemini 2:27 am (P), 5:27 am (E)

18 MO 2 MR ★

Communication is an uphill battle, aside from a short respite around suppertime. Left-brain logic is lacking but right brain intuition is brilliant!

Victoria Day (Canada)

Moon in Gemini • Void 10:57 am (P), 1:57 pm (E)

19 TU 3 MR

You'll do your best work early, when a group or colleague has your back. After that, you're on your own and might even feel abandoned.

Moon Void in Gemini • Moon enters in Cancer
6:56 am (P), 9:56 am (E)

20 WE 1 MR

This morning serves up a big cup of feelings, mostly unpalatable. By tonight, you decide on a different menu, either on your own or with a loved one's help.

Moon in Cancer • Void 5:36 pm (P), 8:36 pm (E)

21 TH 1 P MR ★

Something's got to go, whether material, attitudinal or emotional. Move on, willingly. If not, choices will be made for you "for your own good."

Sun enters Gemini

Moon Void in Cancer • Moon enters Leo 2:42 pm (P), 5:42 pm (E)

22 FR 2 MR

Somebody is peddling a good story about going down a better road. Maybe it's you. The outlook is brightening, but clouds are still on the horizon.

Moon in Leo

23 SA 2 MR

Many people have their blinders on, seeing only their side, their needs, their pain. They're good at articulating it, too. So why not ask for what you want?

Moon in Leo • Void 3:50 am (P), 6:50 am (E)

24 SU 2 MR

It's a good day to enjoy a hobby, sports or entertainment with friends or your circle of nurturing supporters, as long as there's no ambitious agenda.

Shavou'ot, Pentecost

MAY 18-24 HIGHLIGHTS

The Taurus New Moon is just past midnight Monday (E) [Sunday 9:13 pm (P); Monday 12:13 am (E)]. Thankfully, a central trait of this sign is patience, and we'll need a lot of it! The New Moon ushers in a six-week period of an ongoing interplanetary abrasion that indicates difficulties with self-approval or with relationships, possibly due to ego or a conflict in values. (See Star Pages for May 27.) There will be numerous times when confidence, or its absence, makes or breaks interactions. Each week brings variations according to whatever planets are contacted by the main culprits. This week, there are two. The first relates to power, sharing, intimacy and letting go. The prime time of impact is Thursday. The second is associated with boundaries, maturity, responsibilities and respect, also strongly in effect during the day Thursday and again Friday evening. During the first half of these six weeks, the communication planet compounds our challenges by backtracking, which inclines people to ruminate in their internal dialog without expressing their thoughts externally. An argumentative edge further gums up the works Monday and again Saturday. We hardly get a break all week, aside from a brief window of less stress Tuesday morning.

Astro-Overview: *The main feature of the New Moon Monday (E) is the Moon and Sun semisquare Venus, ruler of the New Moon's sign, Taurus. Across the week, these three tussle with Saturn and Pluto (approaching their June 20 semisquare). Thursday, the Sun is sesquiquadrate Pluto and Venus is opposite Pluto. The Moon passes Venus, amplifying these aspects that day. Also Thursday, the Sun enters Gemini and Jupiter is quincunx Pluto, part of Fingers of God June 2-8. Obviously, Thursday is the most intense day this week! Friday night is tough, too, when the Moon prods the Sun's opposition to Saturn. Within a few hours, Venus is sesquiquadrate Saturn. Meanwhile Mercury turns Retrograde Monday for a backtrack in the sign it rules, Gemini (see Star Pages), and Jupiter is biquintile Chiron, also on Monday. The other aspects this week involve Mars: harmonizing with the Nodes Friday, semisquare Eris Saturday and trine Ceres Sunday.*

Details: *Monday Jupiter biquintile Chiron, Mercury turns Retrograde; Thursday Sun enters Gemini, Jupiter quincunx Pluto, Sun sesquiquadrate Pluto, Venus opposite Pluto; Friday Mars trine North Node & sextile South Node, Sun opposite Saturn; Saturday Venus sesquiquadrate Saturn, Mars semisquare Eris; Sunday Mars trine Ceres*

JULY

SU	M	TU	W	T	F	S
			1	2	3	4
5	6	7	8	9	10	11
12	13	14	15	16	17	18
19	20	21	22	23	24	25
26	27	28	29	30	31	

There's no tougher Mercury Retrograde than when it's in a sign that it rules. Such is the case during the backtrack in Gemini from May 18 to June 11 (see Star Pages).

May

Something crazy or unpredictable is afoot. Keep a loose schedule; social plans could change. By tonight, you may be exhausted, at least mentally.

Memorial Day (U.S.)

Moon Void in Leo • Moon enters Virgo 1:52 am (P)
4:52 am (E) • First Quarter Moon

MR P 1 MO 25

Appreciating cleanliness and order drives many to tidy up their surroundings or repair possessions. Others feel moved to provide kind service.

Moon in Virgo • Void 7:21 pm (P), 10:21 pm (E)

MR 3 TU 26

Discussing finances or a relationship can bring about improvement, although you may have to swallow your pride. Take responsibility for your part.

Moon Void in Virgo • Moon enters Libra 2:42 pm (P), 5:42 pm (E)

★ MR 3 WE 27

We're on track, moving in the right direction. Cooperation is at hand and fruitful ideas emerge in brainstorming. A great day for meetings or socializing!

Moon in Libra

MR 4 TH 28

Self-doubt could easily sabotage you or that task may fall to someone disruptive and discordant. Either way, projection or deception makes matters worse.

Moon in Libra • Void 1:20 pm (P), 4:20 pm (E)

MR P 1 FR 29

We move between hurt and healing and may experience an emotional yo-yo. We should receive adequate support but probably have to provide some, too.

Moon Void in Libra • Moon enters Scorpio 2:34 am (P), 5:34 am (E)

MR 3 SA 30

Whether you feel down or put down, see this as an opportunity to focus on possibilities instead of roadblocks. Watch out for squabbles tonight.

Orthodox Pentecost

Moon in Scorpio

MR 1 SU 31

MAY 25-31 HIGHLIGHTS

From May 21 to June 21, we have a trio of planets in Gemini, a sign of conversations, socializing and flitting about locally. The Sun is there along with Gemini's ruling planet, Mercury (visiting longer than usual due to its Retrograde), and another quick planet that loves speed and action. Think of the song Lot of Livin To Do from Bye Bye Birdie: "places to go, people to see." There's so much that interests us and we want to experience it all! As we zip around in a hurry, we need to watch out for accident potential, which is high Monday and made worse by an additional danger of spacing out or being sidetracked. The second peril is present again all day and night Friday (the toughest day this week), as well as Sunday morning. Swiftness alone is risky Wednesday morning and Thursday afternoon, although at this latter time, a positive pattern in place should afford some protection. Being short with people and spending impulsively or unwisely are problematic Monday and Friday. Friday and Sunday, those with a good nature may be imposed upon by others, and lovers may experience misunderstandings. However, it's easy to reassure one another Tuesday evening and midday Thursday. Remember to stop and smell the roses once in a while!

Astro-Overview: *Venus and the Sun are semisquare Wednesday, scraping against other planets all week. The Sun semisquares and Venus squares Uranus Monday, exaggerated by the First Quarter Moon. Friday, they gang up on Eris (Venus, square; the Sun, semisquare). Mercury passes Mars Wednesday on its way to semisquare Venus and conjunct the Sun Saturday. Since it's Retrograde, Mercury is square Neptune Friday, copied by the Sun Sunday as Venus semisquares Neptune. Mercury is semisquare Eris then. Mars, a little ahead of the Sun, squares Neptune Monday. It was trine Ceres last Sunday. First Mercury and then the Sun trine Ceres Saturday, on either side of their conjunction. The other links this week are positive: Venus trine Chiron Wednesday and the Sun trine and sextile the Nodes Thursday.*

Details: *Monday Sun semisquare Uranus, Venus square Uranus, Mars square Neptune; Wednesday Mercury conjunct Mars, Venus semisquare Sun, Venus trine Chiron; Thursday Sun trine North Node & sextile South Node; Friday Mercury square Neptune, Venus square Eris, Sun semisquare Eris; Saturday Mercury trine Ceres, Mercury semisquare Venus, Mercury conjunct Sun, Sun trine Ceres; Sunday Venus sesquiquadrate Neptune, Sun square Neptune, Mercury semisquare Eris*

▶ See p. 3 for meaning of symbols ★, **MR, VR, P.**

The boldness of asking deep questions may require unforeseen flexibility if we are to accept the answers.

Brian Greene

| MAY | | | | | | | JUNE | | | | | | |
SU	M	TU	W	T	F	S	SU	M	TU	W	T	F	S
					1	2							
3	4	5	6	7	8	9	1	2	3	4	5	6	
10	11	12	13	14	15	16	7	8	9	10	11	12	13
17	18	19	20	21	22	23	14	15	16	17	18	19	20
24	25	26	27	28	29	30	21	22	23	24	25	26	27
31							28	29	30				

Moon in Scorpio • Void 4:02 am (P), 7:02 am (E)
Moon enters Sagittarius 11:40 am (P), 2:40 pm (E)

01 MO 2 MR

Although we'd like to look on the bright side, realism intrudes and does not confirm our hopes. Treat this like a wake-up call to see what needs to change.

Moon in Sagittarius • Full Moon (Dyad Moon)
Void 11:00 pm (P)

02 TU 1 MR ★

A dream could be revealing this morning, or a nightmare acts as a warning. Assess what is doable versus what is asking too much of yourself or another.

Moon in Sagittarius, Void (P) • Void 2:00 am (E)
Moon enters Capricorn 5:52 pm (P), 8:52 pm (E)

03 WE 2 MR

Make your wants and needs known. How else can someone help? Not that offers come pouring in, but if you don't speak up, you're really on your own.

Moon in Capricorn

04 TH 2 MR

Aside from a spell of warmth midday, the mood is businesslike today and down-right brusque tonight. Make adjustments early to delegate or define a task.

Moon in Capricorn • Void 3:55 am (P), 6:55 am (E)
Moon enters Aquarius 10:03 pm (P)

05 FR 3 MR ★

We scramble to fix something this morning, though we may encounter opposition or an unruly interruption. Happily, there are laughs along the way.

World Environment Day

Moon in Aquarius (P), Void in Capricorn (E)
Moon enters Aquarius 1:03 am (E)

06 SA 3 MR

Friendly cooperation and stimulating conversation combine in a caring climate, making this a good day for meetings, group activities or social get-togethers.

Moon in Aquarius • Void 7:32 am (P), 10:32 am (E)

07 SU 3 MR

Energy is high early (the best part of the day) and we're itching to do something creative or physical. Later, irritations arise and we'd rather be alone.

JUNE 01-07 HIGHLIGHTS

Beginning last week, misconceptions, deceptions and misunderstandings cloud communications, peaking at the Full Moon Tuesday [9:20 am (P), 12:20 pm (E)]. The problems are not just what's going on between people, they even stem from between our own ears! In some situations, there's too much information. In other cases, there are missing pieces. We can't get a clear picture and we don't know whom to trust. We'll just have to take some things on faith. Fortunately there are two positive configurations at the Full Moon. One helps us listen to one another with care and try to work as a team. The other provides intuition and inspiration along with an optimistic outlook and a bit of luck. Still, we feel the weight of serious circumstances that require effort and resourcefulness to alter for the better. Although we'll encounter detours en route to solutions, we have the energy to work on the heavy issues and aren't afraid to examine them. By later in the week, someone takes the lead to deal with them. A general atmosphere of friendly and humanitarian caring prevails across the week. An uptick in fun and originality for the next two months starts Friday and immediately sets us to making plans and envisioning what we would like to manifest.

Astro-Overview: *Not only is Mercury Retrograde, but it's still in a square with Neptune at the Full Moon Tuesday and joins in the T-square the Sun-Moon opposition forms with Neptune. Eris is close to the midpoint of the Mercury-Neptune square, semisquare each. Mars, ruler of Tuesdays, has a big day Tuesday: quincunx Pluto to make a Finger of God with the Mars sextile to Jupiter (exact Friday). The Mars-Jupiter sextile is also part of an imprecise Fire Grand Trine/Kite with Uranus and the Full Moon in Sagittarius. Another (slightly tighter) Grand Trine, in Air signs, forms between Mercury and the Sun with the North Node and Ceres. Mercury is trine the North Node Wednesday, as the Sun was last Thursday. (Ceres and the North Node were exactly trine May 12.) Ceres turns Retrograde overnight Tuesday, embraced by positive aspects. Like Mars, the Sun is in a Finger of God with Jupiter and Pluto (which were quincunx May 21) from this Friday to next Monday. Venus enters Leo Friday and is trine Saturn the next day.*

Details: *Tuesday Mars quincunx Pluto; Tuesday (P)/Wednesday (E) Ceres turns Retrograde; Wednesday Mercury trine North Node & sextile South Node; Friday Venus enters Leo, Sun quincunx Pluto, Mars sextile Jupiter; Saturday Venus trine Saturn*

JULY

SU	M	TU	W	T	F	S
			1	2	3	4
5	6	7	8	9	10	11
12	13	14	15	16	17	18
19	20	21	22	23	24	25
26	27	28	29	30	31	

Mars and the Sun, traveling close together, make back to back Finger of Gods with Jupiter and Pluto (see June 1-7 Astro-Overview and the Star Pages for June 2-8).

Think big and expect to be surprised by the visions you conjure up. Review them judiciously. Some may not be realistic; others could be dazzling.

Moon Void in Aquarius • Moon enters Pisces 1:17 am (P), 4:17 am (E)

★ MR 2 MO 08

If you feel unappreciated or used, it seems easier to let a slight slide. However, defending yourself increases confidence. Just don't go on offense.

Moon in Pisces • Third Quarter Moon
Void 11:09 am (P), 2:09 pm (E)

MR 2 TU 09

Sweet talk takes you where you want to go, or at least heads you in that direction. It's a good day to discuss values or assess the worth of something.

Moon Void in Pisces • Moon enters Aries 4:15 am (P), 7:15 am (E)

★ MR 3 WE 10

An imbalance between self-concern and consideration for others leads to strained relations. Kindness and better listening improve situations.

Moon in Aries • Void 4:44 pm (P), 7:44 pm (E)

★ MR 2 TH 11

Things seem difficult because they are. Adversity builds strength. Innovative thinking yields answers; practicality and creativity pitch in.

Moon Void in Aries • Moon enters Taurus 7:17 am (P), 10:17 am (E)

★ P 1 FR 12

We're working on a turn-around, which shows promise early. Later, we hit an impasse that requires agility and imagination to circumvent.

Moon in Taurus • Void 3:07 pm (P), 6:07 pm (E)

2 SA 13

Competition is fierce this morning, though we're up to the task and aim at high standards. Tonight, we're reminded we're all only human.

Flag Day

Moon Void in Taurus • Moon enters Gemini 10:52 am (P), 1:52 pm (E)

★ 2 SU 14

JUNE 08-14 HIGHLIGHTS

If there is something that you want to promote about yourself, such as your accomplishments or creations (which could include your children), this is the week to do so. Inventiveness is in the air and you might come up with a great new idea. Thursday is a prime day for such an inspiration (as was last Sunday). Prior to Thursday (when Mercury finishes its Retrograde), you may resurrect a notion from the past to work on once again. Self-assurance is strong most of the week, although not so much on Friday, when doubts can creep in or emotional wounds strike, particularly if the barb is from someone you love. That's a day when it takes extra effort but you should be able to repair hurt feelings in relationships or straighten out a matter concerning finances or possessions. Be careful not to force the need for a patch-up Friday by instigating an argument between Tuesday and then. Over the weekend, the potential for altercations continues but without help to smooth ruffled feathers (except to a minor degree Saturday night). Throughout the week, there is a need to stand up for yourself and fortunately, the capacity to do so is present, although boundaries are quite flexible and leniency will exact a price, especially Thursday morning.

Astro-Overview: *Venus and the Sun, still semisquare, make concurrent hard aspects: Friday to Chiron (Venus, sesquiquadrate; the Sun, square) scratched by the Moon, to Mars (Venus, semisquare Saturday night; the Sun, conjunct Sunday, when both sextile Eris) and to Ceres Sunday night (Venus, opposite; the Sun, sesquiquadrate). Venus sextiles Mercury Wednesday and the North Node Friday, boosted by the Moon Wed. The Sun sextiles Jupiter Monday and Uranus Wed. Mars also sextiles Uranus (Tues.), squares Chiron (Thurs.) and semisquares Venus (Sat.). Mercury semisquares Uranus Tues. night and Sunday, on either side of turning Direct Thursday. Neptune turns Retrograde Friday. Sunday, Saturn re-enters Scorpio.*

Details: *Monday Sun sextile Jupiter; Tuesday Mars sextile Uranus; Tuesday (P)/Wednesday (E) Mercury semisquare Uranus; Wednesday Mercury sextile Venus, Sun sextile Uranus; Thursday Mercury turns Direct, Mars square Chiron; Friday Neptune turns Retrograde, Venus sextile North Node & trine South Node, Venus sesquiquadrate Chiron, Sun square Chiron; Saturday Venus semisquare Mars; Sunday Mercury semisquare Uranus, Sun conjunct Mars, Sun sextile Eris, Mars sextile Eris, Saturn re-enters Scorpio, Venus opposite Ceres; Sunday (P) Sun sesquiquadrate Ceres*

▶ See p. 3 for meaning of Moon Void. **29**

Never make your home in a place. Make a home for yourself inside your own head. That way it will go with you wherever you journey.
Tad Williams

	MAY							JUNE					
SU	M	TU	W	T	F	S	SU	M	TU	W	T	F	S
					1	2		1	2	3	4	5	6
3	4	5	6	7	8	9	7	8	9	10	11	12	13
10	11	12	13	14	15	16	14	15	16	17	18	19	20
17	18	19	20	21	22	23	21	22	23	24	25	26	27
24	25	26	27	28	29	30	28	29	30				
31													

Moon in Gemini

15 MO 3

Humor and perspective help as we try to slough off slights and put on a happy face when associates don't seem to have their usual regard for us.

Moon in Gemini • New Moon • Void 7:18 am (P), 10:18 am
Moon enters Cancer 3:51 pm (P), 6:51 pm (E)

16 TU 2 P ★

Whatever happens, view it as for your own good. Instead of assigning blame, see where you can learn something more about yourself or another person.

Moon in Cancer

17 WE 2

Feelings flow freely. Healing is possible, especially if you can let something go and restructure on a firmer foundation or aim in a better direction.

Moon in Cancer • Void 10:52 pm (P)
Moon enters Leo 11:22 pm (P)

18 TH 2

Overpowering emotions may lead you to be irrational on this crazy and chaotic day. Attempt to get grounded via exercise, yoga, gardening or art.

First day of Ramadan

Moon in Leo (P), in Cancer (E) • Void 1:52 am (E)
Moon enters Leo 2:22 am (E)

19 FR 3

A sunny outlook and a happy morning enable us to weather minor bumps from afternoon into evening. Teamwork and ingenuity move projects forward.

Juneteenth

Moon in Leo

20 SA 2 ★

Seeing the big picture and being open to risk or experimentation can assist you in getting over hurdles or keep you from going down the wrong road.

Moon in Leo • Void 9:09 am (P), 12:09 pm (E)
Moon enters Virgo 9:59 am (P), 12:59 pm (E)

21 SU 3 ★

Obstinacy puts a damper on the morning; adaptability saves the rest of the day. Except for a few selfish souls, most people are in a congenial mood.

Father's Day, Summer Solstice, Litha

JUNE 15-21 HIGHLIGHTS

All June, the level of impatience and irritability is higher than usual. For a couple weeks already and continuing this week, grouchiness is apt to be expressed verbally. Starting Sunday, the waterworks turn on, producing tears. Somewhat on Monday and definitely Tuesday, many people feel unloved, unlovable or unloving. Caring concern for or from others seems missing or discouraged by an unreceptive mood. With this condition in effect at the New Moon Tuesday [7:05 am (P), 10:05 am (E)], there is a hangover effect the next four weeks. The factor indicating lack of support dissipates before the Summer Solstice Sunday [9:38 am (P), 12:38 pm (E)] and does not impact the upcoming season. However, difficulty with affection and crankiness, along with stubbornness, remain in place and color the next three months. (Be on guard for them around July 30, August 6 and August 31.) Luckily, a fortuitous configuration in place at both the New Moon and Solstice brings cooperation, friendliness, good listening and understanding of one another. Still, a major source of friction and frustration has the second of three peaks Saturday (see the Star Pages), intensified Wednesday night and again Sunday morning, making it last for the whole summer, as well.

Astro-Overview: *This week, what the planetary activity lacks in quantity, it gains in intense quality. A potent, difficult aspect between two slow planets occurs Saturday: Saturn semisquare Pluto. The Moon aggravates them Wednesday night and Sunday morning, when the Summer Solstice propels their trials through the coming season. The Sun and Mars are still together and semisquare Venus. Sunday to Monday, the Sun is sesquiquadrate Ceres, as Mars is early Monday. (Venus opposed Ceres last Sunday.) Tuesday morning is the exact Venus-Sun semisquare, magnified as the Moon joins the Sun for a New Moon then. Wednesday to Thursday, Mercury is in soft aspects with the Nodes, boosted by the Moon Friday. Sunday Mercury repeats two aspects it made twice before in its Retrograde cycle: trine Ceres and semisquare Eris. An Air Grand Trine between Mercury, the North Node and Ceres is present at both the New Moon and the Solstice. (The South Node makes it a Kite.)*

Details: *Monday (E) Sun sesquiquadrate Ceres; Monday Mars sesquiquadrate Ceres; Tuesday Venus semisquare Sun; Wednesday (P)/ Thursday (E) Mercury trine North Node & sextile South Node; Saturday Saturn semisquare Pluto; Sunday Sun enters Cancer, Mercury trine Ceres, Mercury semisquare Eris*

JULY

SU	M	TU	W	T	F	S
			1	2	3	4
5	6	7	8	9	10	11
12	13	14	15	16	17	18
19	20	21	22	23	24	25
26	27	28	29	30	31	

A harmonious connection boding good fortune from out of the blue occurs June 22 (see Star Pages), close enough to the Summer Solstice to extend its blessings through the upcoming season.

June

Inventiveness or uniqueness pays off in unexpected, practical ways. Friends or colleagues prove beneficial, though you'll have to lead the way.

Moon in Virgo

★ **3 MO 22**

Work on getting over hurts, or at least don't rub salt into your wounds with worries or fears. Believe that you can improvise, take risks and succeed.

Moon in Virgo • Void 10:12 pm (P) • Moon enters Libra 10:41 pm (P)

★ **3 TU 23**

The importance and extent of relationships is emphasized, including your relationship with yourself. You'll find out on whom you can count.

St. Jean-Baptiste Day (Quebec)

Moon in Libra (P), in Virgo (E) • Void 1:12 am (E)
Moon enters Libra 1:41 am (E) • First Quarter Moon

★ **2 WE 24**

Determine what you want more of as well as what you want to be rid of. It's okay, even necessary, to look at this with a self-centered eye.

Moon in Libra • Void 4:22 pm (P), 7:22 pm (E)

★ **3 TH 25**

Who knows you better than you? By understanding your motivations and emotional underpinning, you can push yourself to get what you seek.

Moon Void in Libra • Moon enters Scorpio 10:57 am (P), 1:57 pm (E)

★ **3 FR 26**

We're more sensitive than usual to interpersonal imbalances and strive to keep ego out of the equation. We can bring out the best in everyone without harming anyone.

Moon in Scorpio

★ **3 SA 27**

The time for repair and restitution has arrived. Karmic chickens come home to roost: rewards are received and punishment is meted out.

Moon in Scorpio • Void 6:50 pm (P), 9:50 pm (E)
Moon enters Sagittarius 8:21 pm (P), 11:21 pm (E)

2 SU 28

JUNE 22-28 HIGHLIGHTS

Acknowledging a smidgen of hesitation or doubt, we plunge into the week with buoyant optimism Monday. Possibilities present themselves and more than a little luck comes our way. Tuesday, it could seem like we're harvesting a strange crop, but a good one. Still, we'll probably shake our heads in amazement. By the weekend, we'll be believers. This is a week for a transformation or release. We can make significant progress if we combine the right elements. We are also moved to address situations that are exaggerated or have become overgrown to head them in a different direction. Key times for this are Wednesday, Thursday and Saturday. On Sunday, we see clearly how to throttle back and put circumstances in order, drawing lines if necessary. Thursday to Saturday is also a time to draw something from our heart or creative depths into manifestation, employing assertion and confidence. Yet in the midst of these positive developments, we are more aware than usual of what pains us or is lacking in our life, especially regarding nurturing we'd like to receive or give. This is reinforced Tuesday morning and Wednesday. An answer could be to expand our circle of support instead of relying on the usual people, perhaps looking to our guides and angels.

Astro-Overview: *After one of the year's toughest aspects (last Saturday's Saturn-Pluto semisquare) comes one of the nicest, Jupiter trine Uranus, for the third time Monday. What a switch from last year's square! Now we get happy surprises instead of magnified weirdness. And this week is riddled with Quintile Triangles. The Sun is pulling away from Mars but each forms a QT with the Ceres-Uranus quintile (exact Monday). Thursday, Jupiter is biquintile Pluto and in a brief QT with the Moon Friday afternoon/evening. Also Thursday, Saturn is biquintile Eris, in a QT with the Sun overnight Friday. In other action, Chiron turns Retrograde Wednesday, and the Sun and Jupiter, semisquare Saturday, make hard aspects with the Nodes.*

Details: *Monday Jupiter trine Uranus, Ceres quintile Uranus; Tuesday Sun biquintile Ceres, Mercury square Neptune, Sun quintile Uranus; Wednesday Chiron turns Retrograde, Mars enters Cancer; Thursday Jupiter biquintile Pluto, Saturn biquintile Eris, Jupiter semisquare North Node & sesquiquadrate South Node; Friday Mars biquintile Ceres; Friday (P)/ Saturday (E) Sun biquintile Saturn; Saturday Sun quintile Eris, Sun square North Node & South Node, Mars quintile Uranus, Sun semisquare Jupiter; Sunday (P) Venus trine Uranus*

In every conceivable manner, the family
is link to our past, bridge to our future.
Alex Haley

	JUNE							**JULY**					
SU	M	TU	W	T	F	S	SU	M	TU	W	T	F	S
	1	2	3	4	5	6				1	2	3	4
7	8	9	10	11	12	13	5	6	7	8	9	10	11
14	15	16	17	18	19	20	12	13	14	15	16	17	18
21	22	23	24	25	26	27	19	20	21	22	23	24	25
28	29	30					26	27	28	29	30	31	

Moon in Sagittarius

29 MO 2 ★

You receive or send mixed messages about a relationship or money this morning. A friend bolsters your confidence afterward. Still, an acrid taste lingers.

Moon in Sagittarius • Void 11:18 am (P), 2:18 pm (E)

30 TU 3 ★

High hopes early about love or finances put yesterday's qualms to rest. Before long, new concerns arise about how much care to invest in a situation.

Moon Void in Sagittarius • Moon enters Capricorn 2:11 am (P), 5:11 am (E) • Full Moon (Mead Moon)

01 WE 3 ★

Make adjustments to keep circumstances (or tempers) from being blown out of proportion. Empathy is strong. Work hard and sacrifice to be of help.

Canada Day

Moon in Capricorn

02 TH 2

Time is a finite commodity. Try to balance your personal agenda against others' needs without guilt or suffering. Bright ideas spark unusual solutions.

Moon in Capricorn • Void 3:38 am (P), 6:38 am (E)
Moon enters Aquarius 5:21 am (P), 8:21 am (E)

03 FR 3 ★

So many lack so much that it's mentally exhausting to contemplate what you could or should do for them. See the big picture and heed your own requirements.

Independence Day (U.S.) observed

Moon in Aquarius

04 SA 1

It's not that we don't want commitment. We just want to be sure our requests and desires are met, whether that means being in a relationship or without one.

Independence Day (U.S.)

Moon in Aquarius • Void 5:32 am (P), 8:32 am (E)
Moon enters Pisces 7:23 am (P), 10:23 am (E)

05 SU 3

A stubborn stand-off could come early. Soon after, flexibility increases but not enough that people will give in regarding their personal wishes.

JUNE 29-JULY 05 HIGHLIGHTS

This week is Independence Day and it's a toss-up whether more people want to be mated or free. Times have been tough lately for love. A shift is on deck, hopefully mostly positive. We're at the start of three-plus months when we will make revisions in relationships. This week, the primary indicator of affections plays a starring role, although the plot has adversities. On Monday or Tuesday, something unusual happens suddenly, setting a good tone. However, an adjustment needs to be made. Monday presents the first opportunity for it but if we miss that, there will be other moments Wednesday to Saturday. Trust is all-important and that comes glaringly to light at the Full Moon Wednesday [7:20 pm (P), 10:20 pm (E)]. We need to be pro-active in our own interest, without adversely impacting someone else. Finding balance is key. Past hurts come up for review and repair Friday. (The topics might be about friendship, self-sacrifice or communication more than romance.) A fitting time for a heart-to-heart talk comes Saturday night into Sunday morning, possibly precipitated by a tiff. By Sunday, we'll recognize where everyone stands. It's good to identify what reality is, even if there's something aggravating about it. Then we know what to work on.

Astro-Overview: *Venus is instrumental this week, activating the June 22 Jupiter-Uranus trine (trine Uranus Mon., conjunct Jupiter Wed.), wrangling with the Nodes Mon., and sextile Mercury Sunday (both aspect Eris Fri. to Sat., boosted by the Moon Sat. night). The Nodes get a T-square from Mars Thurs., irritated by the Moon midday Wed.(Grand Cross) and Saturday. Mercury makes soft aspects with Uranus Thurs. and Jupiter Fri., and tangoes with the Ceres-Chiron semisquare Fri. morning. The Moon joins Ceres that night. The Jupiter-Chiron quincunx Tues. is in a quick Finger of God with the Moon Thurs. afternoon. The Sun-Neptune trine Wed. is the only noteworthy aspect at the Full Moon that night (Moon sextiles Neptune). Mars semisquares Jupiter Sunday.*

Details: *Monday (E) Venus trine Uranus; Monday Venus semisquare No. Node & sesquiquadrate So. Node; Tuesday Jupiter quincunx Chiron; Wednesday Venus conjunct Jupiter, Sun trine Neptune; Thursday Mars square No. Node & So. Node, Mercury sextile Uranus; Friday Ceres semisquare Chiron, Mercury sesquiquadrate Ceres, Mercury square Chiron, Mercury sextile Jupiter, Venus trine Eris; Saturday Mercury sextile Eris; Sunday Mercury sextile Venus, Mars semisquare Jupiter; Sunday (P) Sun sesquiquadrate Saturn*

AUGUST

SU	M	TU	W	T	F	S
						1
2	3	4	5	6	7	8
9	10	11	12	13	14	15
16	17	18	19	20	21	22
23	24	25	26	27	28	29
30	31					

Venus entered the shadow of its upcoming Retrograde June 21. (See 2015 On a Page, p. 61, and the Star Pages for June 29.)

June-July

Strong leadership is necessary to effect major changes. Today could be a time for action or planning and assigning tasks. Invite empathy into the process.

Moon in Pisces

2 MO 06

It's tempting to ignore reality rather than face hard challenges. Some people are stuck in their own viewpoint and can't see what others notice.

Moon in Pisces • Void 7:36 am (P), 10:36 am (E)
Moon enters Aries 9:37 am (P), 12:37 pm (E)

3 TU 07

Put faith in yourself or a higher power - or both - to endure today's tribulations. Expect extremes, a gamut of emotions and by tonight, a shock.

Moon in Aries • Third Quarter Moon

★ **1 WE 08**

Enjoy a smooth day for once, a perfect time to complete projects or make a sale. There are no impediments, and patience and kindness prevail.

Moon in Aries • Void 6:47 am (P), 9:47 am (E)
Moon enters Taurus 12:49 pm (P), 3:49 pm (E)

4 TH 09

Any caring concern for others early fades fast in the face of individuals' wants, which dominate the day. Someone may methodically make a power grab.

Moon in Taurus

★ **3 FR 10**

Disagreements underscore the need for boundaries in relationships but no one wants to budge, until tonight when there is a chance for wiggle room.

Moon in Taurus • Void 2:52 pm (P), 5:52 pm (E)
Moon enters Gemini 5:16 pm (P), 8:16 pm (E)

1 SA 11

A cacophony of chatter makes it hard to plead your case. There's rebellion in the ranks and a "grown-up in the room" is needed to mediate.

Moon in Gemini

3 SU 12

JULY 06-12 HIGHLIGHTS

Across the week, we find ourselves paying attention to personal situations and fiscal or political issues from the past several years. The Sun links to a major planetary harbinger of transition that brought many crises and developments from 2012 through earlier this year. (A new factor involved now is the planet of karmic consequences.) In addition, there is a connection between the Third Quarter Moon Wednesday and the Lunar Eclipse Full Moon on October 8, 2014 (see Moon Family table, p. 69). Circumstances that peaked then are due for a denouement now. From Friday to Sunday, the quick planet associated with news passes by the planets in USA's birth chart related to monetary and foreign matters. Many people continue to address pain about a lack of support that hit home last Friday. There are reminders of it Monday night and Thursday night. Sunday night, we may see some relief or feel a better interpersonal balance. A brief two-week immersion into feelings strongly impacting thoughts and communication starts Wednesday, turning our heads in a different direction Saturday morning. Wednesday and Friday morning, sympathies are easily aroused. We act willingly on them Wednesday, but Friday morning, selfishness or rivalry stands in the way.

Astro-Overview: Saturn was semisquare Pluto June 20 and will be again on August 13. Monday, the Sun is sesquiquadrate Saturn and opposite Pluto, magnified by the Moon at Wednesday's Third Quarter phase. The Uranus-Pluto square has widened so the Sun doesn't square Uranus until Sunday. Still one could say these three are in a wide T-square throughout the week. Mercury enters Cancer Wednesday, ending its long visit to Gemini. Mars, now trailing behind the Sun, is trine Neptune this Wednesday like the Sun was last Wednesday. Jupiter is trine Eris Friday. When the Moon joins Eris in Thursday's wee hours to amplify this trine, most people will sleep through it and not get embroiled in a chaotic mess. The Nodes receive a T-square from Mercury Saturday and a trine and sextile from Ceres Sunday. The Moon triggers the July 3 Ceres-Chiron semisquare twice, Monday night as it passes Chiron and overnight Thursday to Friday, when it is square Ceres and semisquare Chiron.

Details: Monday (E) Sun sesquiquadrate Saturn; Monday Sun opposite Pluto; Wednesday Mercury enters Cancer, Mars trine Neptune; Friday Jupiter trine Eris; Saturday Mercury square North Node & South Node; Sunday Sun square Uranus, North Node trine Ceres & South Node sextile Ceres

---

▶ See p. 3 for meaning of Moon Void.

The love of family and the admiration of friends is much more important than wealth and privilege.

Charles Kuralt

Moon in Gemini • Void 8:31 pm (P), 11:31 pm (E)
Moon enters Cancer 11:14 pm (P)

13 MO 3

A big mouth or quick temper could provoke trouble. Conversely, too much leniency may cause problems. Speaking from the heart with love is the way to go.

Moon in Cancer (P), Moon Void in Gemini (E)
Moon enters Cancer 2:14 am (E)

14 TU 2 ★

Strong emotions are on display, not all of them pretty. Boundaries, respect and fairness figure in. Tonight, sympathy and understanding win out.

Bastille Day

Moon in Cancer • New Moon

15 WE 1 P ★

The focus is on how we express what is important to us. How we go after that impacts others. It's time to move past outworn ways and circumstances.

Moon in Cancer • Void 4:24 am (P), 7:24 am (E)
Moon enters Leo 7:15 am (P), 10:15 am (E)

16 TH 3

Intense interconnection the past couple days may have been stifling. Standing apart now can feel isolating or it might affirm individual strength.

Moon in Leo

17 FR 1

Insecurity surfaces, possibly spawned by a disturbing dream or sleepless night. Such a lack of assurance affects interactions throughout the day.

Eid al-Fitr

Moon in Leo • Void 2:41 pm (P), 5:41 pm (E)
Moon enters Virgo 5:47 pm (P), 8:47 pm (E)

18 SA 2 ★

Confidence returns this morning. By evening, we realize it needs to be tempered by humility. Watch out for words blurted in haste or annoyance.

Moon in Virgo

19 SU 2 ★

An argumentative mood is made worse by judgments and a lack of empathy. Something must be said to instigate corrective measures, just maybe not so harshly.

JULY 13-19 HIGHLIGHTS

A New Moon offers a chance to initiate new activities and embrace a fresh mindset. That's especially true of the New Moon Wednesday [6:24 pm (P), 9:24 pm (E)], when the planets of action and thought team up and align with the planet that transforms and spirals us to a higher level. These three intertwine intensely with two more planets in a potent pattern that looks like a trapezoid. It may be laying a trap for us. Anything we undertake in the coming four-week cycle is best done with careful planning and a cautious approach, taking into account values, finances, relationships and karma. The components of this configuration occur from Tuesday to Thursday, with most exact on Wednesday, a very powerful day! Monday and Tuesday, we tend to be unrealistic and expect too much. On a somewhat similar note, we might be fooling ourselves (or one another) Friday and Sunday. On any of these days, though it's not easy, we may be able to orient wishful thinking toward positive visualization to manifest desires or contribute to improvement or a healing. A surprise factor throws a little chaos into the mix late Wednesday and could bring outright pandemonium Sunday. It's not a boring week. Likewise, the month ahead marches to a booming beat.

Astro-Overview: *Last month, Mercury, Mars and the Sun were all in Gemini at the same time. They're all in Cancer July 8 to 22. The Sun and Moon are square Eris and Uranus, trine Chiron and sesquiquadrate Neptune at Wednesday's New Moon. The more important action then is a rapid-fire mishmash of planets: Mercury is conjunct Mars and both are opposite Pluto, semisquare Venus and sesquiquadrate Saturn, all in less than 24 hours! Saturn remains in a tight semisquare with Pluto (exact 6/20 & 8/13, on either side of Saturn's Direct station 8/2). Mercury is flying along at 2º per day! It's semisquare Jupiter and trine Neptune Monday, square Uranus Saturday and trine Chiron Sunday. Venus enters Virgo Saturday and Eris turns Retrograde Sunday.*

Details: *Monday Mercury semisquare Jupiter, Mercury trine Neptune, Sun trine Chiron; Tuesday Venus square Saturn, Mars sesquiquadrate Saturn; Wednesday Venus semisquare Mars, Mars opposite Pluto, Venus sesquiquadrate Pluto, Mercury sesquiquadrate Saturn, Mercury opposite Pluto, Mercury semisquare Venus; Thursday (P)/Friday (E) Mercury conjunct Mars, Sun square Eris; Friday Sun sesquiquadrate Neptune; Saturday Venus enters Virgo, Mercury square Uranus; Sunday Mercury trine Chiron, Eris turns Retrograde*

AUGUST

SU	M	TU	W	T	F	S
						1
2	3	4	5	6	7	8
9	10	11	12	13	14	15
16	17	18	19	20	21	22
23	24	25	26	27	28	29
30	31					

Rarely do so many planets push each other's buttons simultaneously as the rumble at the July 15 New Moon. One planet repeats some blows in its Retrograde cycle over the next three months.

July

We need to ameliorate a disordered situation, but neither the left nor right brain works very well, though both are quite active. Wait until tomorrow.

Moon in Virgo

1 MO 20

Excellent teamwork, cooperation and strategic planning yield significant progress on current projects. It's also a great day to start something new.

Moon in Virgo • Void 3:07 am (P), 6:07 am (E)
Moon enters Libra 6:23 am (P), 9:23 am (E)

5 TU 21

Emotional attachments make it hard to let go but you're pushed to purge in some way. Clear clutter, streamline paperwork or organize files or possessions.

Sun enters Leo

Moon in Libra

★ 2 WE 22

If someone tries to make you doubt yourself this morning, you'll bounce back and forge ahead, changed for the better. Tonight brings affection and aid.

Moon in Libra • Void 11:12 am (P), 2:12 pm (E) • Moon enters
Scorpio 7:07 pm (P), 10:07 pm (E) • First Quarter Moon (P)

3 TH 23

Much like yesterday, we have another rough morning, followed by a better evening. At first, we feel like we're on our own; later, it's a different story.

Moon in Scorpio • First Quarter Moon (E)

2 FR 24

Exercise caution in physical activities and near electricity today and late tomorrow. This afternoon, look for a breakthrough or turnaround in feelings.

Moon in Scorpio

★ VR 2 SA 25

Long-distance connections offer benefits while closer exchanges may be hurtful or misinterpreted. Be agile to react to sudden developments.

Parents' Day

Moon in Scorpio • Void 2:14 am (P), 5:14 am (E)
Moon enters Sagittarius 5:24 am (P), 8:24 am (E)

★ VR P 3 SU 26

JULY 20-26 HIGHLIGHTS

Astro-Overview: *It's an important week for the Sun. Mercury joins our star Thursday, shortly after each enters the sign the Sun rules, Leo. Ahead of that, both are square Eris and sesquiquadrate Neptune, triggering their ongoing semisquare (the Sun, last week; Mercury, Monday) and trine Saturn (the Sun, Tuesday; Mercury, Wednesday). Later, both oppose Ceres (Mercury, Friday; the Sun, Saturday). Mercury is sextile/trine the Nodes Saturday and sesquiquadrate Chiron Sunday (as the Sun will be next week). Mars touches the long-term Chiron-Uranus semisextile with a square to Uranus Saturday and a trine to Chiron Sunday (in a Grand Trine with the Moon Saturday night). Two planets turn Retrograde this weekend: Venus, Saturday and Uranus, Sunday. The Moon joins the North Node Tuesday, enhancing its loose trine to Ceres.*

A disruptive influence that brought difficulties this past Thursday, Friday and Sunday still holds sway Monday, with a brief hangover effect early this Thursday. Some people could experience a conflict between their personal interests and what seems best for the general population. Or a clash in belief systems might spark disagreements. Another possibility is an overall sense of confusion or disorientation. As is so often the case, good communication makes all the difference. At least, we know our own minds well and have a lot of self-respect now, especially Thursday. We're likely to have to speak up on our behalf then and we won't be shy about it. A cold tone mars Friday morning; people seem aloof and disconnected. Perhaps it's simply time to begin working on greater discrimination in our social ties. For a week starting Saturday, and again for a month from Oct. 8 to Nov. 8, our celestial instructions are to separate the wheat from the chaff in relationships. We'll eject some folks from our fold and lay down the law with others. Our social window is open briefly Sunday afternoon, but by that evening, we withdraw. Maybe there are wounds that need to be licked, either alone or in a private conversation with a close confidante.

Details: *Monday Mercury square Eris, Mercury sesquiquadrate Neptune; Tuesday Sun trine Saturn; Wednesday Mercury trine Saturn, Sun enters Leo; Thursday Mercury enters Leo, Mercury conjunct Sun; Friday Mercury opposite Ceres; Saturday Sun opposite Ceres, Venus turns Retrograde, Mars square Uranus, Mercury sextile North Node & trine South Node; Sunday Mars trine Chiron, Mercury sesquiquadrate Chiron, Uranus turns Retrograde*

Happiness is a by-product of what we share with others.

Douglas M. Lawson

Moon in Sagittarius

27 MO **3** VR

Enthusiasm needs direction or wheels are simply spinning. Tonight, just when you think you won't get what you want, along comes a nice surprise.

Moon in Sagittarius • Void 6:36 am (P), 9:36 am (E)
Moon enters Capricorn 11:47 am (P), 2:47 pm (E)

28 TU **3** VR

Willing workers make a good dent in the morning's big agenda. This evening, the need for a shift to respond to limitations becomes apparent.

Moon in Capricorn

29 WE **1** VR

When people are forced to deal with pain, difficulty or conflict today, they feel useful and see their strength, empowering them to let go and move on.

Moon in Capricorn • Void 11:50 am (P), 2:50 pm (E)
Moon enters Aquarius 2:40 pm (P), 5:40 pm (E)

30 TH **2** VR

Morning and evening, you'll need your wits about you and have to fight the tendency to slip into a fog. A window of clarity opens in the afternoon.

Moon in Aquarius • Full Moon (Corn Moon)

31 FR **1** VR ★

Fun with friends goes a long way toward making us feel better about whatever ails us. Tonight, feed your head with something stimulating and inspiring.

Moon in Aquarius • Void 3:02 pm (P), 6:02 pm (E)
Moon enters Pisces 3:36 pm (P), 6:36 pm (E)

01 SA **1** VR

We find where our limits lie when we try to shift perspective assimilating hard-to-swallow information. There's no "spoonful of sugar" at hand.

Lammas, Lughnassad, Civic Holiday (Canada)

Moon in Pisces

02 SU **3** VR ★

Early-risers start the day with stress and need to blow off steam after. Everyone wants an escape, whether a fantasy, hobby or activities with comrades.

Friendship Day

JULY 27-AUGUST 02 HIGHLIGHTS

Some would call the Full Moon Friday [3:43 am (P), 6:43 am (E)] - the second this month - a blue moon. However, the original definition is a fourth Full Moon in a three-month season. With the Sun in Leo and the Moon in Aquarius, there is competition between pursuing personal pleasures versus involvement with friends or a group, though one could combine the two. The strongest connections the Moon and Sun make at this cycle's peak are to a factor that points out hurts and how to heal them. The Moon is part of a brief lucky triangle Friday morning that breaks down barriers and supports taking calculated risks. A long-term influence in place for much of 2015 challenges us to soften the hard edges of difficult, selfish people or learn to accept them the way they are. In the approach to the Full Moon, the planet of anger and action steps into the process, suggesting to do something rather than stew in irritated juices. Friday, the planet of affection returns to a more joyful sign after a quick foray into a criticizing sign, and heads for a reunion next Tuesday with the planet of expansion and optimism. But hearts (and minds) are not all that open now and Saturday night, the planet of blockages is at a standstill, making us feel stymied.

Astro-Overview: *The Sun is sextile the North Node and trine the South Node Monday. Mercury is pulling ahead of the Sun and makes a semisquare to the North Node and sesquiquadrate to the South Node Saturday. (There's a 15º difference in these aspects.) The Sun is sesquiquadrate Chiron Wednesday and still in the range of influence for this link at the Full Moon Friday morning, when the Moon semisquares Chiron. Mars is square Eris Wednesday and sesquiquadrate Neptune Friday, activating the ongoing Neptune-Eris semisquare. Retrograde Venus re-enters Leo Friday. The Moon opposes Venus and Jupiter Saturday afternoon (the low-point of the week) and in between is square Saturn and semisquare Pluto (stimulating the Saturn-Pluto semisquare, as it also does midday Wednesday). Overnight Saturday night, Saturn turns Direct, basically motionless for days before and after. The week ends with a mentally stimulating Mercury-Uranus trine.*

Details: *Monday Sun sextile North Node & trine South Node; Wednesday Sun sesquiquadrate Chiron, Mars square Eris; Thursday Mars sesquiquadrate Neptune; Friday Venus re-enters Leo; Saturday Mercury semisquare North Node & sesquiquadrate South Node; Saturday (P)/Sunday (E) Saturn turns Direct; Sunday Mercury trine Uranus*

SEPTEMBER

SU	M	TU	W	T	F	S
		1	2	3	4	5
6	7	8	9	10	11	12
13	14	15	16	17	18	19
20	21	22	23	24	25	26
27	28	29	30			

Finances and relationships are bumpy now and need better definition, especially August 3–5.

July-August

Is bigger really better? Not now. Down-size and simplify, aiming to benefit from "less is more." Yet do try to satisfy personal desires tonight.

Moon in Pisces • Void 1:35 pm (P), 4:35 pm (E)
Moon enters Aries 4:24 pm (P), 7:24 pm (E)

★ VR **3** MO **03**

The need to share and contribute has stiff competition from the equally strong pull to go after what you want for yourself. By tomorrow, the latter wins.

Moon in Aries

★ VR P **1** TU **04**

You're quite convincing, talking yourself into having your way. It's called rationalization. After, would you like to guilt-trip yourself, too?

Moon in Aries • Void 4:29 pm (P), 7:29 pm (E)
Moon enters Taurus 6:29 pm (P), 9:29 pm (E)

VR **2** WE **05**

If you're careful about respect and boundaries and employ empathy, diplomacy won't have to get you out of the pickle into which stubbornness put you.

Moon in Taurus • Third Quarter Moon

VR P **2** TH **06**

See if you can start the day with a vow to be flexible, fix what you can and not force what you can't change. Try a team approach and delegation.

Moon in Taurus • Void 9:46 pm (P)
Moon enters Gemini 10:40 pm (P)

★ VR **2** FR **07**

Vent your complaints. This may not change anything, but you'll feel better with it off your chest. You're likely to find a sympathetic ear.

Moon in Gemini (P), in Taurus (E) • Void 12:46 am (E)
Moon enters Gemini 1:40 am (E)

★ VR **1** SA **08**

You feel stronger today, maybe even feisty, and better able to solve problems or step out of harm's way. Be in touch with those you love.

Moon in Gemini

VR **3** SU **09**

AUGUST 03-09 HIGHLIGHTS

Astro-Overview: *Saturn and Pluto have been traveling in a semisquare (exact 6/20 and 8/13). Meanwhile Jupiter comes into a square with Saturn (Monday) and sesquiquadrate with Pluto (Tuesday). All of this would be tough enough, but Venus joins in, conjunct Jupiter and sesquiquadrate Pluto Tuesday, then square Saturn Wednesday. As it did last Saturday, the Moon gives them all a kick Tuesday afternoon and Friday night. Then Mercury passes Venus Thursday and immediately is square Saturn and sesquiquadrate Pluto, moving on to join Jupiter Friday before entering Virgo. Ceres moves into a sextile with Saturn (exact August 11-12), to which Mars connects this week with a trine to Saturn (exact Thursday morning, turned in a quick Grand Trine by the Moon midday Monday) and an opposition to Ceres Friday, before entering Leo Saturday.*

Details: *Monday Jupiter square Saturn, Ceres re-enters Capricorn, Mercury trine Eris; Tuesday Jupiter sesquiquadrate Pluto, Venus conjunct Jupiter, Venus sesquiquadrate Pluto; Wednesday Venus square Saturn; Thursday Mars trine Saturn, Mercury conjunct Venus, Mercury square Saturn, Mercury sesquiquadrate Pluto; Friday Mercury conjunct Jupiter, Mars opposite Ceres, Mercury enters Virgo; Saturday Mars enters Leo*

In the classic "uphill battle" in Greek mythology, Sisyphus rolls a boulder to the top of a rise, only to watch it tumble down and he has to push it up again, ad infinitum. This week won't be as bad as that. However, at certain points, it contains heaping portions of stagnation and frustration, especially in communications and matters of the heart. Serious concerns blot out prospects for light-hearted enjoyment, particularly Tuesday, Thursday and Friday night. A brief burst of inspiration or a positive vision comes midday Monday but not enough to sustain us across the week's rocky terrain. Tuesday has what should be one of the year's most buoyant planetary pair-ups. Yet it comes mired in an overload of responsibilities and we seem to have to shoulder the weight on our own. This results in feeling that whatever we do (and action is unavoidable), it won't be right or enough. We could gain some perspective Wednesday (if we don't over-think matters), only to face another onslaught Thursday. At least, we're persistent then and Friday, another tough day, when the help we need might be offered but only if we plead. Saturday, we seek space to catch our breath. Sunday, we finally get a chance to recharge our spent batteries.

▶ See p. 3 for meaning of Moon Void.

Parenting is not telling your child what to do when he or she misbehaves. Parenting is providing the conditions in which a child can realize his or her full human potential.

Gordon Neufeld

Moon in Gemini • Void 4:45 am (P), 7:45 am (E)
Moon enters Cancer 5:08 am (P), 8:08 am (E)

10 MO 2 VR

You care so much about loved ones that it's uncomfortable to turn the focus onto your needs, but it's unwise to ignore these. Find a way to speak up.

Moon in Cancer

11 TU 2 VR ★

Worry or insecurity adds to problems early. Get someone experienced to bring expertise to the situation. Tonight, an odd turn brings improvement.

Moon in Cancer • Void 10:44 am (P), 1:44 pm (E)
Moon enters Leo 1:52 pm (P), 4:52 pm (E)

12 WE 2 VR ★

Once we realize moaning accomplishes nothing, we examine how better organization greases wheels. A burst of energy allows us to enjoy the evening.

Moon in Leo

13 TH 3 VR ★

A major alteration is needed to set circumstances in order. You might be certain you can deal with it on your own, but it's great when someone else pitches in.

Moon in Leo • New Moon • Void 9:36 pm (P)

14 FR 3 VR

Listen to the passion in your heart. It will give rise to the will power and courage to determine and then go after what, or whom, you love.

Moon in Leo, Void (P) • Void 12:36 am (E)
Moon enters Virgo 12:45 am (P), 3:45 am (E)

15 SA 3 VR ★

If you're in a work mode, you can concentrate on a task, headed toward the finish line or a key milestone. Tonight, criticism raises hackles.

Moon in Virgo

16 SU 2 VR

We're keenly aware of competition or rivals, turning our analytical skills to detailed comparisons. This may arouse irritation at our shortcomings.

AUGUST 10-16 HIGHLIGHTS

The 40-day backtrack of the planet of finances and relationships (halfway over Saturday) asks us to review what is most important to us and ensure we make a place for it in our lives. Many people seek adjustments in partnerships to achieve more self-satisfaction. Also on the docket is control of monetary matters, which was topsy-turvy last week and needs additional attention Tuesday morning and Thursday. We're motivated to address these issues further in the coming 4-week cycle that starts with the Leo New Moon Friday [7:53 am (P), 10:53 am (E)]. Planetary connections then indicate that individual development and personal desires seem more important than commitment to a significant other. Inventiveness and originality come to our aid. Friends and people we know though groups bolster confidence. Yet we still feel an anchor slowing us down. It would help to lighten the load and get rid of any extraneous goods or feelings that we haven't already purged this summer. Anything we don't rectify now will present itself again in the following lunar cycle. Handling it then will be more difficult. That New Moon is an intense solar eclipse and two current influences (one which eases the process and one which gives us a good kick) won't be present.

Astro-Overview: *The Sun and Venus each trine Eris on either side of their conjunction Saturday. The Sun is trine Uranus Thursday (as Venus will be next week). The Moon joins the Sun and Venus in their trines to Uranus and Eris at Friday's New Moon. The Sun and Moon tussle with the Nodes Monday, whereas Mars links nicely with them Thursday. Sunday night, the Moon irritates Mars and Chiron as they form a sesquiquadrate. Mercury has a tough week: sesquiquadrate Uranus Monday, pricking the Neptune-Eris semisquare Wednesday, then Saturday sesquiquadrate Ceres, ending with a nice trine to Pluto. Jupiter enters Virgo Tuesday for the next thirteen months. Saturn is sextile Ceres Tuesday night and then makes a final semisquare to Pluto Thursday.*

Details: *Monday Mercury sesquiquadrate Uranus, Sun semisquare North Node & sesquiquadrate South Node; Tuesday Jupiter enters Virgo; Tuesday (P)/Wednesday (E) Ceres sextile Saturn; Wednesday Mercury sesquiquadrate Eris, Mercury opposite Neptune; Thursday Sun trine Uranus, Mars sextile North Node & trine South Node, Saturn semisquare Pluto; Friday Venus trine Eris; Saturday Mercury sesquiquadrate Ceres, Venus conjunct Sun, Mercury trine Pluto; Sunday Sun trine Eris; Sunday (P) Mars sesquiquadrate Chiron*

SEPTEMBER

SU	M	TU	W	T	F	S
		1	2	3	4	5
6	7	8	9	10	11	12
13	14	15	16	17	18	19
20	21	22	23	24	25	26
27	28	29	30			

The balance between work and fun is tipping toward the work end of the scale. On August 11 (see the Star Pages), a 13-month opportunity begins for finding benefit through service to others.

Everyone is in a helpful mood, treating others with caring and respect. Teamwork, cooperation and diplomacy smooth interactions and endeavors.

Moon in Virgo • Void 10:16 am (P), 1:16 pm (E)
Moon enters Libra 1:22 pm (P), 4:22 pm (E)

★ VR 4 MO 17

Not that it will be easy, but one can negotiate power struggles by probing into what each participant wants and seeking a compromise to satisfy requests.

Moon in Libra

★ VR 2 TU 18

This morning is great for meetings and contacting friends or associates to coordinate creative activities. Later, distrust or competition blocks harmony.

Moon in Libra • Void 7:56 am (P), 10:56 pm (E)

★ VR 3 WE 19

Something critical or hurtful is apt to be blurted in haste, bursting a bubble. By tonight, a sweet apology or warm embrace may ease the sting.

Moon Void in Libra • Moon enters Scorpio 2:24 am (P), 5:24 am (E)

VR 2 TH 20

Bossy types who want to hold the reins and be in charge of everything could have a comeuppance, or at the least, find their efforts go unappreciated.

Senior Citizens Day (U.S.)

Moon in Scorpio

VR 1 FR 21

Try to let it go and move on after feathers are ruffled midday. This evening is cheerier but ambitious plans may not live up to expectations.

Moon in Scorpio • First Quarter Moon • Void 12:31 pm (P), 3:31 pm (E)
Moon enters Sagittarius 1:41 pm (P), 4:41 pm (E)

VR 2 SA 22

Grumbling and complaints are par for the bumpy course today. Compliments and affection might turn them around before all is said and done.

Sun enters Virgo

Moon in Sagittarius

★ VR 2 SU 23

We're in one of the smoother lunar cycles of the year and despite the continuing back-up of the planet in charge of monetary and relationship matters, this should be a relatively good week, especially at the start. From Monday to Tuesday, there's another of those magic triangles that help us use our talents and urge intentions into being. This one involves the planet of manifestation combined with the communication planet and a dwarf planet that asks us to stand on our own and be assertive. If we need to use our wits in a verbal match or debate, they'll be razor sharp. Still, we need to be respectful, of course. Our ability to do so is apt to be tested Tuesday evening and again Friday (the toughest day this week) and Saturday. Thursday, we are aware of a lack or we have a painful conversation, accompanied by ideas of how to solve a problem. Saturday, a strong stubborn streak could impede progress, but determination is strong then and we strive to push something toward completion. Frequently at a First Quarter Moon, we round a bend and forge ahead in an altered direction. Anyone traveling Saturday night should allow extra time for a slow-down. The high-point of the week is Wednesday morning, when there is a pleasant social surprise.

AUGUST 17-23 HIGHLIGHTS

Astro-Overview: *The Mars-Chiron sesquiquadrate in Monday's wee hours was more noticeable last Sunday night and is again when an echo comes Thursday. What we detect to begin the week is the Quintile Triangle made by Mercury Monday and Tuesday with the Saturn-Eris biquintile, which will be exact Sept. 5. Wednesday is another of the many semisextiles between Chiron and Uranus (see Long-Term Influences, p. 74), as well as the week's best aspect, a Venus-Uranus trine, enhanced by the Moon that morning. Mercury opposes Chiron early Thursday, then semisquares Mars late Saturday night. The Moon aggravates them Thursday afternoon and evening. For its final act in the sign it rules, Leo, the Sun is sesquiquadrate Pluto and square Saturn Friday, snagged into the Saturn-Pluto semisquare, which was exact last week. The Moon harshly aspects all three Tuesday night and midday Saturday. Sunday, the Sun enters Virgo.*

Details: *Monday (E) Mars sesquiquadrate Chiron; Monday Mercury quintile Saturn; Tuesday Mercury bi-quintile Eris; Wednesday Chiron semisextile Uranus, Venus trine Uranus; Thursday Mercury opposite Chiron; Friday Sun sesquiquadrate Pluto, Sun square Saturn; Saturday (P)/Sunday (E) Mercury semisquare Mars; Sunday Sun enters Virgo*

*Pride makes us artificial and
humility makes us real.*

Thomas Merton

AUGUST							SEPTEMBER						
SU	M	TU	W	T	F	S	SU	M	TU	W	T	F	S
						1		1	2	3	4	5
2	3	4	5	6	7	8	6	7	8	9	10	11	12
9	10	11	12	13	14	15	13	14	15	16	17	18	19
16	17	18	19	20	21	22	20	21	22	23	24	25	26
23	24	25	26	27	28	29	27	28	29	30
30	31

Moon in Sagittarius • Void 3:04 pm (P), 6:04 pm (E)
Moon enters Capricorn 9:22 pm (P)

24 MO 2 VR ★

Your priorities could be off course and off-putting. Don't rush and overlook important details or miss the bigger picture. Search for the gems.

Moon in Capricorn (P), Void in Sagittarius (E)
Moon enters Capricorn 12:22 am (E)

25 TU 3 VR

We awake hopeful, though not unrealistic if we aim correctly. By implementing a positive vision, we can accomplish much and make a difference.

Moon in Capricorn

26 WE 3 VR

Your thinking cap is on straight, enriched by ingenuity. As long as self-importance doesn't get in the way, it will be a very productive day.

Women's Equality Day

Moon in Capricorn • Void 12:20 am (P), 3:20 am (E)
Moon enters Aquarius 1:03 am (P), 4:03 am (E)

27 TH 3 VR ★

Friends are the bridge over troubled waters early, though someone may experience alienation. Tonight we're more inclusive and thrill-seeking.

Moon in Aquarius

28 FR 1 VR

People don't see eye-to-eye this morning. Watch for a stubborn stand-off, followed by a retreat into individual corners. Later, we wash our hands of it.

Moon in Aquarius • Void 12:03 am (P), 3:03 am (E) • Moon enters
Pisces 1:51 am (P), 4:51 am (E) • Full Moon (Harvest Moon)

29 SA 2 VR

Our scales swing as we seesaw back and forth between judging and accepting. Anyone who is extremely selfish will likely end up feeling guilty.

Moon in Pisces • Void 11:53 pm (P)

30 SU 4 VR

The planets are low-key and so are we. It's a calm and peaceful day, a time to re-group, lick wounds and emerge refreshed, grateful for one's blessings.

AUGUST 24-30 HIGHLIGHTS

Minds are very fertile this week. We'll see what we grow in our mental gardens. As the week begins, we're intent on setting things in order for a substantive harvest. This could include weeding out something unwanted. We focus this energy mostly on work or ways we are of service. Once the planet of thought shifts into a relationship-oriented sign Thursday, we're more interested in our liaisons. Initially, we must face what is inequitable Friday. By Saturday, we look to get a handle on partnerships and orient them in the direction of fairness and harmony (re-examining them next Monday). Self-assurance should be strong, especially Wednesday. However, the potential exists for people to be highly critical then, whether this appears in the form of berating oneself or via judgment of or by others, particularly for what is different or non-mainstream. The Full Moon Saturday [11:35 am (P), 2:35 pm (E)] highlights that we're in a lengthy period when outcasts and loners need sympathy and help. (See Sept. 8 in the Star Pages.) There may be a big deal about their suffering. They might contend they want to try to make it on their own, but they do need assistance. With the Sun in Virgo and the Full Moon in Pisces, multiple offers of aid appear.

Astro-Overview: As often happens, the most active planet this week is Mercury (the quickest planet after the Moon). Monday, Mercury is trine Ceres, then Wednesday it's sextile Saturn, stimulating the Ceres-Saturn sextile of Aug.12. The Moon boosts them Wednesday night. After entering Libra Thursday, Mercury is semisquare Venus Friday. On either side of this aspect, both Venus and Mercury connect with the Nodes (emphasized by the Moon overnight Monday, early Friday morning and next Monday). The Sun is conjunct Jupiter Wednesday and sesquiquadrate Uranus Friday. (The Jupiter-Uranus sesquiquadrate is Sept. 2.) The Moon aspects all three at the Full Moon Saturday. In addition, the Moon is two degrees from a conjunction to Neptune and semisquare to Eris. (The Sun aspects both next Monday.) With the Sun and Jupiter across from the Moon, the Full Moon foreshadows the Jupiter-Neptune opposition and Jupiter-Eris sesquiquadrate (both exact on Sept. 17).

Details: Monday Mercury trine Ceres, Venus semisquare North Node & sesquiquadrate South Node; Wednesday Mercury sextile Saturn, Sun conjunct Jupiter; Thursday Mercury enters Libra; Friday Mercury semisquare Venus, Sun sesquiquadrate Uranus; Saturday Mercury conjunct North Node & opposite South Node

---

OCTOBER

SU	M	TU	W	T	F	S
				1	2	3
4	5	6	7	8	9	10
11	12	13	14	15	16	17
18	19	20	21	22	23	24
25	26	27	28	29	30	31

August-September

The tug o' war between giving others attention or help and wanting it ourselves puts a strain on relationships and shows people's true colors.

Moon in Pisces, Void (P) • Void 2:53 am (E)
Moon enters Aries 1:33 am (P), 4:33 am (E)

★ VR 1 MO 31

A strong urge for autonomy, exacerbated by impulsiveness, could entice one to eschew obligations, but there's no escape from the resulting karma.

Moon in Aries • Void 9:37 am (P), 12:37 pm (E)

★ VR 2 TU 01

Ideas, though grand, may not be all that impractical. However, they do need a thorough vetting, without glossing over details, before proceeding.

Moon Void in Aries • Moon enters Taurus 2:02 am (P), 5:02 am (E)

★ VR 2 WE 02

A good dose of aggravation provides motivation to change our orientation. Still, old habits act as inertia, slowing us and making it hard to change.

Moon in Taurus

VR 2 TH 03

Wheels are turning in your head, opening your eyes to something out of the ordinary. You'll need to discern whether it's true or fooling you.

Moon in Taurus • Void 3:20 am (P), 6:20 am (E)
Moon enters Gemini 4:48 am (P), 7:48 am (E)

VR 1 FR 04

With a little forethought (and unless doubt creeps in), you'll know the right things to say to express love and healing to inspire positive changes.

Moon in Gemini • Third Quarter Moon
Void 4:04 pm (P), 7:04 pm (E)

★ VR 3 SA 05

A nurturing bond (familial or otherwise) spurs a turning point as we try to bring order to chaos or, conversely, shake up what is too staid and stuffy.

Moon Void in Gemini • Moon enters Cancer 10:40 am (P), 1:40 pm (E)

★ 1 SU 06

AUG. 31–SEPT. 06 HIGHLIGHTS

We've probably had about enough of reviewing relationships and making adjustments, revisiting old hurts and issues, and trying to get resolution about them. The push for this hits a natural end-point Sunday, although there will be lingering effects the next four to six weeks. Finances have been adjusted, as well, and we're poised to make progress in that department. We're especially antsy Monday to Tuesday, wondering when we can get a move on. We see the light at the end of the tunnel Saturday. Still, we won't have a sense of much forward motion the next couple weeks. Then the pace picks up around the equinox. Monday through Friday, we're busy assessing and making judgments about independence versus dependence and who needs help or who can provide it. Some people only need a shot of confidence to shift from the receiving end to the giving side of the spectrum. Others fiercely proclaim self-sufficiency, even if resisting outside input is to their detriment. On the weekend, strength, maturity and good boundaries contribute to a feeling of security and the ability to handle whatever curve balls come our way. Self-love is another factor that makes all the difference. We may find this crucial ingredient right under our own roof.

Astro-Overview: *The Sun completes aspects Monday (sesquiquadrate Eris and opposite Neptune) that were forming at last Saturday's Full Moon. The Moon pesters these planets Tuesday evening and Friday night, also bothering Thursday's Sun-Ceres sesquiquadrate then. Overnight Monday, Venus joins Mars. The Moon helps us catch their power Saturday. As Venus did last week, Mars links to the Nodes in Friday's wee hours, noticed more with a Moon contact Sunday. The biggest item this week is Jupiter sesquiquadrate Uranus Wednesday. The last time they clashed was in a square in the Cardinal Grand Cross of April, 2014. Developments now may connect to events then. Saturn and Eris are biquintile Saturday (in a quick Quintile Triangle with the Moon Sunday night), reinforcing strides made Aug. 17-18 in their QT with Mercury. The Sun trines Pluto Saturday, sparked by the Moon next Monday. Venus returns to forward motion Sunday.*

Details: *Monday Sun sesquiquadrate Eris, Sun opposite Neptune; Monday (P)/Tuesday (E) Venus conjunct Mars; Wednesday Jupiter sesquiquadrate Uranus; Thursday Sun sesquiquadrate Ceres; Friday Mars semisquare North Node & sesquiquadrate South Node; Saturday Saturn biquintile Eris, Sun trine Pluto; Sunday Venus turns Direct*

▶ See p. 3 for meaning of Moon Void.

Service to others is the rent you pay for your room here on earth.
Muhammad Ali

AUGUST						
SU	M	TU	W	T	F	S
						1
2	3	4	5	6	7	8
9	10	11	12	13	14	15
16	17	18	19	20	21	22
23	24	25	26	27	28	29
30	31					

SEPTEMBER						
SU	M	TU	W	T	F	S
		1	2	3	4	5
6	7	8	9	10	11	12
13	14	15	16	17	18	19
20	21	22	23	24	25	26
27	28	29	30			

Moon in Cancer

07 MO 2

Forceful words could push someone past a limit. If delivered with tenderness, the same message serves its purpose and builds a bond.

Labor Day (U.S. & Canada)

Moon in Cancer • Void 6:28 pm (P), 9:28 pm (E)
Moon enters Leo 7:36 pm (P), 10:36 pm (E)

08 TU 2 ★

You may feel you have to sacrifice your wants to fulfill another person's, but it's not an either/or situation. Ingenuity offers a win-win answer.

Moon in Leo

09 WE 1 ★

Enthusiasm can't compensate for low energy early. Later, people play the Devil's Advocate to turn a conversation's direction or present both sides.

Moon in Leo

10 TH 4

Excitement permeates the atmosphere from morning until evening. We're confident, feeling charged and up to whatever competition or tasks we face.

Moon in Leo • Void 6:03 am (P), 9:03 am (E)
Moon enters Virgo 6:55 am (P), 9:55 am (E)

11 FR 2

Try not to start the day with a negative attitude despite an uphill struggle. By tonight, a weird turn of events has a fortunate outcome, or so it seems.

Patriot Day (U.S.)

Moon in Virgo • Solar Eclipse New Moon (P)

12 SA 2 ★

Criticism trumps empathy, if you're not mindful. It's tough to be diplomatic and let irritations slide, but judgments aren't the route to improve circumstances.

Moon in Virgo • Solar Eclipse New Moon (E) • Void 7:08 pm (P),
10:08 pm (E) • Moon enters Libra 7:41 pm (P), 10:41 pm (E)

13 SU 4 ★

Care and support lay the foundation for greater harmony in the weeks ahead, when cooperation and mutual assistance should succeed over selfishness.

Grandparents' Day (U.S.)

SEPTEMBER 07-13 HIGHLIGHTS

Often people require awareness and effort to balance or blend a soft side and a hard side. Different situations respond better to one or the other approach. A person can show too much weakness or too much strength. This week and next, it's hard to know how to act in this regard, particularly on both Tuesdays. This Tuesday, additional challenges come from impatience and focusing on oneself. On both Tuesdays, nurturing instincts are emphasized and the question is whether to aim these at personal needs or put the attention on a significant other. Self-concern definitely steals the spotlight Thursday; it's not even a contest. Wednesday, Friday morning and Saturday, discussions dig deeply into how power and resources are shared. Other topics are finances, sex and reproduction. Strong opinions are expressed and stubbornness is likely. A big astrological event is this weekend: a Solar Eclipse New Moon [Saturday 11:41 pm (P), Sunday 2:41 am (E)] in Virgo. This major beginning is in the sign of service and helping others, as well as health-consciousness. In the coming month, we concentrate on healing, whether physically, emotionally or spiritually. Old wounds may be examined in a new light and a fresh start can be made to relieve current pain.

Astro-Overview: *The Neptune-Eris semisquare is exact Tuesday for the second of three times. The Moon gives them a shove that morning and again next Tuesday evening. Mars trines Uranus Tuesday and Eris Sunday night, highlighted by the Moon Thursday for a fiery burst of energy. Mercury, square Pluto Wednesday and semisquare Saturn Saturday, accentuates the August 13 Saturn-Pluto semisquare. The Moon pumps them up Monday opposing Pluto and again early Friday morning. The North and South Nodes, which show where in the zodiac eclipses can occur, will shift into Virgo and Pisces, respectively, October 9 (see the Star Pages). This weekend's New Moon is the first eclipse in Virgo since February 2008. The Sun and Moon are quincunx Uranus and opposite Chiron, underscoring the Chiron-Uranus semisextile, which occurs 37 times 2009-2048, most recently August 19. They are also (more widely) trine Ceres. At the eclipse, Saturn is less than two degrees from sextile to the North Node and trine to the South Node (exact Sept. 26).*

Details: *Tuesday Neptune semisquare Eris, Mars trine Uranus; Wednesday Mercury square Pluto; Saturday Sun opposite Chiron, Mercury semisquare Saturn; Saturday (P)/Sunday (E) Solar Eclipse New Moon; Sunday (P) Mars trine Eris*

OCTOBER

SU	M	TU	W	T	F	S
					1	2	3
4	5	6	7	8	9	10
11	12	13	14	15	16	17
18	19	20	21	22	23	24
25	26	27	28	29	30	31

There is not much of a break, only a space of eleven days, between the end of Venus Retrograde (Sept. 6) and the beginning of another Mercury Retrograde (Sept. 17).

September

Pause to reflect on requests for backing, your own and the needs of others. How much energy must be devoted? Are appropriate boundaries in place?

Rosh Hashanah

Moon in Libra

★ 2 MO 14

Take a moment this morning to convey a thoughtful message. Later, people get wrapped up in their own world, whether their work, misery or adversaries.

Moon in Libra • Void 9:22 pm (P)

2 TU 15

Is adequate attention being given to or received from a partner or teammate? A lack, even if imagined rather than real, spawns hurt or sparks criticism.

Mexican Independence Day

Moon in Libra, Void (P) • Void 12:22 am (E)
Moon enters Scorpio 8:43 am (P), 11:43 am (E)

★ 1 WE 16

You feel something needs to change, either on the job or in your private life. Realizing now is not the best period to push for it, you resign yourself to waiting.

Constitution Day (Citizenship Day) (U.S.)

Moon in Scorpio

★ MR P 1 TH 17

This morning, there's a lot of sharing, with mutual responsibility and service. Then aggression and power struggles rumble until calm finally descends.

Moon in Scorpio • Void 12:49 pm (P), 3:49 pm (E)
Moon enters Sagittarius 8:32 pm (P), 11:32 pm (E)

MR 3 FR 18

Our minds and/or actions are scattered helter-skelter in a morass of confusion that becomes irritating. The fix is to slow down and address one thing at a time.

Moon in Sagittarius

MR 1 SA 19

Optimism skyrockets; enthusiasm and energy peak. We strive to stretch our reach and risk trying a new activity, though there may be a measure of fear to get past.

Moon in Sagittarius

MR 3 SU 20

The Libra time of year starts Sept. 23. Already we're embroiled in relationship examinations that will increase over the coming weeks. The planet of thought and communication begins a three-week backward step Thursday, extending its visit to Libra, the sign of love, marriage and partnership. While there, it works to uncover what's been hidden and explain the psychology of our interactions with the people we hold most dear. (See Sept. 9 in the Star Pages.) Adjustments to the direction of liaisons come Wednesday and again Thursday evening, when extreme emotions enter in. Balancing individual desires against a significant other's is at the heart of the matter. There may be a connection at these times to occurrences around June 29 and August 24. The issue of being pushy versus yielding mentioned in last week's Highlights continues, under a magnifying glass Wednesday night, Thursday and Saturday. How much or how well we nurture or need nurturing is emphasized Monday and Friday. Also Monday as well as Tuesday night, we're concerned about our level of independence and autonomy. Thursday night, an extended period begins of being more serious about fulfilling an urge for freedom and adventure. Sunday is a great day for plans along that line.

SEPTEMBER 14-20 HIGHLIGHTS

Astro-Overview: *Moving forward again now, Venus repeats Wednesday the semisquare to the North Node and sesquiquadrate to the South Node that it made June 29 and August 24. The Moon amplifies these aspects Thursday evening. Mars and Jupiter both aspect Eris, Mars in a trine Monday and Jupiter in a sesquiquadrate Thursday. Wednesday night, Jupiter opposes Neptune, putting pressure on the Neptune-Eris semisquare, still tightly in orb. The Moon nicks all three Tuesday night and again Saturday. Ceres turns Direct Monday and promptly receives a trine from the Sun Friday, which the Moon boosts that afternoon. Mercury turns Retrograde Thursday and Saturn re-enters Sagittarius that night for a long visit. Venus is approaching a repeat of its trines to Uranus (exact next Tuesday) and Eris (exact Sept. 29), so as the Moon transits Sagittarius, it creates a Fire Grand Trine with them Sunday morning to afternoon.*

Details: *Monday (E) Mars trine Eris; Monday Ceres turns Direct; Wednesday Venus semisquare North Node & sesquiquadrate South Node; Wednesday (P)/Thursday (E) Jupiter opposite Neptune; Thursday Mercury turns Retrograde, Jupiter sesquiquadrate Eris, Saturn re-enters Sagittarius; Friday Sun trine Ceres; Sunday (P) Mercury semisquare Saturn*

▶ See p. 3 for meaning of symbols ★, **MR**, **VR**, **P**.

Health is the greatest gift, contentment the greatest wealth, faithfulness the best relationship.
Buddha

Moon in Sagittarius • First Quarter Moon • Void 1:59 am (P),
4:59 am (E) • Moon enters Capricorn 5:33 am (P), 8:33 am (E)

21 MO 1 MR

Responsibility weighs heavily on our shoulders. It's motivational but not joyful. We may wish we could escape it and we're happy when we hit the pillow tonight.

International Day of Peace

Moon in Capricorn • Void 4:13 pm (P), 7:13 pm (E)

22 TU 2 MR

Grumbling and displeasure early on dissipate when hopes rise for solutions and improvements, though impatient types will still be disappointed.

Moon Void in Capricorn
Moon enters Aquarius 10:51 am (P), 1:51 pm (E)

23 WE 3 MR ★

Yesterday's complaints may resurface today but most people feel good enough about themselves they won't be bothered. Cooperation is much better.

Autumn Equinox, Mabon, Yom Kippur, Eid al-Adha, Sun enters Libra

---

Moon in Aquarius • Void 9:02 pm (P)

24 TH 2 MR ★

A careful examination, perhaps rethinking what's been addressed before, shows a different way of looking at a topic. Equality could be at issue.

Moon in Aquarius, Void (P) • Void 12:02 am (E)
Moon enters Pisces 12:44 pm (P), 3:44 pm (E)

25 FR 1 P MR ★

The going is slow; it feels like we're getting nowhere. People are crabby and stubborn this morning and aloof or unavailable tonight. Rely on yourself.

Native American Day (CA & WA)

Moon in Pisces • Void 9:32 am (P), 12:32 pm (E)

26 SA 3 MR ★

Any moaning is over early. The rest of the day, we use positive visualization to make a difference. A steady hand on the rudder keeps us from drifting off course.

Moon Void in Pisces • Moon enters Aries 12:29 pm (P),
3:29 pm (E) • Lunar Eclipse Full Moon (Blood Moon)

27 SU 4 MR ★

After a lazy or relaxing morning, energy first floats, then soars. We're more interested in our own pursuits than what others want, which might make waves.

SEPTEMBER 21-27 HIGHLIGHTS

Autumn is official Wednesday morning [1:21 am (P), 4:21 am (E)] and it looks like a weird one. (See Seasonal Synopses, p. 75.) A point showing our direction for growth reaches the equinox degree, greeting the Sun as it enters Libra. It signals that our mission for the season is to truly balance our own concerns with those of others and compromise so everyone has a fair shot. However, the most self-oriented planet exerts strong influence, locked in a snarl that inclines people to battle for dominance. Perhaps venting frustrations allows us to address the causes better. In addition, the ruler of the sign of love and harmony is wide open to the vagaries of the planet of the unexpected and a pattern impacting how people support one another puts us under duress. Behavior in relationships has an important impact during this period between eclipses, when energies are intensified and volatile. Karma is at play. Knowing that could keep us on track. We need to be wary that imagination doesn't over-inflate matters. Big changes are in the air; we're at a turning point. Something must be left behind to make way for the new. A key culmination is illuminated by the Lunar Eclipse Full Moon Sunday [7:50 pm (P), 10:50 pm (E)] (see the Star Pages).

Astro-Overview: *What a crazy, stressful week! The Sun enters Libra Wednesday two days before Pluto's Direct station Friday. Then comes Sunday's Lunar Eclipse Full Moon. Retrograde Mercury and Mars, semisquare Wednesday, weave a gnarly tangle with Saturn and Pluto (separating from their Aug. 13 semisquare). Mercury is semisquare Saturn Monday (see Sept. 7-13 Astro-Overview) and square Pluto Thursday, a repeating aspect in this Retrograde cycle (see Star Pages for Sept. 9). Mars is sesquiquadrate Pluto Monday and, after entering Virgo Thursday, is square Saturn Friday night, hours after the Pisces Moon drenches them in a T-square. The Moon also disturbs this discordant quartet Tuesday morning and next Monday. The Nodes and Saturn have a third warm embrace Saturday (see the Star Pages).*

Details: *Monday (E) Mercury semisquare Saturn; Monday Mars sesquiquadrate Pluto; Tuesday Venus trine Uranus; Wednesday Sun enters Libra, Mercury semisquare Mars, Sun sextile Saturn; Wednesday (P)/ Thursday (E) Sun conjunct North Node & opposite South Node; Thursday Mercury square Pluto, Mars enters Virgo; Thursday (P)/Friday (E) Pluto turns Direct; Friday Mars square Saturn; Saturday Saturn sextile North Node & trine South Node; Sunday Lunar Eclipse Full Moon*

NOVEMBER

SU	M	TU	W	T	F	S
1	2	3	4	5	6	7
8	9	10	11	12	13	14
15	16	17	18	19	20	21
22	23	24	25	26	27	28
29	30					

September-October

Everyone's in a rush and haste is making waste every which way. Any caution in place this morning and afternoon is thrown to the wind by tonight.

Moon in Aries

MR 2 MO 28

Sukkot begins

You crave a freewheeling feeling but loyalties and obligations rope you down. This evening's me time is superseded by having to help someone in need.

Moon in Aries • Void 12:45 am (P), 3:45 am (E)
Moon enters Taurus 11:57 am (P), 2:57 pm (E)

MR 2 TU 29

Circumstances beyond your control intrude this afternoon, interrupting what is otherwise quite a pleasant day. Late tonight, rain heads for your parade.

Moon in Taurus

★ **MR 3 WE 30**

Morning and evening, we analyze our actions, resulting in dissatisfactions. But this afternoon, brilliance shines, wisdom triumphs and magic is possible.

Moon in Taurus • Void 3:44 am (P), 6:44 am (E)
Moon enters Gemini 1:03 pm (P), 4:03 pm (E)

★ **MR 2 TH 01**

Any sunny outlook early is soon engulfed in an overcast of sour attitude, bogged down by minutiae. Focusing on what's worse doesn't lead us to what's better.

Moon in Gemini

MR 1 FR 02

Communication and cooperation are elevated when an element of fun or creativity is introduced. Tonight, emotions are tense and strained between mates.

Moon in Gemini • Void 10:18 am (P), 1:18 pm (E)
Moon enters Cancer 5:22 pm (P), 8:22 pm (E)

MR 3 SA 03

The morning is graced with caring and lending a hand. Though some of that largess spills over into the evening, it can't overpower a begrudging sense of duty.

Moon in Cancer • Third Quarter Moon

MR 3 SU 04

Though the Sun in Libra period is known for peace and love, we're not at our most amorous this fall, diminishing the affection we show others and even - perhaps most importantly - ourselves. Tuesday to Thursday and Sunday are frosted by this chilling effect, which is even more potent next week. Talking through problems may help but could easily descend into repetition of old dialogues. A shake-up in the status quo is brewing. The ways this might manifest will be more evident in about three weeks. Already people are poised to jump the gun, though, particularly Monday night and throughout Thursday. These are times when tempers are on edge and the chance for mishaps increases. While we should always pay special attention to our words and movement during Retrogrades of Mercury (which governs all forms of communication and ground transportation), these are moments to really watch one's mouth and step. Judgment, criticism and egocentrism interfere when we seek or offer support Tuesday to Friday. Encouragement might come out sounding more like preaching or bragging, or aim to fill a self-serving agenda. Take advantage of a brief mental highpoint Thursday afternoon, good for brainstorming, and latch onto a tender moment Sunday morning.

SEPT. 28-OCTOBER 04 HIGHLIGHTS

Astro-Overview: *Venus and the Sun hone in on their Oct. 7 semisquare, triggered by Mercury Tuesday (semisquare Venus) and Wednesday (conjunct the Sun). Most people will be asleep when the Moon annoys these three overnight Wednesday, but not when it stirs up the Venus-Sun abrasion at Sunday's Third Quarter Moon. The Saturn-Uranus sesquiquadrate (exact Oct. 22) is heating up, goosed by Mars' square to Saturn last Friday and sesquiquadrate to Uranus this Thursday (signaling accident potential). They rattle as the Moon bumps them from afternoon to evening Monday and again Thursday night. Ceres is sesquiquadrate Jupiter overnight Wednesday, foreshadowed by a slap from the Moon early Tuesday, reprised Friday morning. Overshadowed by this strong turbulence, Venus is trine Eris Tuesday for the third time (see July 3 in the Star Pages). The Moon joins Eris in Tuesday's wee hours and sextiles it and Venus early Saturday. The Moon forms a quick Mystic Rectangle with Saturn and the Nodes Thursday afternoon and trines Neptune early Sunday, offering brief relief.*

Details: *Tuesday Venus trine Eris, Mercury semisquare Venus; Wednesday Mercury conjunct Sun; Wednesday (P)/Thursday (E) Ceres sesquiquadrate Jupiter; Thursday Mars sesquiquadrate Uranus*

    ▶ See p. 3 for meaning of Moon Void.   **45**

Love is like quicksilver in the hand.
Leave the fingers open, and it stays.
Clutch it, and it darts away.

Dorothy Parker

SEPTEMBER							OCTOBER						
SU	M	TU	W	T	F	S	SU	M	TU	W	T	F	S
			1	2	3	4	5					1	2	3
6	7	8	9	10	11	12	4	5	6	7	8	9	10
13	14	15	16	17	18	19	11	12	13	14	15	16	17
20	21	22	23	24	25	26	18	19	20	21	22	23	24
27	28	29	30				25	26	27	28	29	30	31

Moon in Cancer • Void 4:04 am (P), 7:04 am (E)

05 MO 1 MR

A moody Monday finds many singing the blues, feeling put upon or put down. A jittery, irritated edge starts the day and attitudes plummet from there.

World Habitat Day

Moon Void in Cancer
Moon enters Leo 1:31 am (P), 4:31 am (E)

06 TU 2 P MR

The pendulum swings out to the farthest point in relationship or monetary affairs, making us anxious. At least, our thinking is grounded.

Moon in Leo • Void 2:10 pm (P), 5:10 pm (E)

07 WE 1 MR ★

Self-concern is at the center of all forms of exchange, in some instances in healthy ways and in other cases, dysfunctionally. Look for this in the news, too.

Moon Void in Leo
Moon enters Virgo 12:50 pm (P), 3:50 pm (E)

08 TH 2 MR ★

This afternoon, heartfelt service and fondness for accuracy are the best today can offer. Otherwise, we're annoyed by criticism or too many details.

Moon in Virgo • Void 3:12 pm (P), 6:12 pm (E)

09 FR 3 ★

High standards and expectations produce complaints. Stop and view situations fairly. An unexpected boon lifts spirits this afternoon, bringing a turn-around.

Moon Void in Virgo

10 SA 1

We start the day vulnerable. Then harmony is upset by judgments (of oneself or a partner) for violating boundaries or principles. Support arrives late on the scene.

Moon Void in Virgo
Moon enters Libra 1:45 am (P), 4:45 am (E)

11 SU 3 ★

The strength of a bond is re-established through honest discourse to find compromise or take a break. It's practical to clear the decks and prepare for a new chapter.

OCTOBER 05-11 HIGHLIGHTS

Challenges continue in the Libra arena of close interpersonal interactions. Since Libra's ruling planet also governs finances, they could take a hit, too. Most days this week are tainted: Monday (late) through Thursday and Saturday. Stress arises from a poor sense of self-worth on the part of either partner. There's good news, though. Communication mix-ups decrease in quantity or intensity as Mercury's Retrograde in Libra concludes Thursday. Mercury's one connection, Tuesday, brings realism and clarity. The sign-pair indicating areas slated for growth and release leaves the Libra/Aries polarity Friday. This should diminish relationship conflicts or their resulting karma. Before relief sets in, there's another tug on the planetary knot that pits us between being pushy and lenient. The pull comes from the planet of aggression and impatience, jarring us Monday through Wednesday and again early Friday. Fortunately, an upbeat planet has two positive links at the end of the week (both bolstered by the Moon Friday afternoon). It strokes the planet of surprises Friday for luck. Sunday, it combines with the planet of transformation to ease the process of any current transitions. Their blend is also fortuitous for financial and health matters.

Astro-Overview: *Venus and the Sun are semisquare Wednesday, before Venus re-enters Virgo Thursday. They tango with the Saturn-Pluto semisquare Tuesday (aspecting Pluto) and Saturday (aspecting Saturn). The Moon scratches all four Thursday and next Monday, when Uranus is also involved (receiving aspects from the Sun Sunday and Venus next Monday). Mercury's last aspect while Retrograde is sextile Saturn Tuesday, lit up by the Moon early that day. Friday, Mercury turns Direct. Mars opposes Neptune Tuesday and is sesquiquadrate Eris Wednesday, kicking the Neptune-Eris semisquare, still in orb. The Moon messes with all three midday Monday and early Friday. The Nodes enter new signs Friday. Jupiter is biquintile Uranus Friday and trine Pluto Sunday. The Moon joins Jupiter Friday afternoon, blessing both aspects.*

Details: *Monday (P)/Tuesday (E) Venus sesquiquadrate Pluto; Tuesday Sun square Pluto, Mercury sextile Saturn, Mars opposite Neptune; Wednesday Mars sesquiquadrate Eris, Venus semisquare Sun; Thursday Venus re-enters Virgo; Friday Mercury turns Direct, Jupiter biquintile Uranus, North Node enters Virgo & South Node enters Pisces; Saturday Sun semisquare Saturn, Venus square Saturn; Sunday Jupiter trine Pluto, Sun opposite Uranus*

NOVEMBER

SU	M	TU	W	T	F	S
1	2	3	4	5	6	7
8	9	10	11	12	13	14
15	16	17	18	19	20	21
22	23	24	25	26	27	28
29	30					

The earth-Sun and Moon-earth orbits intersect at two points, the North Node and South Node, which show where eclipses occur. On October 9, they move into new signs (see the Star Pages).

October

The urge to embrace conflicts with a desire for space. Inequity erects a barrier to negotiation or cooperation. It might be best to walk away for the moment.

Columbus Day (U.S.), Native Americans Day (SD), Thanksgiving (Canada)

Moon in Libra • New Moon
Void 5:06 pm (P), 8:06 pm (E)

1 MO 12

Key people aren't there for us. It might be they're just busy but it smarts as if they're showing a cold shoulder. Maybe we'll learn a lesson from it.

Navaratri

Moon Void in Libra
Moon enters Scorpio 2:38 pm (P), 5:38 pm (E)

2 TU 13

Things have turned around for the better since yesterday. Armed with drive and inspiration, we accomplish a lot. It's a good day for organizing and purging.

Al-Hijra/Muharram (Islamic New Year)

Moon in Scorpio • Void 5:58 pm (P), 8:58 pm (E)

4 WE 14

We're stymied as we try to get a project off the ground. All the pieces are not yet in place and something hidden is causing a problem. Persistence will uncover it.

Moon Void in Scorpio

2 TH 15

Chaos stops by for an uninvited visit. You think things are under control early. That illusion is soon dispelled. Try to regain equilibrium ahead of a crazy evening.

National Boss Day

Moon Void in Scorpio • Moon enters
Sagittarius 2:18 am (P), 5:18 am (E)

P 1 FR 16

Too much on the TO DO list may be an exercise in frustration. We're distracted on tangents until afternoon. Then high energy carries us over the finish line.

Sweetest Day

Moon in Sagittarius

2 SA 17

A wide view makes it clear which of multiple choices to pursue today. Rather than going solo, it likely involves teamwork and being of service to others.

Moon in Sagittarius • Void 1:48 am (P), 4:48 am (E)
Moon enters Capricorn 11:52 am (P), 2:52 pm (E)

3 SU 18

The four-week cycle beginning at Monday's New Moon in Libra [5:06 pm (P), 8:06 pm (E)] could be make-it-or-break-it time for some couples. The planet most indicative of separation, as well as fierce independence and rebellion, is in a stand-off with the Sun and Moon. All three clash with the love planet, which is also under pressure from the planet of restrictions and limitations. There will be tests, including examination of past transgressions. The piper is coming to be paid. At least we're in a mindset to face reality. Interchange could include the same topics this Tuesday as were discussed last Tuesday. Some partners may offer forgiveness while others think they're better off by themselves. Things hit a peak Friday, when projection and misperception sully the conversation. Improvement may not come until next week. Actions are exaggerated from Tuesday to Saturday. At best, these will express as helpfulness on a grand scale (most likely on Wednesday, the easiest day this week); at worst, as a tirade of finger-pointing (perhaps midday Tuesday or Saturday morning). Positive outcomes from such confrontations are processing pain to move beyond it and relinquishing attempts to control one's mate or run the show in a relationship.

OCTOBER 12-18 HIGHLIGHTS

Astro-Overview: *The key features of the New Moon Monday involve the Sun-Venus semisquare exact last week. The Moon is likewise semisquare Venus and opposite Uranus (as the Sun was last Sunday). Venus is still in its square to Saturn from last Saturday, while Saturn nears a sesquiquadrate to Uranus (exact Oct. 22). Venus is sesquiquadrate Uranus this Monday. Next Venus steps into the Neptune-Eris semisquare Friday to Saturday, as the Sun does Thursday to Friday. The Moon pinches these four Friday evening. Mars joins Jupiter Saturday, repeating Wednesday and Thursday, respectively, Jupiter's biquintile to Uranus and trine to Pluto of last week. The Moon is friendly to Mars, Pluto and Jupiter Wednesday afternoon to evening. Thursday, Mars is also sesquiquadrate Ceres. Slower Jupiter, traveling at about the same rate as Ceres, made this aspect Oct. 1 and will again Nov. 10. Both last and this Tuesday, Mercury (now Direct) is sextile Saturn.*

Details: *Monday Venus sesquiquadrate Uranus; Tuesday Mercury sextile Saturn; Wednesday Mars biquintile Uranus; Thursday Mars sesquiquadrate Ceres, Sun sesquiquadrate Neptune, Mars trine Pluto; Friday Sun opposite Eris, Venus opposite Neptune; Saturday Venus sesquiquadrate Eris, Mars conjunct Jupiter*

▶ See p. 3 for meaning of symbols ★, **MR, VR, P.**

If we do an eye for an eye and a tooth for a tooth, we will be a blind and toothless nation.
Martin Luther King Jr.

Moon in Capricorn

19 MO 3

A purposeful approach yields optimum results. Alterations are required along the way but these are handled without difficulty. There might be an upset late, though.

Moon in Capricorn • First Quarter Moon • Void 1:31 pm (P), 4:31 pm (E) • Moon enters Aquarius 6:38 pm (P), 9:38 pm (E)

20 TU 2

Uncertainty mars the morning. Agreeing on plans is a struggle this afternoon and easier in early evening. Later, objections and arguments resume.

Moon in Aquarius

21 WE 3

We're on firm intellectual footing and see circumstances realistically. Most folks are friendly and cooperative, making this a good day for meetings or socializing.

**Moon in Aquarius • Void 9:22 pm (P)
Moon enters Pisces 10:18 pm (P)**

22 TH 1 P ★

People waffle and change their minds. They don't want to be pinned down and recoil at the enforcement of rules, wanting others to get off their case.

**Moon in Pisces (P), in Aquarius (E) • Void 12:22 am (E)
Moon enters Pisces 1:18 am (E)**

23 FR 3 ★

Emotions are strong today and something goes over the top, whether it's affection and offers for assistance or discontent that pushes for change.

Ashura, Sun enters Scorpio

**Moon in Pisces • Void 4:18 am (P), 7:18 am (E)
Moon enters Aries 11:22 pm (P)**

24 SA 2

We feel each other's pain or maybe we harm one another. Either way, we're not in a world of hurt alone. We could put caring into constructive service.

United Nations Day, Make a Difference Day

**Moon in Aries (P), Void in Pisces (E)
Moon enters Aries 2:22 am (E)**

25 SU 3 ★

Our energy is high today. We're in GO mode to do a lot, especially if there's someone special with whom to do it. But tonight, closeness is not a comfort.

OCTOBER 19-25 HIGHLIGHTS

As the famous Ecclesiastes verse tells us, "to everything, there is a season;" a time to create order, a time when order breaks down; seasons when things grow and when they wilt. Of course, plants go to seed in fall and Scorpio (which the Sun enters Friday) is the sign of death and regeneration. This fall, decay occurs across the board, symbolically. Flourishing is stunted, largely due to disagreement on basic values. This is painfully apparent Thursday to Saturday. Furthermore, we're at a point of re-thinking what constitutes order and authority. Discussions this week (especially Thursday and late Sunday) about who has power and how it's wielded could hark back to situations last December or this past May (see Oct. 22 in the Star Pages). Leaders of all types are criticized more than praised. In personal lives, elders and marital partners suffer a lack of respect. People gripe, displeased with the way things are and have been. They're hungry for change but disinclined to take the time to strategize the best structure for it. They just want a quick fix. Overwhelmed by problems, many fail to grasp brief chances to make practical headway Tuesday evening and Friday night, or to have productive, peaceful conversations Wednesday afternoon.

Astro-Overview: *The Sun and Venus, still semisquare, hit on Ceres (the Sun, Thursday; Venus, Saturday) and Jupiter (the Sun, Friday, after entering Scorpio, and Venus, Sunday), before their sesquiquadrate Nov. 10. The Moon aggravates all four Tuesday and Friday night. Thursday, Mercury squares Pluto (see Star Pages for Sept. 9), bumped by the Moon that evening and Monday morning. Also Monday, the Moon boosts Pluto's trine from Venus (exact Friday) and recent trines from Jupiter and Mars. Saturn and Uranus are sesquiquadrate Thursday, poked by the Moon Monday night and early Friday. Mercury stings them Sunday (opposite Uranus) and next Monday (semisquare Saturn), when the Moon scrapes them all. A Mars-Chiron opposition early Friday is felt more as the Moon prods it Tuesday night. Ceres and the Nodes link nicely Friday, enhanced by the Moon Tuesday evening.*

Details: *Thursday Saturn sesquiquadrate Uranus, Sun square Ceres, Mercury square Pluto; Friday Venus trine Pluto, Mars opposite Chiron, Sun enters Scorpio, North Node trine & South Node sextile Ceres, Sun semisquare Jupiter; Saturday Venus sesquiquadrate Ceres; Sunday Venus conjunct Jupiter, Mercury opposite Uranus; Sunday (P) Sun sesquiquadrate Chiron, Mercury semisquare Saturn*

DECEMBER

SU	M	TU	W	T	F	S
		1	2	3	4	5
6	7	8	9	10	11	12
13	14	15	16	17	18	19
20	21	22	23	24	25	26
27	28	29	30	31		

October-November

We're ready to floor the accelerator but the light is red. Impatience might be placated by maturity. Pushy people topple those who yield or are weak.

Moon in Aries • Void 5:25 am (P), 8:25 am (E)
Moon enters Taurus 11:07 pm (P)

P 1 MO 26

Probing deep into emotional waters raises the specter of drowned pain. Everyone needs a hug today or at least some sympathy and sage advice.

Moon in Taurus (P), Void in Aries (E) • Moon enters
Taurus 2:07 am (E) • Full Moon (Snow Moon)

★ **2 TU 27**

When someone is selfish, others can chide him or let it slide. Discussing the matter might be difficult or delicate but that's no excuse to ignore it.

Moon in Taurus • Void 8:20 am (P), 11:20 am (E)
Moon enters Gemini 11:24 pm (P)

2 WE 28

Tough topics must be addressed, calling for diplomacy and tact, but these don't come to our aid immediately, especially if distrust interferes.

Moon in Gemini (P), Void in Taurus (E)
Moon enters Gemini 2:24 am (E)

2 TH 29

You can't help but put your own agenda at the top of your list. So much else needs to be done, you might feel guilty about it. Don't be so hard on yourself.

Moon in Gemini • Void 7:52 pm (P), 10:52 pm (E)

2 FR 30

Surrender to imagination and escape into fantasy. Doing so releases pent-up feelings. Enjoy food and fun with family or friends who are like family.

Halloween, All Hallows' Eve, Samhain

Moon Void in Gemini • Moon enters Cancer
2:09 am (PDT), 5:09 am (EDT)

4 SA 31

Though we don't necessarily understand exactly what another person is experiencing, we can promote each other's healing through affection and encouragement.

All Saints' Day, Dia de los Muertos, Daylight Saving Time ends at 2 am

Moon in Cancer • Void 7:35 pm (PST), 10:35 pm (EST)

★ **2 SU 01**

The conundrums of last week continue Monday and Thursday morning, turning conversations to contemplating the cutting edge versus established ways of doing things. Wednesday and Thursday, minds focus on striking a balance between people with greed and people in need. Of course, the main event of the week is the Full Moon Tuesday [5:05 am (P), 8:05 am (E)]. With the Sun in transitional Scorpio and the Moon in intractable Taurus, change is definitely needed but meets with resistance. There's a feeling of deterrence instead of determination to forge ahead. Maybe we're unsure or disagree about what improvements to make or how to go about implementing them. Possibly resentment and hurt feelings stand in the way. We are willing to assist others (unless we need support ourselves), but people are mostly interested in acting on their passions, whether those are romantic, artistic or charitable. The Full Moon is close enough to Halloween to provide an ample glow, brightening evening festivities and revelers will enjoy that the holiday is on a Saturday this year. That night, conditions are right for pretending and portraying roles, as well as creating illusions. It's a very good party night, as long as you're careful about being "under the influence."

OCT. 26-NOVEMBER 01 HIGHLIGHTS

Astro-Overview: *The Saturn-Uranus sesquiquadrate (exact Oct. 22) is in Mercury's crosshairs (opposite Uranus, semisquare Saturn) overnight Sunday to Monday, instantly shot by the Moon passing Uranus that morning. Wednesday, Mercury pummels the Neptune-Eris semisquare (sesquiquadrate Neptune, opposite Eris). The Moon gives them a slap Monday and Thursday afternoon. Tuesday's Full Moon finds the Moon tangled in trying aspects between the Sun, Venus, Mars, Chiron and Ceres (which enters Aquarius that day). Jupiter is nearly in the web, as well. The various components are exact from last week to next, getting a clang from the Full Moon's gong. The Moon makes another series of harsh aspects with this gang Friday. The Sun does have one nice aspect this week, a trine to Neptune, exact Friday. The Full Moon enhances this with a sextile to Neptune, and then the Moon pampers both Saturday night. Mercury finishes its long visit in Libra, departing for Scorpio Sunday night.*

Details: *Monday (E) Sun sesquiquadrate Chiron, Mercury semisquare Saturn; Tuesday Venus opposite Chiron, Ceres enters Aquarius; Wednesday Mercury sesquiquadrate Neptune, Mercury opposite Eris; Friday Sun semisquare Mars, Sun trine Neptune; Sunday (P) Mercury enters Scorpio*

▶ See p. 3 for meaning of Moon Void. **49**

*Unlike fine wine, bottled up emotions
do not taste better with time.*

Glenn Ridless

OCTOBER

SU	M	TU	W	T	F	S
			1	2	3
4	5	6	7	8	9	10
11	12	13	14	15	16	17
18	19	20	21	22	23	24
25	26	27	28	29	30	31

NOVEMBER

SU	M	TU	W	T	F	S
1	2	3	4	5	6	7
8	9	10	11	12	13	14
15	16	17	18	19	20	21
22	23	24	25	26	27	28
29	30

Moon Void in Cancer • Moon enters Leo 7:48 am (P), 10:48 am (E)

02 MO 2 ★

Good thing you have a lot of spine now because slights and barbs (some quite clever) will be lobbed about. Yet there's plenty of heart shining through.

All Souls' Day

Moon in Leo • Third Quarter Moon
Void 5:46 pm (P), 8:46 pm (E)

03 TU 1 P ★

Awareness of what ails you or is going awry must precede repair or restitution. You may be told pointblank or there will be in-your-face signs you can't miss.

Election Day (U.S.)

Moon Void in Leo
Moon enters Virgo 6:22 pm (P), 9:22 pm (E)

04 WE 2

Morning is discombobulated, though not disastrously so. The rest of the day is good for wrapping up a creative project: sorting, organizing, discarding, etc.

Moon in Virgo

05 TH 2 ★

Shakespeare's "I must be cruel, only to be kind," applies today. Add, "I must be bossy, only to make you change," another version of "This is for your own good."

Guy Fawkes Day

Moon in Virgo

06 FR 2

Looking through a divine lens, you see a wider view. Check how your everyday work fits into your overall spiritual mission. If it doesn't, figure out how it could.

Moon in Virgo • Void 4:47 am (P), 7:47 am (E)
Moon enters Libra 7:14 am (P), 10:14 am (E)

07 SA 4

You may have to attend to some work early but the majority of the day is likely to be earmarked for socializing or doing something to benefit someone else.

Moon in Libra • Void 6:42 pm (P), 9:42 pm (E)

08 SU 2 ★

Though the day begins sweetly (great for a breakfast date!), a sudden shift throws you off kilter. Straightening out the mess consumes you through the evening.

NOVEMBER 02-08 HIGHLIGHTS

If you have an ugly or dangerous growth in your body, you cut it off or out. Likewise, when something unhealthy arises in your life, you reach a realization it has got to go. That comes up the first half of this week. It might be a situation at work or in a close relationship. The planet of relating joins the planet of new activity Monday in a sign that inclines us to be more choosy about the people we love. This is reinforced overnight Friday to Saturday morning. We've just come through the main Libra time of year and a key indicator for growth and karma was in Libra from spring of 2014 until Oct.9. This focused us on relationships, balance, fairness and harmony. Sometimes we learn about these through their opposite or absence. This week, no planets are in Libra until the weekend, when the Moon welcomes the sign's ruling planet for a period of rebalancing. Our attention turns to wounds we suffered and the healing we need to do, beginning with excising the source. Scorpio time is designed for taking out the garbage and starting fresh. Our determination to do so is boosted Tuesday and Thursday night. Friday, new inspiration arrives and quickly we connect with people who can be instrumental in refining our affections or healing our heart.

Astro-Overview: *At last week's Full Moon, Ceres and Chiron were becoming entwined and Jupiter was nearly involved. Now the knot is tied. Jupiter is opposite Chiron Tuesday and Ceres is semisquare Chiron Thursday. (Next Tuesday, Ceres is sesquiquadrate Jupiter.) Mercury enters Scorpio in Monday's wee hours and aspects these three from late Monday to Tuesday morning. The Moon shoves all four Monday and the main threesome again very early Friday. (By then, Mercury has scooted out of orb of the trio.) A Sun-Pluto sextile late Thursday night is instantly stroked by the Moon. The Sun quickly tangoes with the Nodes. Mercury is trine Neptune Friday. After joining Mars Monday evening, Venus breezes by the North Node overnight Friday and enters the sign it rules, Libra, Sunday morning.*

Details: *Monday (E) Mercury enters Scorpio; Monday Venus conjunct Mars, Mercury square Ceres; Tuesday Mercury semisquare Jupiter, Mercury sesquiquadrate Chiron, Jupiter opposite Chiron; Thursday Jupiter quincunx Uranus, Ceres semisquare Chiron, Sun sextile Pluto; Thursday (P)/Friday (E) Sun semisquare North Node & sesquiquadrate South Node; Friday Mercury trine Neptune; Friday (P)/Saturday (E) Venus conjunct North Node & opposite South Node; Sunday Venus enters Libra*

DECEMBER

SU	M	TU	W	T	F	S
		1	2	3	4	5
6	7	8	9	10	11	12
13	14	15	16	17	18	19
20	21	22	23	24	25	26
27	28	29	30	31		

A special type of triangle called a Finger of God conducts us via odd detours to a destination that seems cosmically ordained. There are two of these Nov. 9-13 (see the Star Pages).

Enhanced problem-solving abilities and careful analysis lead you to correct action. Something needs to reach closure before you can move ahead.

Moon Void in Libra
Moon enters Scorpio 8:02 pm (P), 11:02 pm (E)

★ **3 MO 09**

Yesterday, you were sure where to head. Today, you're second-guessing yourself. Be confident and trust your intelligence and instincts.

Moon in Scorpio

★ **2 TU 10**

Let one thing go and something better comes along. Follow your heart and attractions. Friends or associates are happy to provide support.

Veterans Day (U.S.), Remembrance Day (Canada)

Moon in Scorpio • New Moon

4 WE 11

An odd line of thinking brings you to a moment of brilliance. Tonight is great for socializing but you may be drained if you overextend yourself.

Moon in Scorpio • Void 6:54 am (P), 9:54 am (E)
Moon enters Sagittarius 7:14 am (P), 10:14 am (E)

★ **3 TH 12**

Multi-tasking is distracting and trying to accomplish too much zaps your energy. A balanced pace is the way to go, and delegate what you can.

Moon in Sagittarius • Void 7:18 pm (P), 10:18 pm (E)

★ **3 FR 13**

Might as well allow time for getting sidetracked cause that's very probable. Try not to let that irritate you. Maybe you should say NO.

Sadie Hawkins Day

Moon Void in Sagittarius
Moon enters Capricorn 4:21 pm (P), 7:21 pm (E)

2 SA 14

Your ingenuity comes to the rescue (possibly more than once) as you find solutions. Yet you wear your power well and manage to maintain humility.

Moon in Capricorn

★ **3 SU 15**

The past few weeks, we've had difficulty getting things to grow the way we want them to. We might have done weeding and pruning to help the process. This week, we start to move past that sluggishness. By the end of next week, we should see progress. Wednesday to Thursday is an appropriate time to assess what is most valuable or lucrative and invest in that (after the New Moon). We may also have felt last week that our luck went on vacation or became strange in some way. This week, a rather unusual pattern puts us through twists and turns but in the end, things turn out alright. Since the influence of whatever is in effect at the New Moon Wednesday [9:47 am (P), 12:47 pm (E)] extends its impact over the coming four-week cycle, we'll have ample opportunity to get back on track. Monday, we get a bright idea for an improvement and how to implement it. In the next step (beginning this weekend), we have the chance to bring special talents to our most unique, individual endeavors. This turn in luck will help those move forward, too. Our attention is drawn to ways in which we can be innovative and reach a wider audience with what we want to communicate. We should find there's less competition and better cooperation from Nov. 12 to Dec. 4.

NOVEMBER 09-15 HIGHLIGHTS

Astro-Overview: *The last aspects Mars has in Virgo before entering Libra Thursday are conjunct the North Node Monday and a semisquare Tuesday from Mercury, which is semisquare the North Node that morning. Mercury and the Sun are trine Chiron and sextile Jupiter (still roughly opposite), echoed by the Moon at Wednesday's New Moon. Last week's Jupiter-Uranus quincunx draws the Mercury and Sun sextiles into Fingers of God (see the Star Pages), also in place at the New Moon, extending their influence over the next month. By the end of the week, Mercury and the Sun are biquintile Uranus, part of Quintile Triangles with Ceres (see next week). Venus is trine Ceres and sextile Saturn ahead of their sextile Nov. 22.*

Details: *Monday Sun trine Chiron, Sun quincunx Uranus, Mars conjunct North Node & opposite South Node; Tuesday Mercury semisquare North Node & sesquiquadrate South Node, Mercury sextile Pluto, Mercury semisquare Mars, Ceres sesquiquadrate Jupiter, Sun sextile Jupiter; Wednesday Venus trine Ceres; Thursday Mercury trine Chiron, Mercury quincunx Uranus, Mars enters Libra; Friday Venus sextile Saturn, Mercury sextile Jupiter; Saturday (P)/Sunday (E) Sun quintile Ceres; Sunday Sun biquintile Uranus; Sunday (P) Mercury quintile Ceres*

▶ See p. 3 for meaning of symbols ★, **MR**, **VR**, **P**.

We have just enough religion to make us hate, but not enough to make us love one another.

Jonathan Swift

Moon in Capricorn • Void 12:53 pm (P), 3:53 pm (E)
Moon enters Aquarius 11:24 pm (P)

16 MO 3 ★

We remain hopeful this morning, despite uncertainties and impediments. Later, our positive expectations, will power and originality pay off.

Moon in Aquarius (P), Void in Capricorn (E)
Moon enters Aquarius 2:24 am (E)

17 TU 3 P ★

Everyone is a bit of a natural psychologist or sleuth today, seeking a deeper meaning or understanding of one's relationship to others or to assets.

Moon in Aquarius • First Quarter Moon (P)

18 WE 2 ★

This is a DYI day: do it yourself. Offers of assistance are unlikely. You want everything done your way anyway and no one can do that better than you-know-who.

Moon in Aquarius • First Quarter Moon (E) • Void 12:19 am (P),
3:19 am (E) • Moon enters Pisces 4:21 am (P), 7:21 am (E)

19 TH 2

Worries got you down? Check if there's merit to your concerns; they might stem from projection or insecurity. The picture looks different tonight.

Moon in Pisces

20 FR 2 ★

Good instincts present solutions to a problem early. Later, information comes to light which makes people question their values, net worth or self-worth.

Moon in Pisces • Void 5:23 am (P), 8:23 am (E)
Moon enters Aries 7:12 am (P), 10:12 am (E)

21 SA 3

Re-orienting objectives boosts confidence. See how a partner or teammate can figure into plans. Ask for advice from someone older and wiser.

Moon in Aries • Void 11:16 am (P), 2:16 pm (E)

22 SU 2 ★

People are bustling about, doing their own business and not too concerned about anybody else, though they might experience a moment of guilt over that.

Sun enters Sagittarius

NOVEMBER 16-22 HIGHLIGHTS

Fertile minds conceive forward-leaning notions as the week begins. By Tuesday, there may be a winner among them to work toward manifesting - if the resources and human-power can be mustered. There's no guarantee of that, at least not yet and maybe not for some time. More than one vision may be left on the drawing board this year into next due to obstacles and limitations (see Nov. 29 in the Star Pages). We get our first tastes of the associated frustration Monday morning, Wednesday and Thursday. Respect is meager and boundaries are porous at these times, too. (Saturday night is better for blending firmness and gentleness.) Communication is more important than usual this week, bouncing between being smooth and bumpy. Monday afternoon and Saturday morning are the easiest times. Tuesday, Thursday evening, Friday night and Sunday, disagreements over who's in charge hinder getting along. It's a hard week for relationships; a whole lot of talking that gets partners nowhere. However, hidden information could come to light and bring a shift by the weekend. More openness is sorely needed. We'll be more inclined to be candid (possibly even blunt) once the communication planet and the Sun enter Sagittarius (Friday and Sunday, respectively).

Astro-Overview: *Tuesday's Ceres-Uranus quintile is in consecutive Quintile Triangles made by the Sun (last Sunday) and Mercury (this Monday), augmented by the Moon as it passes Ceres Tuesday morning. Mercury and the Sun are conjunct Tuesday, duplicating several aspects this week. Both semisquare Venus Tuesday. Mercury is sextile and trine the Nodes Thursday, as the Sun is Friday; all are caressed by the Moon Saturday morning. Mercury is semisquare Pluto Thursday, like the Sun is early Saturday. In between, Venus squares Pluto Friday. Mercury enters Sagittarius Friday; the Sun follows suit on Sunday. Mercury is sesquiquadrate Uranus Saturday; the Sun, not until next Tuesday. Neptune turns Direct Wednesday. Ceres and Saturn are sextile Sunday.*

Details: *Monday (E) Mercury quintile Ceres; Monday Mercury biquintile Uranus; Tuesday Mercury semisquare Venus, Ceres quintile Uranus, Mercury conjunct Sun, Venus semisquare Sun; Wednesday Neptune turns Direct; Thursday Mercury sextile North Node & trine South Node, Mercury semisquare Pluto; Friday Sun sextile North Node & trine South Node, Mercury enters Sagittarius, Venus square Pluto; Saturday Sun semisquare Pluto, Mercury sesquiquadrate Uranus; Sunday Ceres sextile Saturn, Sun enters Sagittarius*

DECEMBER

SU	M	TU	W	T	F	S
			1	2	3	4	5
6	7	8	9	10	11	12
13	14	15	16	17	18	19
20	21	22	23	24	25	26
27	28	29	30	31		

The real and the unreal square off on Thanksgiving in the first of three instances of a major clash between the planets of fact and fiction, part of a cycle that dates back to 1989.

November

You really need the extra patience available today. A relationship with a lover, friend or co-worker causes anxiety. Remain calm and be diplomatic.

Moon Void in Aries • Moon enters Taurus
8:26 am (P), 11:26 am (E)

2 MO 23

This afternoon into early evening is as good as it gets this week. Use the upbeat energy, innovation and practicality then to your best advantage.

Moon in Taurus • Void 5:26 pm (P), 8:26 pm (E)

3 TU 24

Your mind is quick and fruitful but the ideas generated may not be feasible, or at least not at this time. Don't rush into sudden expenditures or disclosures.

Moon Void in Taurus • Moon enters Gemini 9:15 am (P),
12:15 pm (E) • Full Moon (Oak Moon)

★ P **2 WE 25**

Big dreams can lead to big disappointments. Keep your feet on the ground and examine situations using both your head and your heart.

Thanksgiving (U.S.)

Moon in Gemini • Void 7:35 pm (P), 10:35 pm (E)

★ **2 TH 26**

This low-key day is a good time to recuperate after the hyper-tense Full Moon. Be with supportive and nurturing people (maybe your family or maybe not).

Moon Void in Gemini • Moon enters Cancer
11:27 am (P), 2:27 pm (E)

2 FR 27

Delusions about finances, possessions or a loved one are slated to be dispelled, perhaps with an abrupt loss. However, this may work out okay in the long run.

Moon in Cancer

★ **1 SA 28**

On this extremely tough day, be thankful if your problems are only minor. No matter what, be gentle with yourself. Don't add self-injury to circumstantial insult.

First Sunday of Advent

Moon in Cancer • Void 4:46 pm (P), 7:46 am (E)
Moon enters Leo 4:47 pm (P), 7:47 pm (E)

P **1 SU 29**

A Full Moon is a culmination, a peak. If the Moon stimulates other planets, whatever they represent is intensified. The Full Moon Wednesday [2:44 pm (P), 5:44 pm (E)] brings out the best of a beneficial pattern and the downside of a deleterious one. The friendly influence runs from last Sunday through Wednesday, while the difficult connections kick in Wednesday and rumble through Sunday, reverberating for some time to come. Attention centers on the planet of responsibility, restrictions, maturity and manifestation and the planet of communication. Both are in each formation. We'll learn a lot about limitations and consequences. The first grouping includes the planet of initiation and action, helping us move pragmatic plans along. (This is not the week to start something; moments of favorable planetary ties are too close to times of difficult ones.) Pride and a need for approval (from oneself or others) interfere with ambitions. A further impediment to accomplishing goals comes from a trend of late for entropy to predominate. (That's nature's tendency for all systems and organisms to break down over time, gradually declining into disorder.) The planet of chaos is also in this mix. And an indicator of pain or injury is emphasized.

NOVEMBER 23-29 HIGHLIGHTS

Astro-Overview: *Venus and the Sun punch Uranus to start this crazy week, magnified by harsh links from Wednesday's Full Moon. The end of the week is worse! A Saturn-Neptune square (Thursday) is in a nasty web of hard aspects Wednesday to Sunday involving Mercury, Venus, the Sun and Eris (still semisquare Neptune). Luckily, a few positive Saturn aspects provide a little sanity. A smooth triangle of trines and sextiles between Ceres, Saturn and Mars is enhanced by Mercury joining Saturn. The Full Moon forms a Grand Trine/Kite with them. Amidst all this, Chiron semisextiles Uranus Wednesday and turns Direct Friday night.*

Details: *Monday Venus opposite Uranus; Monday (P)/Tuesday (E) Mars sextile Saturn; Tuesday Sun sesquiquadrate Uranus, Mercury conjunct Saturn; Tuesday (P)/Wednesday (E) Mars trine Ceres, Mercury square Neptune; Wednesday Mercury sextile Ceres, Mercury sesquiquadrate Eris, Mercury sextile Mars, Chiron semisextile Uranus; Thursday Saturn square Neptune, Venus semisextile Jupiter; Friday (P)/Saturday (E) Chiron turns Direct; Saturday Venus sesquiquadrate Neptune, Venus semisquare Saturn, Venus opposite Eris; Sunday Sun square Neptune, Sun conjunct Saturn, Sun sesquiquadrate Eris, Saturn sesquiquadrate Eris*

If it were not for hope, the heart would break.
Greek proverb

NOVEMBER							DECEMBER						
SU	M	TU	W	T	F	S	SU	M	TU	W	T	F	S
1	2	3	4	5	6	7					1	2	3
8	9	10	11	12	13	14	4	5	6	7	8	9	10
15	16	17	18	19	20	21	11	12	13	14	15	16	17
22	23	24	25	26	27	28	18	19	20	21	22	23	24
29	30						25	26	27	28	29	30	31

Moon in Leo

30 MO 3

High energy and excitement make for a lively day! Though work isn't necessarily the focus, some people may find fun or joy in it, or a creative way to go about it.

Moon in Leo • Void 7:09 pm (P), 10:09 pm (E)

01 TU 3

Enthusiastic discussions this morning reveal surprising information or an innovation. Generosity warms relations from afternoon through a social evening.

AIDS Awareness Day

Moon Void in Leo • Moon enters Virgo 2:09 am (P), 5:09 am (E) • Third Quarter Moon (P)

02 WE 1

An irritating interruption early leads to a tangent, from which you can't easily return to your original intentions. The day erodes into disorder by night.

Moon in Virgo • Third Quarter Moon (E) Void 8:59 pm (P), 11:59 pm (E)

03 TH 2

People are in a helpful, productive mood most of the day. Some may dwell on burdens or feel pulled in too many directions. Most have a smile by bedtime.

Moon Void in Virgo Moon enters Libra 2:34 pm (P), 5:34 pm (E)

04 FR 3 ★

A myriad of details to juggle could fray nerves unless efficiency or assistance intervenes. By afternoon, inspiration strikes and confidence increases.

Moon in Libra

05 SA 3

Camaraderie and cooperation infuse an amiable air into the day's activities. However, resentment may seethe tonight, cloaked under a veneer of manners.

Moon in Libra • Void 6:03 pm (P), 9:03 pm (E)

06 SU 2 ★

Hurts lurk around every corner, yet some people skirt today's rough edges by seeing the best in everything and everyone, regardless of the hard reality.

Saint Nicholas Day

NOV. 30-DEC. 06 HIGHLIGHTS

The celestial vibrations are not as intense this week as last week. What a relief! Still, this Wednesday evening, there are echoes of the stress at last Wednesday's Full Moon. Developments from about that time and this past Sunday continue then. The nicest elements of what went on at the Full Moon are also present, resonating Monday and Saturday, although Saturday night is not as pleasant. Pressure rises in relationships then and on Sunday. As often happens, the speedy planet in charge of communication is very active. On its agenda: solving problems (hopefully not creating new ones) and making improvements Tuesday (with a second step in the process Thursday); honest, but annoying, mouthing off Friday; and sparking something creative or spiritual Sunday to next Monday, when there's another of those special talent triangles (see the Star Pages). Willpower, confidence and leadership are fairly strong, particularly Monday, Tuesday and Saturday, but they take a hard hit near the Third Quarter Moon overnight Wednesday. It would be smart to have a plan in mind ahead of time to guide your actions then in the event of any mayhem arising. Beginning Saturday, attractions and affection go to a deeper level, even an extreme, until Dec. 30.

Astro-Overview: *It's rare for four days of a week to have only aspects made by the Moon. However, the Moon is always activating planetary links exact on nearby days. Wednesday evening, the Moon shoves last Sunday's ugly Sun-Saturn-Neptune-Eris mess. Monday and Saturday, the Moon stimulates the best features of last week's Full Moon via favorable connections to Saturn and the Sun (trine last Sunday) and Ceres (sextile the Sun Tuesday), as well as Mars (sextile the Sun Sunday). When the Moon conjuncts Mars Saturday, it also triggers a Mars-Pluto square (exact Sunday) and a Quintile Triangle formed by Mercury from Sunday to next Monday with a Mars-Neptune biquintile exact Friday. Tuesday, Mercury is trine Uranus and square Chiron. Then Mercury is square Jupiter Friday; both are scraped by the Moon as it joins Jupiter Thursday night. Friday, Mercury is trine Eris. Venus enters Scorpio that day, then is sesquiquadrate Chiron (Sunday), both bumped by the Moon Thursday.*

Details: *Tuesday Mercury trine Uranus, Mercury square Chiron, Sun sextile Ceres; Friday Mercury square Jupiter, Mars biquintile Neptune, Venus enters Scorpio, Mercury trine Eris; Sunday Sun sextile Mars, Venus sesquiquadrate Chiron, Mars square Pluto, Mercury quintile Neptune*

JANUARY

SU	M	TU	W	T	F	S
					1	2
3	4	5	6	7	8	9
10	11	12	13	14	15	16
17	18	19	20	21	22	23
24	25	26	27	28	29	30
31						

November-December

A quick mind and strong words are great assets - if you don't jump the gun or ruffle feathers. Consider the impact of what you have to say, then speak with love.

Pearl Harbor Remembrance Day, Hanukkah begins

Moon Void in Libra • Moon enters Scorpio
3:26 am (P), 6:26 am (E)

★ 1 MO 07

True power and leadership lie in knowing how to assess needed changes, create viable plans and inspire others to help implement them. That's a tall order!

Moon in Scorpio • Void 10:39 pm (P)

3 TU 08

Put yourself on the front burner if this is what you need for healing or assistance. If it's just for attention or selfish purposes, others are alienated.

Moon in Scorpio, Void (P) • Void 1:39 am (E)
Moon enters Sagittarius 2:25 pm (P), 5:25 pm (E)

★ 1 WE 09

Humanitarian efforts have an immediate positive karmic payoff. Hard-hearted or egotistical behavior brings no reward and undermines relationships.

Human Rights Day

Moon in Sagittarius

★ 1 TH 10

There's so much to do and you'd probably like it better if you didn't have to go it alone. But you do, at least until evening, when reinforcements arrive.

Moon in Sagittarius • New Moon • Void 8:06 am (P),
11:06 am (E) • Moon enters Capricorn 10:46 pm (P)

1 FR 11

Imagination and vision work hand in hand with practicality and utility. This is a great day for art, entertainment, loving care and a gentle nudge for betterment.

Moon in Capricorn (P), Void in Sagittarius (E)
Moon enters Capricorn 1:46 am (E)

4 SA 12

Proceeding step by step according to a plan keeps you from getting ahead of yourself or going astray. Work within limitations for the best shot at success.

Moon in Capricorn • Void 3:07 pm (P), 6:07 pm (E)

2 SU 13

The last days of a lunar cycle ordinarily are a time for closure and putting matters to rest, more so when the cycle winding down began in the sign of Scorpio, the harbinger of endings. Energy naturally declines in this phase and on Monday and Tuesday, we face a profusion of analysis and processing that likely leaves us feeling drained. There could be a second wind of mental energy late Monday evening, though. Ahead of the New Moon, a situation needs to be addressed or repaired to allow more authenticity or to take advantage of originality and creativity. Appropriate times for this are Tuesday, Wednesday and Thursday night. Beginning Wednesday evening, our minds zero in on goals with more grounded, practical thinking, lasting into January. Some people may be on edge or short-tempered Thursday and again Sunday morning, times when klutziness or accident potential is higher than usual. Relationships may suffer some difficulties Monday and Thursday night. Problems stem from an increase in criticism occurring concurrently with unrealistic expectations. Couples will weather the storm if trust is strong enough between the partners. By the time the New Moon arrives Friday [2:29 am (P), 5:29 am (E)], we're ready to head in a different direction.

DECEMBER 07-13 HIGHLIGHTS

Astro-Overview: The Sagittarius New Moon early Friday emphasizes the Sun's aspects of the week: trine Uranus (Tuesday night) and square Chiron (Wednesday), while Chiron is in another of its many semisextiles to Uranus (most recently exact on 11/25). Uranus and Pluto, still in orb of their multi-year square, are in a T-square with Mars (square Pluto last Sunday, opposite Uranus this Thursday). This is magnified by the Moon Wednesday afternoon to evening and Sunday morning, thus strongly in effect at the New Moon. Mercury opens the week semisquare Ceres Monday morning and Monday night in a T-square with the Nodes, which trade hard aspects with Ceres early Wednesday. This quartet is pinched by the Moon early Tuesday morning and Friday night to Saturday morning. Wednesday night, Mercury enters Capricorn. Venus is semisquare Jupiter Thursday night and trine Neptune overnight Thursday to Friday.

Details: Monday Mercury semisquare Ceres, Mercury square North & South Nodes, Mercury quintile Mars; Tuesday Sun trine Uranus; Wednesday North Node sesquiquadrate & South Node semisquare Ceres, Sun square Chiron, Mercury enters Capricorn; Thursday Mars opposite Uranus, Venus semisquare Jupiter; Thursday (P)/Friday (E) Venus trine Neptune

▶ See p. 3 for meaning of symbols ★, **MR**, **VR**, **P**.

The best use of laws is to teach men to trample bad laws under their feet.
Wendell Phillips

| NOVEMBER | | | | | | | | DECEMBER | | | | | |
SU	M	TU	W	T	F	S		SU	M	TU	W	T	F	S
									1	2	3	4	5
1	2	3	4	5	6	7							
8	9	10	11	12	13	14		6	7	8	9	10	11	12
15	16	17	18	19	20	21		13	14	15	16	17	18	19
22	23	24	25	26	27	28		20	21	22	23	24	25	26
29	30							27	28	29	30	31	

Moon Void in Capricorn
Moon enters Aquarius 4:59 am (P), 7:59 am (E)

14 MO 1 P

Faith and understanding are today's saving graces amidst doubts and criticism. If you're pushy, you'll turn people away just when you need them most.

Moon in Aquarius • Void 11:17 pm (P)

15 TU 3 ★

Know your strengths and be confident putting them to good use. You'll draw support from friends and associates, though you're quite capable on your own.

Moon in Aquarius, Void (P) • Void 2:17 am (E)
Moon enters Pisces 9:45 am (P), 12:45 pm (E)

16 WE 1

Hints about something hidden are upsetting early. Later, watch your feet; you could trip, actually or symbolically. Tonight's dreams show fears to eradicate.

Moon in Pisces

17 TH 4

Pool resources to compensate for what some people lack. Empathy and innovation team up to foster improvements. Hurting hearts are healed.

Moon in Pisces • First Quarter Moon • Void 7:14 am (P), 10:14 am (E) • Moon enters Aries 1:26 pm (P), 4:26 pm (E)

18 FR 1

This morning calls for selfless acts and remembering how everyone's interconnected. Later, a personal relationship needs reparations.

Moon in Aries

19 SA 3

Constructive suggestions are not taken well if delivered with a lot of "shoulds." Lead by example, showcasing your unique abilities.

Moon in Aries • Void 2:01 pm (P), 5:01 pm (E)
Moon enters Taurus 4:13 pm (P), 7:13 pm (E)

20 SU 1 P

The give-and-take feels like one person is doing most of the giving and the other, most of the taking. A cool head is needed to quell quarrels.

DECEMBER 14-20 HIGHLIGHTS

In the Sagittarius time of year, we often overload our plates, literally at Thanksgiving and figuratively during the month the Sun is in this sign of excess. When enough is enough, we remember the wisdom of simplicity and minimalism that we forgot in our zeal to go for it all. Monday, disorder (or worse) associated with overdoing grabs our attention; we might back off then and there. If not, Friday's First Quarter Moon is an apt time to round the bend. Likely arenas for snags from superfluous conditions are finances, relationships, work, health and helping those in need. There's pressure to make a difference somehow, but can it be done without overextending? Again, Monday is a key time, especially after the morning. Finances look bright Thursday, which is also a fine day for career matters, romance, creativity and charity. A partnership might take a significant step forward then. Self-interest is strong Tuesday (a good day to be seen in one's best light) and Sunday, when too much focus on oneself causes trouble. Saturday brings answers to problems, probably by revealing the roots of the matter. Be especially cautious Wednesday afternoon to evening and Saturday night, when rushing causes difficulty or hasty words can't be retracted.

Astro-Overview: *Monday morning, the Sun is square Jupiter and less than two hours later, trine Eris. Jupiter is quincunx Eris Tuesday. The Moon stimulates these aspects late Tuesday night, when it's sextile Eris and the Sun. The first of these sextiles creates a Finger of God with Jupiter. Friday morning, the Sun squares the Nodes as the Moon passes the South Node at the First Quarter Moon. Mercury is sextile Neptune Monday, on break until it's conjunct Pluto Saturday (squared by the Moon that day) and square Uranus Sunday. Venus has a scrape with the Nodes Monday, then is square Ceres Thursday, when it's also sextile Pluto. Immediately, the Moon reinforces them and boosts Venus's trine to Chiron (exact Saturday) and Mercury's sextile to Chiron (exact next Monday). Mars slams into the Neptune-Eris semisquare Sunday, kicked by the Moon early that morning.*

Details: *Monday Sun square Jupiter, Sun trine Eris, Mercury sextile Neptune, Venus semisquare North Node & sesquiquadrate South Node; Tuesday Jupiter quincunx Eris; Thursday Venus square Ceres, Venus sextile Pluto; Friday Sun square North & South Nodes; Saturday Venus trine Chiron, Mercury conjunct Pluto; Sunday Mars sesquiquadrate Neptune, Mars opposite Eris, Mercury square Uranus*

JANUARY

SU	M	TU	W	T	F	S
					1	2
3	4	5	6	7	8	9
10	11	12	13	14	15	16
17	18	19	20	21	22	23
24	25	26	27	28	29	30
31						

This won't be just any old Christmas. A Full Moon brings a climax with a weird twist as the wildcard planet, Uranus, pivots and one of the year's dominant themes is reprised.

December

This is a productive day if distractions and sidetracks are avoided. Smart remedies and healing words smooth the way, but assistance might be lacking.

Winter Solstice, Yule, Sun enters Capricorn

Moon in Taurus

★ **3 MO 21**

Another day when we get a lot done, this time with help. An inclination to be of service combines with persistence and a drive to achieve completion.

Moon in Taurus • Void 6:26 am (P), 9:26 am (E)
Moon enters Gemini 6:31 pm (P), 9:31 pm (E)

★ **3 TU 22**

People are superficially sociable but there's an underlying sense of separateness that leaves us hungry for meaningful contact or support.

Mawlid al-Nabi (Muhammad's Birthday)

Moon in Gemini

1 WE 23

A day of mixed signals: fondness is present but somewhat overshadowed by bustling efficiency and a focus on personal agendas. Try doing tasks in tandem.

Christmas Eve

Moon in Gemini • Void 12:04 pm (P), 3:04 pm (E)
Moon enters Cancer 9:26 pm (P)

3 TH 24

Confusion in the morning converts to clarity by afternoon. Still, there are odd occurrences all day. Sentimentality and withholding affection coexist.

Christmas

Moon in Cancer (P), Void in Gemini (E) • Moon enters
Cancer 12:26 am (E) • Full Moon (Wolf Moon)

★ **P 2 FR 25**

Closeness grows by supporting each other, emotionally or financially. Boundaries prevent a feeling of being saddled with someone else's burdens.

Boxing Day, Kwanzaa begins

Moon in Cancer • Void 7:36 pm (P), 10:36 pm (E)

P 3 SA 26

Something weighs heavily on your mind, perhaps a painful situation, diminishing the joy or relaxation you wanted and needed from this day of rest.

Moon Void in Cancer
Moon enters Leo 2:31 am (P), 5:31 am (E)

1 SU 27

"Season's Greetings" warm us at this chilly time of year, which can be emotionally rather cool. Monday, the Sun enters Capricorn, a sign of stiff formality, business-like rather than mushy. While love is generally shared widely at Christmastime, not all the planets cooperate in that regard. Wednesday, a dwarf planet associated with nurturance gets frosty from the Capricorn Sun's icicles and a connection to an aloof planet that puts distance between people. A long-term link that diffuses sympathy via a dose of self-absorption is exact Monday night and painfully visible Friday, when flaws are uncloaked. On the day of the Full Moon [Friday, 3:12 am (P), 6:12 am (E)], a planet of individuality in a solo sign stands still, exerting extra influence. The only planet in the sign of relating has a me-first quality and lines up with the most selfish dwarf planet. Luckily, these tendencies are counterbalanced by several factors. There are planetary combinations signifying a helpful, affectionate nature and a desire to make a positive difference. A team-up of beneficial planets opens hearts and pours out generosity (most evident Saturday afternoon to evening). And Cancer, the Full Moon's sign, promotes family closeness and expressing feelings.

DECEMBER 21-27 HIGHLIGHTS

Astro-Overview: Monday night is the final Neptune-Eris semisquare, an aspect in effect most of 2015. Early Friday, Mercury squares Eris and semisquares Neptune. That afternoon, it trines Jupiter. Mercury is sextile Chiron Monday. Sunday night, it's semisquare Saturn and friendly to the Nodes. Saturday, the Moon accents Mercury's weekend aspects and a Venus-Jupiter sextile (exact Thursday). The Sun enters Capricorn Monday night, then semisquares Ceres Wednesday. That's a tight aspect at Friday's Full Moon, which also features a Sun-Neptune sextile (exact next Tuesday). Wednesday, Ceres sextiles Uranus, which turns Direct Friday night. A Mars-Saturn semisquare Saturday is trampled by the Moon that night. Saturday, Venus hugs the Nodes and the Moon gives them a goodnight kiss.

Details: Monday Mercury sextile Chiron, Sun enters Capricorn; Monday (P)/Tuesday (E) Neptune semisquare Eris; Wednesday Ceres sextile Uranus, Sun semisquare Ceres; Thursday Venus sextile Jupiter; Friday Mercury square Eris, Mercury semisquare Neptune, Mercury trine Jupiter, Uranus turns Direct; Saturday Mars semisquare Saturn, Venus sextile North Node & trine South Node; Sunday Mercury semisquare Saturn; Sunday (P) Mercury trine North Node & sextile South Node

---

▶ See p. 3 for meaning of Moon Void.

57

Moon in Leo

28 MO 2

Don't be thrown off when some people enjoy shaking things up just for fun or the shock value. Your own pleasure-seeking may divert you from duties tonight.

Moon in Leo • Void 9:38 am (P), 12:38 pm (E)
Moon enters Virgo 10:58 am (P), 1:58 pm (E)

29 TU 2

Resist reacting impulsively to something said (especially in haste or anger) or to whatever seems amiss in monetary or romantic matters. Have faith.

Moon in Virgo

30 WE 2 ★

Be choosy to whom you offer assistance or from whom you accept it. Integrity and principles are important. Don't rush a decision this afternoon.

Moon in Virgo • Void 9:33 pm (P)
Moon enters Libra 10:41 pm (P)

31 TH 3

You might follow the Chinese custom: clean house ahead of a new year. It's a good day for helpful gestures and for analysis if you're guided by tried-and-true values.

New Year's Eve

Moon in Libra (P), in Virgo (E) • Void 12:33 am (E)
Moon enters Libra 1:41 am (E) • Third Quarter Moon (P)

01 FR 3 ★

Social interactions from morning 'til night are very pleasant. You may get a little angst comparing your experiences to friends' lives and judging yourself.

New Year's Day

Moon in Libra • Third Quarter Moon (E)
Void 8:23 am (P), 11:23 am (E)

02 SA 2 ★

We may be withdrawn today or want our space, until we perk up for a close comrade. Tonight, we team up to escape via sports or entertainment.

Moon Void in Libra
Moon enters Scorpio 11:36 am (P), 2:36 pm (E)

03 SU 2 ★

Deep thoughts or discussions reveal what can be done to make improvements or clear the decks for a lighter load going forward. Creativity flows!

DEC. 28, '15-JAN. 03, '16 HIGHLIGHTS

To plan for the coming year, it's useful to set a course by reviewing the year gone by. Thursday is appropriate for this, not just according to the calendar, but also since the planets then support a wide-angle view and directional analysis. If conditions seem hairy regarding finances or relationships, the challenges are likely only transitory. From Tuesday night to Thursday (with an echo Saturday morning), the planet in charge of these key areas briefly jolts the waning struggle between two slow planets which have been fomenting major change since 2011. As we move into 2016, their stand-off weakens. If you've accomplished needed revisions in these areas, you've done your work and present situations need not color your decisions for the future greatly. Gut instincts are trustworthy Tuesday and Wednesday; check what they say and follow their advice. The same days, ignore your mind, which leaps to conclusions or leads you to argue with yourself indecisively. Soon Mercury will be Retrograde and you may change your mind anyway. Many circumstances begin shifting now as three quick planets change signs. As this week moves into the next, a beneficial pattern gives us confidence that our actions will proceed along the path of least resistance.

Astro-Overview: *Mercury harmonizes with the Nodes early Monday. A Mercury-Mars square on Tuesday is shot by the Moon Sunday as it passes Mars, also triggering a Quintile Triangle Mars makes with the Sun and South Node from Saturday through next Tuesday. Three of the quick planets enter new signs this week, two with two-part visits due to Retrogradation. Venus enters Sagittarius Wednesday and will not go Retrograde in 2016. Mercury will soon and Mars will in April. Mercury enters Aquarius Friday (turning Retrograde next Tuesday) and Mars enters Scorpio Sunday. The Uranus-Pluto square that just won't quit is pestered by Venus (semisquare Pluto overnight Tuesday, sesquiquadrate Uranus Thursday). The Moon bothers these three Tuesday and Saturday. The Sun has just one aspect, a sextile to Neptune Tuesday.*

Details: *Monday (E) Mercury trine North Node & sextile South Node; Tuesday Sun sextile Neptune, Mercury square Mars; Tuesday (P)/Wednesday (E) Venus semisquare Pluto, Venus enters Sagittarius; Thursday Venus sesquiquadrate Uranus; Friday Mercury enters Aquarius; Friday (P)/Saturday (E) Sun quintile Mars; Sunday Mars enters Scorpio; Monday (Jan. 4) Sun quintile South Node; Tuesday (Jan. 5) Mercury turns Retrograde, South Node biquintile Mars*

2016 Calendar

JANUARY
SU	M	TU	W	T	F	S
					1	2
3	4	5	6	7	8	9
10	11	12	13	14	15	16
17	18	19	20	21	22	23
24	25	26	27	28	29	30
31						

FEBRUARY
SU	M	TU	W	T	F	S
	1	2	3	4	5	6
7	8	9	10	11	12	13
14	15	16	17	18	19	20
21	22	23	24	25	26	27
28	29					

MARCH
SU	M	TU	W	T	F	S
		1	2	3	4	5
6	7	8	9	10	11	12
13	14	15	16	17	18	19
20	21	22	23	24	25	26
27	28	29	30	31		

APRIL
SU	M	TU	W	T	F	S
					1	2
3	4	5	6	7	8	9
10	11	12	13	14	15	16
17	18	19	20	21	22	23
24	25	26	27	28	29	30

MAY
SU	M	TU	W	T	F	S
1	2	3	4	5	6	7
8	9	10	11	12	13	14
15	16	17	18	19	20	21
22	23	24	25	26	27	28
29	30	31				

JUNE
SU	M	TU	W	T	F	S
			1	2	3	4
5	6	7	8	9	10	11
12	13	14	15	16	17	18
19	20	21	22	23	24	25
26	27	28	29	30		

JULY
SU	M	TU	W	T	F	S
					1	2
3	4	5	6	7	8	9
10	11	12	13	14	15	16
17	18	19	20	21	22	23
24	25	26	27	28	29	30
31						

AUGUST
SU	M	TU	W	T	F	S
	1	2	3	4	5	6
7	8	9	10	11	12	13
14	15	16	17	18	19	20
21	22	23	24	25	26	27
28	29	30	31			

SEPTEMBER
SU	M	TU	W	T	F	S
				1	2	3
4	5	6	7	8	9	10
11	12	13	14	15	16	17
18	19	20	21	22	23	24
25	26	27	28	29	30	

OCTOBER
SU	M	TU	W	T	F	S
						1
2	3	4	5	6	7	8
9	10	11	12	13	14	15
16	17	18	19	20	21	22
23	24	25	26	27	28	29
30	31					

NOVEMBER
SU	M	TU	W	T	F	S
		1	2	3	4	5
6	7	8	9	10	11	12
13	14	15	16	17	18	19
20	21	22	23	24	25	26
27	28	29	30			

DECEMBER
SU	M	TU	W	T	F	S
				1	2	3
4	5	6	7	8	9	10
11	12	13	14	15	16	17
18	19	20	21	22	23	24
25	26	27	28	29	30	31

2016 Moon Phases

NEW

1/9 • 2/8 • **3/8** • 4/7 • 5/6 • 6/4 • 7/4 • 8/2 • **9/1** • 9/30 • 10/30 • 11/29 • 12/29

FIRST QUARTER

1/16 • 2/15 • 3/15 • 4/13 • 5/13 • 6/12 • 7/11 • 8/10 • 9/9 • 10/9 • 11/7 • 12/7

FULL

1/23 • 2/22 • **3/23** • 4/22 • 5/21 • 6/20 • 7/19 • 8/18 • **9/16** • 10/16 • 11/14 • 12/13

THIRD QUARTER

1/2 • 1/31 • 3/1 • 3/31 • 4/29 • 5/29 • 6/27 • 7/26 • 8/24 • 9/23 • 10/22 • 11/21 • 12/20

Dates based on Eastern time zone. Eclipses are shown in bold type.

2015 On a Page

Janet's Plan-its™

Dates based on North American time zones. May differ from calendars using Greenwich Mean Time.

AR	Aries
TA	Taurus
GE	Gemini
CN	Cancer
LE	Leo
VI	Virgo
LI	Libra
SC	Scorpio
SG	Sagittarius
CP	Capricorn
AQ	Aquarius
PI	Pisces

RETROGRADE MOTION

As we spin, the signs along the zodiac belt and the planets appear to move east to west hour by hour. But over time, the planets move through the signs west to east. The Moon takes two to three days to traverse a sign while Pluto takes over a decade! Each planet (other than the Sun or Moon) appears to stop and reverse its direction from time to time. This is an optical illusion called "Retrograde" motion. Later, it stops a second time and resumes forward (Direct) motion. It hangs out longer at the degrees of these stopping points, called "stations." When that planet, or even another planet, later makes connections ("aspects") to the station degrees, issues that emerged during that Retrograde period are re-visited. Matters associated with the planet are more difficult during the Retrograde phase and are more intense for a few days around the stations.

Planets move through the Retrograde range three times. First they proceed forward through the range of degrees where the backtracking will occur. This is called the entry "shadow" (shaded on the graph). Next, they back up over that degree range in the Retrograde portion of the cycle (marked in black on the graph). Finally, they go forward again through the backtracking range in the exit "shadow" (shaded). Related events can occur during these three phases. We don't feel the effect of the shadows as much as we do the Retrograde itself, but we often sense the slow-down at the stations.

Many people notice the Retrograde of Mercury since it's linked to mix-ups in all forms of communication and local transportation. Anything begun then (or in the entry shadow) is subject to mistakes or revisions. A safer time for contracts, major decisions or beginning new activities is when Mercury is not in the entry shadow or Retrograde. There's less likelihood for revision later for activities initiated during the exit shadow.

Looking at the 2015 Retrograde graph, you can see there is usually one planet (or more) in Retrograde motion. Shadows are always in progress (which is typical). Times of "least resistance" are when no heavenly bodies are Retrograde (which doesn't happen in 2015) or only one is Retrograde: 1/10-1/20, 2/12-3/13, 4/9-4/15 and 12/26-1/4/16. Two are Retrograde 1/21-2/11, 3/14-4/8, 4/16-5/17 and 11/29-12/25. At all other times, three or more are Retrograde. The more that are Retrograde, the more progress is impeded. The highest numbers are six 7/19-7/24, 9/7-9/14 and 9/17-9/25; seven 7/25 and 8/3-9/6 and eight 7/26-8/2. (These numbers include Eris, not shown on the bar chart.)

MOON GROOVES

The degree of New and Full Moons repeats for a period of about six months, moving through consecutive signs. (I coined the term "moon groove" for this phenomenon.) For the next six months or so, the degree of each New and Full Moon decreases one or two degrees each month until another groove ensues. This pattern doesn't conform to a calendar year, so you only can see part of it on the 2015 list.

New Moons occur within one degree of 0° of the signs from September 2014 through March 2015. Full Moons are within one degree of 14° from October 2014 through May 2015. In the next groove, New Moons occur within one degree of 19° of the signs from September 2015 through April 2016 and Full Moons are within one degree of 3° from September 2015 through April 2016.

If you have a planet in your birth chart at a moon groove degree, it receives extra attention during a groove period. If it's accentuated by New Moons, take new action in the area of your life represented by that planet. If Full Moons spotlight your natal planet, matters culminate in a big way over several months regarding the affairs of that planet. In interpreting effects, consider your birth planet's sign, house and aspects. If a New or Full Moon is on your birthday, that's important! If it falls within the period of a moon groove, the emphasis will likely affect you throughout the entire moon groove time frame.

Read more about Moon cycles in Using This Planner (p. 2) and the article on lunar phases (p. 90).

● New Moon   ○ Full Moon   Ⓔ Eclipse   **B** Shadow begins   **R** Retrograde   **D** Direct   **E** Shadow ends

2015 Janet's Plan-its™ On a Page

	MERCURY	VENUS	MARS	CERES	JUPITER	SATURN	CHIRON	URANUS	NEPTUNE	PLUTO	MOON PHASES
(pre-year)					R 12/8/14, 22°38' LE	B 12/8/14, 28°17' SC	D 11/23/14, 13°6' PI	D 12/21/14, 12°34' AR	D 11/16/14, 4°48' PI	B 12/26/14, 12°58' CP	**E** = ECLIPSE
JANUARY	B 1/5, 1°18' AQ R 1/21, 17°5' AQ									(next R shadow) E 1/12, 13°35' CP (prior R shadow)	Full 1/4, 14°31' CN New 1/20, 0°9' AQ
FEBRUARY	D 2/11, 1°18' AQ						B 3/2, 16°56' PI (next R shadow)		B 2/19, 7°1' PI (next R shadow)		Full 2/3, 14°48' LE New 2/18, 29°59' AQ
MARCH	E 3/8, 17°5' AQ			B 3/17, 25°6' CP		R 3/14, 4°56' SG	E 3/15, 17°45' PI (prior R shadow)		E 3/6, 7°36' PI (prior R shadow)		Full 3/5, 14°50' VI New 3/20, 29°27' PI **E**
APRIL					D 4/8, 12°35' LE			E 4/7, 16°30' AR B 4/8, 16°33' AR		R 4/16, 15°33' CP	Full 4/4, 14°24' LI **E** New 4/18, 28°25' AR
MAY	B 5/4, 4°34' GE R 5/18, 13°9' GE										Full 5/3, 13°23' SC New 5/18, 26°56' TA
JUNE	D 6/11, 4°34' GE E 6/26, 13°9' GE	B 6/21, 14°23' LE		R 6/3, 9°13' AQ		R 6/24, 21°33' PI			R 6/12, 9°49' PI		Full 6/2, 11°49' SG New 6/16, 25°7' GE
JULY		R 7/25, 0°46' VI			E 7/6, 22°38' LE			R 7/26, 20°30' AR			Full 7/1, 9°55' CP New 7/15, 23°14' CN Full 7/31, 7°56' AQ
AUGUST	B 8/28, 0°54' LI					D 8/2, 28°17' SC					New 8/14, 21°31' LE Full 8/29, 6°6' PI
SEPTEMBER	R 9/17, 15°55' LI	D 9/6, 14°23' LE		D 9/14, 25°6' CP						D 9/25, 12°58' CP	New 9/13, 20°10' VI **E** Full 9/27, 4°40' AR **E**
OCTOBER	D 10/9, 0°54' LI E 10/24, 15°55' LI	E 10/9, 0°46' VI			B 10/12, 13°15' VI						New 10/12, 19°20' LI Full 10/27, 3°45' TA
NOVEMBER						E 11/8, 4°56' SG	D 11/28, 16°56' PI	D 11/18, 7°1' AR		B 12/28, 14°56' CP (next R shadow)	New 11/11, 19°1' SC Full 11/25, 3°20' GE
DECEMBER	B 12/19, 14°55' CP R 1/5/16, 1°3' AQ	E 12/1, 9°13' AQ			B 12/19, 9°47' SG			D 12/25, 16°33' AR		E 1/15/16, 15°33' CP (prior R shadow)	New 12/11, 19°3' SG Full 12/25, 3°20' CA
(post-year)					R 1/7/16, 23°14' VI	R 3/25/16, 16°24' SG	E 3/19/16, 21°33' PI	E 4/10/16, 20°30' AR	E 3/8/16, 9°49' PI		

MARS DOES NOT GO RETROGRADE IN 2015.

Legend (right margin):
- **E** Shadow ends
- **D** Direct
- **R** Retrograde
- **B** Shadow begins
- **E** Eclipse
- ○ Full Moon
- ● New Moon

The shadows of Chiron, Neptune, Pluto and Eris overlap, creating brief double shadows (darker shading). Eris begins 2015 Retrograde, turning Direct 1/9/15 at 22°5' AR. Its shadows overlap from 3/1 to 5/28 between 22°18' AR and 23°11' AR. Eris turns Retrograde 7/19 at 23°25' AR. It next turns Direct 1/10/16 at 22°18' AR.

How to Read an Ephemeris

Components of the Ephemeris

An ephemeris (eh fem' er iss) is a reference book showing precisely when certain celestial phenomena occur. Janet's Plan-its weekly Highlights and Star Pages list a lot of this data so you only need these pages if you want to explore astrology at a deeper level or identify when influences will impact your individual chart. See Making It Personal (p. 4).

Check the Keywords (p. 98) to see the symbols for the planets, signs, aspects and lunar phases. (NOTE: this ephemeris uses a different symbol for Pluto: ♇.) The time listed is calculated for Greenwich Mean Time (GMT), the worldwide standard in England. To convert to your time zone, subtract 4 hours for Atlantic, 5 hours for Eastern, 6 for Central, 7 for Mountain and 8 for Pacific. During Daylight Saving Time, subtract one hour less.

The twelve equal signs of the zodiac are 30 degrees each, measured in celestial "longitude." The longitude table for each month has columns for various celestial factors and a row for each day. (You can ignore the "Sid. Time" column unless you're calculating a chart "from scratch.") A position is listed in this order: degree, space, minute (1/60th of a degree) and in the case of the Sun and Moon, the second (1/60th of a minute). These are measurements in space, not to be confused with clock time. The minutes (other than for the Sun and Moon) use a decimal fraction. The Moon moves so quickly it's listed at both midnight (0 hr) and noon. The other planets' positions are listed at midnight GMT. When planets are Retrograde as a month begins, the second line of the month says R. The column is shaded when the planet is Retrograde and a D shows the day it turns Direct. The position is also listed for the Moon's North Node. (The South Node is always the same degree and minutes of the opposite sign.) The table shows its "true" position, which alternates between Retrograde (normal for it) and Direct. Many astrologers only use the Mean (average) position for the Nodes, which is always Retrograde.

The Star Pages tell you the day a planet enters a sign. The ephemeris shows the exact minute in the "planet ingress" list at the bottom. A space separates the two months that share the page. The "Astro Data" column on the left tells you when planets turn Retrograde (R) or Direct (D) and when two outer planets have an aspect. The degrees of these phenomena are not listed here, but you can "ballpark" them from the row for the applicable date. (You can ignore the items showing when planets rise above (N) or below (S) the "celestial equator," the middle of the zodiac path.)

The "Last Aspect" and "☽ Ingress" columns list the time that the Moon makes its last aspect in a sign, becoming Void of Course (see Using This Planner, p. 2) and when it enters the next sign, ending the Void period. Janet's Plan-its™ daily entries tell the Void and ingress times. Here you can see the Moon's last aspect, an influence that continues throughout the Void period. The "☽ Phases & Eclipses" box lists the main phases of the Moon: New, First Quarter, Full and Last Quarter. First it states the day of the month, then the time, then the phase, and last the zodiac degree, sign and minutes where it occurs. New and Full Moons that aspect anything in your chart within a couple of degrees can have a big influence for you (see 2015 On a Page, p. 60).

A second "Astro Data" box on the right has information you may not need, like the SVP (related to Indian astrology) and the Julian Day (number of days since the century began). It also lists some useful data: the zodiacal longitude on the first of the month for Eris (the new planet out past Pluto) and the asteroids Pallas Athena, Juno, Chiron and Vesta, along with the Mean (average) position of the Moon's North Node.

Relating the Ephemeris to YOUR Chart

Now that you're familiar with the types of information in the ephemeris, how do you figure out when planets affect YOU? Look for aspects to your birth chart. These occur when a moving ("transiting") planet reaches the same degree as one of your natal planets. To figure out the type of aspect, you'll need to look at the order of the signs in the zodiac, from Aries to Pisces. The aspect depends on the sign of the transiting planet relative to the natal planet: same sign = conjunction; the sign immediately before or after = semisextile; 2 signs before or after = sextile; 3 signs before or after = square; 4 signs before or after = trine; 5 signs before or after = quincunx; 6 signs away = opposition. Another type of aspect occurs when the transiting planet is 1-1/2 signs before or after (semisquare) or 4-1/2 signs before or after (sesquiquadrate). These are harder to spot. Allow up to five degrees leeway (the astrological term is "orb"), although the closer to exact, the stronger the influence.

For example, look at your birthday. The degree of the Sun is the same every year on that date (within a degree). Now you can look for other dates in the year when a planet goes through the same degree of the same sign and you'll know that planet is activating your Sun's potentials, strengthening or adding to how you express your purpose and intentions. If any planet is within 5 degrees of a sign three or six signs away, your Sun is receiving a square or an opposition, and that time frame should hold challenges for you personally; you may not get the glory you deserve around then or be able to wield your usual influence. This same process can be applied to any planet in your chart. Aspects from transiting planets amplify what your natal planet signifies by its sign and house positions and its natal aspects. If the transiting aspect is a helpful one, the outcome should be positive with a smooth experience. If the aspect is a difficult one, then your experience is likely to be more stressful or require you to work harder to obtain a happy result.

Find the planetary stations (or see the graph on 2015 On a Page) and check if any of the planets change direction in an aspect to anything in your chart. If so, you're apt to experience a slow-down in the activities associated with your natal planet when the transit stations. The nature of the transiting planet describes the pressures applying to your life and the type of aspect hints as to whether the experience will be pleasant or trying. For instance, if you receive a square from stationing Saturn, obstacles will slow your progress in the area(s) associated with the receiving planet. If you receive a trine from Jupiter, your path should be nearly bump-free for the part(s) of your life that Jupiter affects. Be sure to look for your natal house starting with the sign that your receiving planet rules. Thus if your Mars receives an aspect, look at your house that starts with Aries. The Keyword list includes sign rulers.

You can use these principles to assess your personal impact from the year's astrological phenomena, noted chronologically in the Star Pages (p. 72) and sorted by zodiac degree on the All Star List (p. 70).

LONGITUDE — January 2015

Day	Sid.Time	☉	0 hr ☽	Noon ☽	True ☊	☿	♀	♂	⚳	♃	♄	♅	♆	♇
1 Th	6 41 20	10♑13 50	20♉37 02	27♉11 38	15♎26.4	23♑39.4	26♑43.3	21♒03.1	26♐53.7	21♌45.5	0♐52.0	12♈36.8	5♓23.1	13♑09.9
2 F	6 45 16	11 14 58	3♊43 32	10♊12 45	15R 19.7	25 14.4	27 58.5	21 50.0	27 18.2	21R 41.0	0 58.0	12 37.4	5 24.6	13 12.0
3 Sa	6 49 13	12 16 06	16 39 18	23 03 12	15 09.8	26 48.9	29 13.7	22 37.0	27 42.6	21 36.4	1 04.0	12 38.0	5 26.1	13 14.1
4 Su	6 53 09	13 17 14	29 24 24	5♋42 53	14 57.4	28 22.7	0♒28.8	23 24.0	28 07.1	21 31.6	1 09.9	12 38.6	5 27.6	13 16.2
5 M	6 57 06	14 18 22	11♋58 36	18 11 32	14 43.2	29 55.7	1 43.9	24 11.0	28 31.5	21 26.6	1 15.8	12 39.3	5 29.2	13 18.3
6 Tu	7 01 02	15 19 30	24 21 43	0♌29 11	14 28.6	1♒27.5	2 59.1	24 57.9	28 55.8	21 21.4	1 21.6	12 40.1	5 30.8	13 20.4
7 W	7 04 59	16 20 38	6♌34 01	12 36 22	14 14.7	2 58.0	4 14.2	25 44.9	29 20.1	21 16.1	1 27.4	12 40.9	5 32.4	13 22.5
8 Th	7 08 55	17 21 46	18 36 25	24 34 27	14 02.7	4 26.8	5 29.3	26 31.9	29 44.4	21 10.6	1 33.1	12 41.7	5 34.1	13 24.6
9 F	7 12 52	18 22 54	0♍30 45	6♍25 43	13 53.4	5 53.5	6 44.3	27 18.9	0♑08.7	21 05.0	1 38.7	12 42.6	5 35.7	13 26.6
10 Sa	7 16 49	19 24 02	12 19 46	18 13 25	13 47.0	7 17.8	7 59.4	28 05.8	0 32.9	20 59.3	1 44.3	12 43.6	5 37.4	13 28.7
11 Su	7 20 45	20 25 10	24 07 12	0♎01 43	13 43.5	8 39.2	9 14.5	28 52.8	0 57.1	20 53.4	1 49.9	12 44.6	5 39.1	13 30.8
12 M	7 24 42	21 26 17	5♎57 36	11 55 30	13D 42.1	9 57.1	10 29.5	29 39.8	1 21.2	20 47.3	1 55.3	12 45.6	5 40.9	13 32.9
13 Tu	7 28 38	22 27 25	17 56 06	24 00 08	13R 42.0	11 11.0	11 44.6	0♓26.7	1 45.3	20 41.1	2 00.7	12 46.7	5 42.6	13 35.0
14 W	7 32 35	23 28 33	0♏08 17	6♏21 13	13 41.9	12 20.1	12 59.6	1 13.7	2 09.4	20 34.8	2 06.1	12 47.9	5 44.4	13 37.0
15 Th	7 36 31	24 29 40	12 39 37	19 04 03	13 40.7	13 23.7	14 14.6	2 00.6	2 33.4	20 28.4	2 11.4	12 49.1	5 46.2	13 39.1
16 F	7 40 28	25 30 48	25 35 02	2♐13 00	13 37.4	14 21.0	15 29.6	2 47.6	2 57.4	20 21.8	2 16.6	12 50.4	5 48.1	13 41.2
17 Sa	7 44 24	26 31 55	8♐58 13	15 50 48	13 31.4	15 11.1	16 44.6	3 34.5	3 21.3	20 15.1	2 21.7	12 51.7	5 49.9	13 43.2
18 Su	7 48 21	27 33 02	22 50 41	29 57 36	13 22.9	15 53.2	17 59.5	4 21.5	3 45.2	20 08.3	2 26.8	12 53.0	5 51.8	13 45.3
19 M	7 52 18	28 34 09	7♑11 04	14♑30 24	13 12.3	16 26.4	19 14.5	5 08.4	4 09.1	20 01.4	2 31.8	12 54.4	5 53.7	13 47.3
20 Tu	7 56 14	29 35 15	21 54 42	29 22 54	13 00.7	16 49.8	20 29.4	5 55.3	4 32.9	19 54.3	2 36.8	12 55.9	5 55.6	13 49.4
21 W	8 00 11	0♒36 21	6♒53 48	14♒26 10	12 49.5	17R 02.8	21 44.3	6 42.2	4 56.6	19 47.2	2 41.6	12 57.4	5 57.5	13 51.4
22 Th	8 04 07	1 37 26	21 58 42	29 30 10	12 39.9	17 04.6	22 59.2	7 29.1	5 20.3	19 40.0	2 46.4	12 58.9	5 59.5	13 53.4
23 F	8 08 04	2 38 30	6♓59 26	14♓25 30	12 32.9	16 55.0	24 14.1	8 16.0	5 44.0	19 32.7	2 51.2	13 00.5	6 01.4	13 55.4
24 Sa	8 12 00	3 39 33	21 47 33	29 04 56	12 28.8	16 33.7	25 28.9	9 02.9	6 07.6	19 25.3	2 55.8	13 02.1	6 03.4	13 57.4
25 Su	8 15 57	4 40 36	6♈17 12	13♈24 05	12D 27.2	16 01.1	26 43.7	9 49.7	6 31.1	19 17.8	3 00.4	13 03.8	6 05.4	13 59.4
26 M	8 19 53	5 41 37	20 25 27	27 21 20	12 27.2	15 17.7	27 58.5	10 36.6	6 54.6	19 10.3	3 04.9	13 05.5	6 07.4	14 01.4
27 Tu	8 23 50	6 42 37	4♉11 52	10♉57 15	12R 27.6	14 24.6	29 13.3	11 23.4	7 18.0	19 02.7	3 09.3	13 07.3	6 09.5	14 03.4
28 W	8 27 47	7 43 36	17 37 47	24 13 45	12 27.2	13 23.3	0♓28.0	12 10.2	7 41.4	18 55.0	3 13.6	13 09.1	6 11.5	14 05.3
29 Th	8 31 43	8 44 34	0♊45 29	7♊13 19	12 24.9	12 15.4	1 42.8	12 56.9	8 04.7	18 47.2	3 17.9	13 11.0	6 13.6	14 07.3
30 F	8 35 40	9 45 30	13 37 34	19 58 30	12 20.0	11 03.0	2 57.4	13 43.7	8 28.0	18 39.5	3 22.1	13 12.9	6 15.7	14 09.2
31 Sa	8 39 36	10 46 26	26 16 24	2♋31 30	12 12.5	9 48.4	4 12.1	14 30.4	8 51.2	18 31.6	3 26.2	13 14.8	6 17.7	14 11.1

LONGITUDE — February 2015

Day	Sid.Time	☉	0 hr ☽	Noon ☽	True ☊	☿	♀	♂	⚳	♃	♄	♅	♆	♇
1 Su	8 43 33	11♒47 20	8♋44 00	14♋54 05	12♎02.7	8♒33.7	5♓26.7	15♓17.1	9♑14.3	18♌23.8	3♐30.2	13♈16.8	6♓19.9	14♑13.0
2 M	8 47 29	12 48 13	21 01 54	27 07 36	11R 51.4	7R 21.1	6 41.3	16 03.8	9 37.4	18R 15.9	3 34.1	13 18.8	6 22.0	14 14.9
3 Tu	8 51 26	13 49 05	3♌11 19	9♌13 09	11 39.7	6 12.2	7 55.9	16 50.5	10 00.4	18 08.0	3 38.0	13 20.9	6 24.1	14 16.8
4 W	8 55 22	14 49 56	15 13 16	21 11 48	11 28.5	5 08.8	9 10.4	17 37.1	10 23.3	18 00.0	3 41.8	13 23.0	6 26.2	14 18.7
5 Th	8 59 19	15 50 45	27 08 55	3♍04 49	11 18.9	4 12.1	10 24.9	18 23.7	10 46.2	17 52.1	3 45.5	13 25.2	6 28.4	14 20.5
6 F	9 03 16	16 51 34	8♍59 45	14 53 57	11 11.5	3 22.8	11 39.4	19 10.3	11 09.0	17 44.1	3 49.1	13 27.4	6 30.6	14 22.4
7 Sa	9 07 12	17 52 21	20 47 46	26 41 33	11 06.6	2 41.7	12 53.8	19 56.9	11 31.7	17 36.1	3 52.6	13 29.6	6 32.7	14 24.2
8 Su	9 11 09	18 53 07	2♎35 42	8♎30 40	11D 04.2	2 08.8	14 08.2	20 43.4	11 54.4	17 28.1	3 56.0	13 31.8	6 34.9	14 26.0
9 M	9 15 05	19 53 53	14 26 57	20 25 06	11 03.8	1 44.2	15 22.5	21 29.9	12 17.0	17 20.2	3 59.3	13 34.2	6 37.1	14 27.8
10 Tu	9 19 02	20 54 37	26 25 40	2♏29 15	11 04.8	1 27.9	16 36.9	22 16.4	12 39.5	17 12.2	4 02.6	13 36.5	6 39.3	14 29.5
11 W	9 22 58	21 55 20	8♏36 30	14 48 01	11 06.1	1D 19.4	17 51.2	23 02.8	13 02.0	17 04.3	4 05.7	13 38.9	6 41.5	14 31.3
12 Th	9 26 55	22 56 02	21 04 27	27 26 23	11R 06.9	1 18.5	19 05.4	23 49.3	13 24.4	16 56.4	4 08.8	13 41.3	6 43.8	14 33.0
13 F	9 30 51	23 56 43	3♐54 25	10♐29 01	11 06.3	1 24.7	20 19.6	24 35.7	13 46.7	16 48.5	4 11.8	13 43.8	6 46.0	14 34.8
14 Sa	9 34 48	24 57 24	17 10 37	23 59 30	11 04.0	1 37.6	21 33.8	25 22.0	14 08.9	16 40.6	4 14.7	13 46.2	6 48.2	14 36.5
15 Su	9 38 45	25 58 03	0♑55 49	7♑59 32	10 59.7	1 56.6	22 48.0	26 08.4	14 31.1	16 32.8	4 17.5	13 48.8	6 50.5	14 38.1
16 M	9 42 41	26 58 40	15 10 27	22 28 07	10 53.8	2 21.3	24 02.1	26 54.7	14 53.1	16 25.1	4 20.2	13 51.3	6 52.7	14 39.8
17 Tu	9 46 38	27 59 17	29 51 53	7♒20 52	10 47.0	2 51.4	25 16.2	27 41.0	15 15.1	16 17.4	4 22.8	13 53.9	6 55.0	14 41.4
18 W	9 50 34	28 59 52	14♒54 03	22 30 12	10 40.3	3 26.3	26 30.2	28 27.2	15 37.0	16 09.7	4 25.3	13 56.6	6 57.2	14 43.1
19 Th	9 54 31	0♓00 26	0♓08 01	7♓46 09	10 34.5	4 05.7	27 44.2	29 13.5	15 58.8	16 02.2	4 27.7	13 59.2	6 59.5	14 44.7
20 F	9 58 27	1 00 58	15 23 14	22 58 02	10 30.4	4 49.2	28 58.1	29 59.6	16 20.6	15 54.7	4 30.0	14 01.9	7 01.8	14 46.3
21 Sa	10 02 24	2 01 28	0♈29 22	7♈56 17	10D 28.3	5 36.6	0♈12.0	0♈45.8	16 42.2	15 47.2	4 32.2	14 04.6	7 04.0	14 47.8
22 Su	10 06 20	3 01 57	15 17 57	22 33 47	10 28.0	6 27.5	1 25.9	1 31.9	17 03.8	15 39.9	4 34.3	14 07.4	7 06.3	14 49.3
23 M	10 10 17	4 02 24	29 43 22	6♉46 28	10 29.0	7 21.6	2 39.7	2 18.0	17 25.2	15 32.6	4 36.3	14 10.2	7 08.6	14 50.9
24 Tu	10 14 14	5 02 49	13♉43 02	20 33 08	10 30.5	8 18.7	3 53.5	3 04.0	17 46.6	15 25.4	4 38.3	14 13.0	7 10.9	14 52.3
25 W	10 18 10	6 03 12	27 16 58	3♊54 50	10R 31.8	9 18.6	5 07.2	3 50.1	18 07.8	15 18.4	4 40.1	14 15.8	7 13.2	14 53.8
26 Th	10 22 07	7 03 33	10♊27 04	16 54 04	10 32.0	10 21.1	6 20.8	4 36.0	18 29.0	15 11.4	4 41.8	14 18.7	7 15.4	14 55.3
27 F	10 26 03	8 03 52	23 16 17	29 34 08	10 30.9	11 26.0	7 34.4	5 22.0	18 50.1	15 04.6	4 43.4	14 21.6	7 17.7	14 56.7
28 Sa	10 30 00	9 04 10	5♋48 05	11♋58 32	10 28.2	12 33.1	8 48.0	6 07.9	19 11.0	14 57.8	4 45.0	14 24.5	7 20.0	14 58.1

Astro Data

	Dy Hr Mn
☽0S	11 4:57
☿R	21 15:55
☽0N	24 8:18
☽0S	7 12:55
☿D	11 14:57
☽0N	20 18:50
♂0N	21 17:29
♀0N	22 15:28
♃⊼♇	27 23:11

Planet Ingress

		Dy Hr Mn
♀	♒	3 14:48
☿	♒	5 1:08
⚳	♑	8 15:24
♂	♓	12 10:20
☉	♒	20 9:43
♀	♓	27 15:00
☉	♓	18 23:50
♂	♈	20 0:11
♀	♈	20 20:05

Last Aspect / ☽ Ingress (January)

Last Aspect Dy Hr Mn			☽ Ingress	Dy Hr Mn
1 12:19	♀	△	♊	1 17:09
3 11:55	♂	△	♋	4 1:07
5 4:53	☉	☍	♌	6 11:03
8 17:05	♂	☍	♍	8 22:58
10 15:46	☉	△	♎	11 11:57
13 9:46	☉	□	♏	13 23:44
15 23:52	☉	⚹	♐	16 8:01
17 19:25	♃	△	♑	18 12:04
19 10:51	♇	☌	♒	20 12:59
22 1:45	♀	☌	♓	22 12:48
23 11:13	♇	⚹	♈	24 13:31
26 14:23	♀	⚹	♉	26 16:37
28 2:18	♃	□	♊	28 22:36
30 9:24	♃	⚹	♋	31 7:09

Last Aspect / ☽ Ingress (February)

Last Aspect Dy Hr Mn			☽ Ingress	Dy Hr Mn
1 13:37	♂	△	♌	2 17:41
4 5:31	♃	☌	♍	5 5:46
6 22:09	♂	☍	♎	7 18:44
9 11:58	☉	△	♏	10 7:05
12 5:32	♂	△	♐	12 16:46
14 15:15	♂	□	♑	14 22:24
16 20:17	♂	⚹	♒	17 0:13
18 23:47	☉	☌	♓	18 23:47
19 23:02	♇	⚹	♈	20 23:13
22 0:36	♃	△	♉	23 0:28
24 2:57	♃	□	♊	25 4:54
26 8:43	♃	⚹	♋	27 12:50

☽ Phases & Eclipses

Dy Hr Mn		
5 4:53	○	14♋31
13 9:46	☾	22♎52
20 13:14	●	0♒09
27 4:48	☽	6♉55
3 23:09	○	14♌48
12 3:50	☾	23♏06
18 23:47	●	0♓00
25 17:14	☽	6♊47

Astro Data

1 January 2015
Julian Day # 42004
SVP 5♓02'56"
GC 27♐02.9 ⚴ 1♐47.3
Eris 22♈05.1R ⚵ 16♌08.5R
⚷ 13♓46.4 ⚶ 15♑13.0
☽ Mean ☊ 14♎56.2

1 February 2015
Julian Day # 42035
SVP 5♓02'51"
GC 27♐03.0 ⚴ 13♐42.9
Eris 22♈07.3 ⚵ 9♌10.7R
⚷ 15♓10.6 ⚶ 1♒40.4
☽ Mean ☊ 13♎17.8

March 2015 LONGITUDE

Day	Sid.Time	☉	0 hr ☽	Noon ☽	True ☊	☿	♀	♂	⚳	♃	♄	♅	♆	♇
1 Su	10 33 56	10♓04 25	18♋05 54	24♋10 36	10♎24.2	13♒42.4	10♈01.5	6♈53.7	19♑31.9	14♌51.2	4♐46.4	14♈27.5	7♓22.3	14♑59.5
2 M	10 37 53	11 04 38	0♌12 59	6♌13 23	10R 19.3	14 53.7	11 14.9	7 39.5	19 52.7	14R 44.7	4 47.7	14 30.5	7 24.5	15 00.8
3 Tu	10 41 49	12 04 49	12 12 08	18 09 30	10 14.1	16 06.8	12 28.3	8 25.3	20 13.3	14 38.3	4 49.0	14 33.5	7 26.8	15 02.1
4 W	10 45 46	13 04 59	24 05 47	0♍01 13	10 09.1	17 21.8	13 41.6	9 11.0	20 33.9	14 32.0	4 50.1	14 36.5	7 29.1	15 03.4
5 Th	10 49 42	14 05 06	5♍56 04	11 50 34	10 04.9	18 38.4	14 54.9	9 56.7	20 54.3	14 25.9	4 51.1	14 39.5	7 31.4	15 04.7
6 F	10 53 39	15 05 11	17 44 56	23 39 27	10 01.9	19 56.7	16 08.1	10 42.4	21 14.6	14 19.9	4 52.0	14 42.6	7 33.6	15 06.0
7 Sa	10 57 36	16 05 15	29 34 21	5♎29 54	10D 00.1	21 16.5	17 21.2	11 28.0	21 34.9	14 14.0	4 52.9	14 45.7	7 35.9	15 07.2
8 Su	11 01 32	17 05 17	11♎26 24	17 24 10	9 59.7	22 37.9	18 34.3	12 13.5	21 55.0	14 08.3	4 53.6	14 48.8	7 38.1	15 08.4
9 M	11 05 29	18 05 17	23 23 32	29 24 53	10 00.3	24 00.7	19 47.3	12 59.0	22 15.0	14 02.8	4 54.2	14 51.9	7 40.4	15 09.6
10 Tu	11 09 25	19 05 15	5♏28 35	11♏35 03	10 01.6	25 24.9	21 00.2	13 44.5	22 34.9	13 57.3	4 54.7	14 55.1	7 42.6	15 10.7
11 W	11 13 22	20 05 12	17 44 45	23 58 07	10 03.2	26 50.5	22 13.1	14 30.0	22 54.6	13 52.1	4 55.1	14 58.3	7 44.9	15 11.8
12 Th	11 17 18	21 05 07	0♐15 38	6♐37 45	10 04.7	28 17.4	23 25.9	15 15.3	23 14.3	13 47.0	4 55.5	15 01.5	7 47.1	15 12.9
13 F	11 21 15	22 05 00	13 04 56	19 37 36	10R 05.6	29 45.7	24 38.7	16 00.7	23 33.8	13 42.0	4 55.7	15 04.7	7 49.3	15 14.0
14 Sa	11 25 11	23 04 52	26 16 07	3♑00 49	10 05.9	1♓15.2	25 51.4	16 46.0	23 53.2	13 37.2	4R 55.8	15 07.9	7 51.6	15 15.0
15 Su	11 29 08	24 04 42	9♑51 54	16 49 29	10 05.3	2 46.0	27 04.0	17 31.3	24 12.5	13 32.6	4 55.8	15 11.1	7 53.8	15 16.0
16 M	11 33 05	25 04 31	23 53 33	1♒03 56	10 04.0	4 18.1	28 16.6	18 16.5	24 31.6	13 28.1	4 55.7	15 14.4	7 56.0	15 17.0
17 Tu	11 37 01	26 04 18	8♒20 17	15 42 05	10 02.4	5 51.5	29 29.1	19 01.7	24 50.6	13 23.9	4 55.5	15 17.7	7 58.2	15 18.0
18 W	11 40 58	27 04 03	23 08 38	0♓39 04	10 00.7	7 26.1	0♉41.5	19 46.8	25 09.5	13 19.7	4 55.2	15 21.0	8 00.4	15 18.9
19 Th	11 44 54	28 03 46	8♓12 24	15 47 28	9 59.2	9 02.0	1 53.9	20 31.9	25 28.3	13 15.8	4 54.8	15 24.3	8 02.5	15 19.8
20 F	11 48 51	29 03 27	23 23 07	0♈58 07	9 58.3	10 39.1	3 06.2	21 17.0	25 46.9	13 12.0	4 54.3	15 27.6	8 04.7	15 20.6
21 Sa	11 52 47	0♈03 06	8♈31 14	16 01 23	9D 58.0	12 17.5	4 18.4	22 02.0	26 05.3	13 08.4	4 53.7	15 30.9	8 06.9	15 21.5
22 Su	11 56 44	1 02 43	23 27 31	0♉48 44	9 58.2	13 57.1	5 30.5	22 47.0	26 23.7	13 05.0	4 53.0	15 34.3	8 09.0	15 22.3
23 M	12 00 40	2 02 18	8♉04 20	15 13 46	9 58.7	15 38.0	6 42.6	23 31.9	26 41.8	13 01.8	4 52.2	15 37.6	8 11.1	15 23.1
24 Tu	12 04 37	3 01 51	22 16 40	29 12 48	9 59.4	17 20.1	7 54.6	24 16.8	26 59.9	12 58.7	4 51.3	15 41.0	8 13.2	15 23.8
25 W	12 08 34	4 01 22	6♊02 10	12♊44 50	10 00.0	19 03.6	9 06.5	25 01.6	27 17.8	12 55.9	4 50.3	15 44.3	8 15.4	15 24.5
26 Th	12 12 30	5 00 50	19 21 01	25 51 03	10 00.4	20 48.3	10 18.3	25 46.4	27 35.5	12 53.2	4 49.3	15 47.7	8 17.4	15 25.2
27 F	12 16 27	6 00 16	2♋15 19	8♋34 16	10R 00.6	22 34.4	11 30.0	26 31.1	27 53.1	12 50.7	4 48.1	15 51.1	8 19.5	15 25.9
28 Sa	12 20 23	6 59 40	14 48 24	20 58 15	10 00.6	24 21.8	12 41.7	27 15.8	28 10.5	12 48.4	4 46.8	15 54.5	8 21.6	15 26.5
29 Su	12 24 20	7 59 02	27 04 20	3♌07 12	10 00.4	26 10.5	13 53.2	28 00.4	28 27.8	12 46.3	4 45.4	15 57.9	8 23.6	15 27.1
30 M	12 28 16	8 58 21	9♌07 23	15 05 23	10 00.3	28 00.5	15 04.7	28 45.0	28 44.9	12 44.3	4 43.9	16 01.3	8 25.7	15 27.7
31 Tu	12 32 13	9 57 38	21 01 42	26 56 48	10D 00.2	29 51.9	16 16.1	29 29.5	29 01.8	12 42.6	4 42.3	16 04.7	8 27.7	15 28.2

April 2015 LONGITUDE

Day	Sid.Time	☉	0 hr ☽	Noon ☽	True ☊	☿	♀	♂	⚳	♃	♄	♅	♆	♇
1 W	12 36 09	10♈56 52	2♍51 08	8♍45 08	10♎00.3	1♈44.7	17♉27.4	0♉14.0	29♑18.6	12♌41.0	4♐40.7	16♈08.2	8♓29.7	15♑28.7
2 Th	12 40 06	11 56 04	14 39 09	20 33 34	10 00.4	3 38.8	18 38.6	0 58.4	29 35.2	12R 39.7	4R 38.9	16 11.6	8 31.7	15 29.2
3 F	12 44 02	12 55 14	26 28 42	2♎24 52	10 00.6	5 34.3	19 49.7	1 42.8	29 51.6	12 38.5	4 37.1	16 15.0	8 33.6	15 29.7
4 Sa	12 47 59	13 54 22	8♎22 21	14 21 23	10R 00.7	7 31.0	21 00.6	2 27.1	0♒07.9	12 37.5	4 35.1	16 18.4	8 35.6	15 30.1
5 Su	12 51 56	14 53 28	20 22 14	26 25 08	10 00.6	9 29.1	22 11.5	3 11.4	0 24.0	12 36.7	4 33.1	16 21.9	8 37.5	15 30.5
6 M	12 55 52	15 52 32	2♏30 18	8♏37 57	10 00.3	11 28.5	23 22.3	3 55.7	0 39.9	12 36.1	4 31.0	16 25.3	8 39.4	15 30.8
7 Tu	12 59 49	16 51 34	14 48 17	21 01 32	9 59.6	13 29.1	24 33.0	4 39.8	0 55.6	12 35.7	4 28.8	16 28.7	8 41.3	15 31.2
8 W	13 03 45	17 50 35	27 17 54	3♐37 36	9 58.6	15 30.9	25 43.6	5 24.0	1 11.2	12D 35.5	4 26.5	16 32.1	8 43.2	15 31.5
9 Th	13 07 42	18 49 33	10♐00 52	16 27 55	9 57.5	17 33.7	26 54.1	6 08.1	1 26.6	12 35.4	4 24.1	16 35.6	8 45.1	15 31.7
10 F	13 11 38	19 48 29	22 58 58	29 34 13	9 56.4	19 37.6	28 04.5	6 52.1	1 41.7	12 35.6	4 21.7	16 39.0	8 46.9	15 32.0
11 Sa	13 15 35	20 47 24	6♑13 52	12♑58 06	9 55.6	21 42.3	29 14.7	7 36.1	1 56.7	12 35.9	4 19.1	16 42.4	8 48.7	15 32.2
12 Su	13 19 31	21 46 17	19 47 01	26 40 44	9D 55.3	23 47.6	0♊24.9	8 20.0	2 11.5	12 36.5	4 16.5	16 45.8	8 50.5	15 32.4
13 M	13 23 28	22 45 09	3♒39 14	10♒42 30	9 55.5	25 53.5	1 35.0	9 03.9	2 26.1	12 37.2	4 13.8	16 49.3	8 52.3	15 32.5
14 Tu	13 27 25	23 43 58	17 50 21	25 02 32	9 56.2	27 59.7	2 44.9	9 47.8	2 40.5	12 38.1	4 11.0	16 52.7	8 54.1	15 32.6
15 W	13 31 21	24 42 46	2♓18 43	9♓38 23	9 57.2	0♉06.0	3 54.8	10 31.6	2 54.7	12 39.1	4 08.1	16 56.1	8 55.8	15 32.7
16 Th	13 35 18	25 41 32	17 00 56	24 25 40	9 58.3	2 12.1	5 04.5	11 15.3	3 08.7	12 40.4	4 05.2	16 59.5	8 57.5	15 32.7
17 F	13 39 14	26 40 17	1♈51 45	9♈18 18	9R 59.0	4 17.7	6 14.1	11 59.0	3 22.5	12 41.9	4 02.2	17 02.9	8 59.2	15R 32.8
18 Sa	13 43 11	27 38 59	16 44 22	24 08 58	9 59.1	6 22.5	7 23.6	12 42.7	3 36.1	12 43.5	3 59.1	17 06.3	9 00.8	15 32.8
19 Su	13 47 07	28 37 40	1♉31 09	8♉50 01	9 58.2	8 26.1	8 32.9	13 26.3	3 49.4	12 45.3	3 55.9	17 09.7	9 02.5	15 32.7
20 M	13 51 04	29 36 19	16 04 43	23 14 31	9 56.3	10 28.3	9 42.2	14 09.8	4 02.6	12 47.3	3 52.7	17 13.0	9 04.1	15 32.6
21 Tu	13 55 00	0♉34 56	0♊18 51	7♊17 13	9 53.7	12 28.8	10 51.3	14 53.4	4 15.5	12 49.5	3 49.3	17 16.4	9 05.7	15 32.5
22 W	13 58 57	1 33 30	14 09 21	20 55 05	9 50.6	14 27.1	12 00.3	15 36.8	4 28.1	12 51.9	3 46.0	17 19.8	9 07.3	15 32.4
23 Th	14 02 54	2 32 03	27 34 24	4♋07 25	9 47.6	16 23.0	13 09.1	16 20.2	4 40.6	12 54.5	3 42.5	17 23.1	9 08.8	15 32.3
24 F	14 06 50	3 30 34	10♋34 24	16 55 39	9 45.1	18 16.2	14 17.8	17 03.6	4 52.8	12 57.2	3 39.0	17 26.4	9 10.3	15 32.1
25 Sa	14 10 47	4 29 02	23 11 38	29 22 48	9D 43.5	20 06.4	15 26.4	17 46.9	5 04.8	13 00.1	3 35.5	17 29.8	9 11.8	15 31.8
26 Su	14 14 43	5 27 28	5♌29 44	11♌33 00	9 43.0	21 53.4	16 34.8	18 30.1	5 16.5	13 03.2	3 31.8	17 33.1	9 13.3	15 31.6
27 M	14 18 40	6 25 52	17 33 12	23 30 56	9 43.5	23 36.9	17 43.1	19 13.3	5 28.0	13 06.4	3 28.2	17 36.4	9 14.7	15 31.3
28 Tu	14 22 36	7 24 14	29 26 50	5♍21 30	9 44.9	25 16.8	18 51.2	19 56.5	5 39.3	13 09.8	3 24.4	17 39.7	9 16.2	15 31.0
29 W	14 26 33	8 22 34	11♍15 32	17 09 28	9 46.6	26 52.8	19 59.2	20 39.6	5 50.3	13 13.4	3 20.6	17 42.9	9 17.5	15 30.7
30 Th	14 30 29	9 20 52	23 03 53	28 59 15	9 48.3	28 24.9	21 07.0	21 22.6	6 01.0	13 17.2	3 16.8	17 46.2	9 18.9	15 30.3

Astro Data

	Dy Hr Mn
♃△♅	3 12:25
☽0S	6 19:28
♄ R	14 15:02
♅□♇	17 2:54
☽0N	20 6:13
☉0N	20 22:45
☿0N	2 6:37
☽0S	3 1:40
♃ D	8 16:57
☽0N	16 16:40
♇ R	17 3:54
☽0S	30 8:46

Planet Ingress

		Dy Hr Mn
☿	♓	13 3:52
♀	♉	17 10:15
☉	♈	20 22:45
☿	♈	31 1:44
♂	♉	31 16:26
⚳	♒	3 12:21
♀	♊	11 15:28
☿	♉	14 22:51
☉	♉	20 9:42

Last Aspect / ☽ Ingress

Last Aspect Dy Hr Mn			☽ Ingress	Dy Hr Mn
28 17:53	♇	☍	♌	1 23:34
3 8:47	☿	☍	♍	4 11:58
5 18:36	♇	△	♎	7 0:52
9 1:24	☿	△	♏	9 13:10
11 19:46	☿	□	♐	11 23:30
13 23:11	♀	△	♑	14 6:40
16 8:02	♀	□	♒	16 10:14
17 18:18	♂	✶	♓	18 10:58
20 9:36	☉	☌	♈	20 10:28
21 22:51	♂	☌	♉	22 10:40
23 14:25	☿	✶	♊	24 13:22
26 12:35	♂	✶	♋	26 19:45
29 1:58	♂	□	♌	29 5:48
30 13:57	♅	△	♍	31 18:12

Last Aspect / ☽ Ingress

Last Aspect Dy Hr Mn			☽ Ingress	Dy Hr Mn
2 9:01	♀	△	♎	3 7:07
4 15:58	♅	☍	♏	5 19:04
7 20:42	♀	☍	♐	8 5:08
9 17:42	☉	△	♑	10 12:47
12 8:15	☿	□	♒	12 17:44
14 19:45	☿	✶	♓	14 20:12
15 21:37	♇	✶	♈	16 21:00
18 18:57	☉	☌	♉	18 21:31
19 23:07	♇	△	♊	20 23:28
22 5:38	♅	✶	♋	23 4:25
24 17:04	☿	✶	♌	25 13:13
27 14:12	☿	□	♍	28 1:07
30 12:23	☿	△	♎	30 14:03

☽ Phases & Eclipses

Dy Hr Mn		
5 18:05	○	14♍50
13 17:48	☾	22♐49
20 9:36	●	29♓27
20 9:45:37	●	T 02'47"
27 7:43	☽	6♋19
4 12:06	○	14♎24
4 12:00	○	T 1.001
12 3:44	☾	21♑55
18 18:57	●	28♈25
25 23:55	☽	5♌27

Astro Data

1 March 2015
Julian Day # 42063
SVP 5♓02'48"
GC 27♐03.1 ⚵ 22♐40.4
Eris 22♈17.8 ⚴ 3♌50.8R
⚷ 16♓49.5 ⚶ 16♒11.7
☽ Mean ☊ 11♎48.8

1 April 2015
Julian Day # 42094
SVP 5♓02'46"
GC 27♐03.1 ⚵ 29♐09.3
Eris 22♈35.8 ⚴ 4♌22.7
⚷ 18♓43.1 ⚶ 1♓34.1
☽ Mean ☊ 10♎10.3

Ephemeris pages reproduced by permission of the publisher: Starcrafts, LLC, 334-A Calef Hwy., Epping, NH 03042. astrocom.com & starcraftspublishing.com

© 2014 Janet Booth | 1-877-293-1607 | JanetsPlan-its.com

Ephemeris pages reproduced by permission of the publisher: Starcrafts, LLC, 334-A Calef Hwy., Epping, NH 03042. astrocom.com & starcraftspublishing.com

LONGITUDE — May 2015

Day	Sid.Time	☉	0 hr ☽	Noon ☽	True ☊	☿	♀	♂	⚳	♃	♄	♅	♆	♇
1 F	14 34 26	10♉19 07	4♎56 02	10♎54 41	9♎49.3	29♉52.9	22♊14.6	22♉05.6	6♒11.5	13♌21.1	3♐12.9	17♈49.4	9♓20.2	15♑29.9
2 Sa	14 38 23	11 17 21	16 55 33	22 58 59	9R 49.1	1♊16.6	23 22.1	22 48.6	6 21.8	13 25.2	3R 08.9	17 52.6	9 21.5	15R 29.5
3 Su	14 42 19	12 15 33	29 05 14	5♏14 34	9 47.5	2 36.1	24 29.4	23 31.4	6 31.7	13 29.5	3 04.9	17 55.8	9 22.8	15 29.0
4 M	14 46 16	13 13 44	11♏27 07	17 43 03	9 44.4	3 51.2	25 36.5	24 14.3	6 41.5	13 33.9	3 00.9	17 59.0	9 24.1	15 28.6
5 Tu	14 50 12	14 11 52	24 02 26	0♐25 18	9 39.7	5 01.9	26 43.4	24 57.1	6 50.9	13 38.5	2 56.8	18 02.2	9 25.3	15 28.1
6 W	14 54 09	15 09 59	6♐51 41	13 21 32	9 34.1	6 07.9	27 50.2	25 39.8	7 00.1	13 43.2	2 52.7	18 05.3	9 26.5	15 27.5
7 Th	14 58 05	16 08 04	19 54 48	26 31 25	9 28.0	7 09.4	28 56.7	26 22.5	7 09.0	13 48.1	2 48.5	18 08.5	9 27.7	15 27.0
8 F	15 02 02	17 06 08	3♑11 18	9♑54 23	9 22.3	8 06.2	0♋03.1	27 05.2	7 17.6	13 53.2	2 44.3	18 11.6	9 28.8	15 26.4
9 Sa	15 05 58	18 04 11	16 40 33	23 29 44	9 17.6	8 58.3	1 09.3	27 47.8	7 26.0	13 58.4	2 40.1	18 14.7	9 29.9	15 25.8
10 Su	15 09 55	19 02 12	0♒21 51	7♒16 48	9 14.4	9 45.6	2 15.3	28 30.3	7 34.1	14 03.8	2 35.9	18 17.7	9 31.0	15 25.1
11 M	15 13 52	20 00 12	14 14 32	21 14 55	9D 12.9	10 28.0	3 21.1	29 12.8	7 41.8	14 09.3	2 31.6	18 20.8	9 32.1	15 24.5
12 Tu	15 17 48	20 58 10	28 17 52	5♓23 14	9 12.9	11 05.6	4 26.7	29 55.3	7 49.3	14 15.0	2 27.2	18 23.8	9 33.1	15 23.8
13 W	15 21 45	21 56 07	12♓30 51	19 40 28	9 13.9	11 38.1	5 32.1	0♊37.7	7 56.5	14 20.8	2 22.9	18 26.8	9 34.1	15 23.0
14 Th	15 25 41	22 54 03	26 51 47	4♈04 28	9R 15.1	12 05.7	6 37.3	1 20.1	8 03.4	14 26.7	2 18.5	18 29.8	9 35.0	15 22.3
15 F	15 29 38	23 51 57	11♈18 05	18 32 06	9 15.6	12 28.3	7 42.2	2 02.4	8 09.9	14 32.9	2 14.1	18 32.7	9 35.9	15 21.5
16 Sa	15 33 34	24 49 51	25 45 57	2♉59 00	9 14.5	12 45.9	8 46.9	2 44.6	8 16.2	14 39.1	2 09.7	18 35.7	9 36.8	15 20.7
17 Su	15 37 31	25 47 43	10♉10 34	17 19 59	9 11.3	12 58.5	9 51.4	3 26.9	8 22.2	14 45.5	2 05.3	18 38.6	9 37.7	15 19.9
18 M	15 41 27	26 45 34	24 26 32	1♊29 33	9 06.0	13 06.1	10 55.7	4 09.0	8 27.8	14 52.1	2 00.9	18 41.5	9 38.6	15 19.1
19 Tu	15 45 24	27 43 23	8♊28 27	15 22 42	8 58.9	13R 08.9	11 59.7	4 51.2	8 33.1	14 58.7	1 56.4	18 44.3	9 39.4	15 18.2
20 W	15 49 21	28 41 11	22 11 53	28 55 41	8 50.7	13 06.9	13 03.5	5 33.3	8 38.1	15 05.6	1 51.9	18 47.1	9 40.1	15 17.3
21 Th	15 53 17	29 38 57	5♋33 55	12♋06 31	8 42.4	13 00.3	14 07.0	6 15.3	8 42.8	15 12.5	1 47.5	18 49.9	9 40.9	15 16.4
22 F	15 57 14	0♊36 42	18 33 33	24 55 12	8 34.9	12 49.2	15 10.3	6 57.3	8 47.1	15 19.6	1 43.0	18 52.7	9 41.6	15 15.5
23 Sa	16 01 10	1 34 25	1♌11 44	7♌23 32	8 28.9	12 34.0	16 13.2	7 39.2	8 51.2	15 26.8	1 38.5	18 55.4	9 42.3	15 14.5
24 Su	16 05 07	2 32 07	13 31 04	19 34 51	8 24.9	12 14.9	17 15.9	8 21.1	8 54.8	15 34.2	1 34.0	18 58.2	9 42.9	15 13.5
25 M	16 09 03	3 29 47	25 35 27	1♍33 29	8D 22.9	11 52.3	18 18.3	9 02.9	8 58.2	15 41.7	1 29.6	19 00.8	9 43.5	15 12.5
26 Tu	16 13 00	4 27 26	7♍29 36	13 24 28	8 22.6	11 26.6	19 20.4	9 44.7	9 01.2	15 49.3	1 25.1	19 03.5	9 44.1	15 11.5
27 W	16 16 56	5 25 03	19 18 44	25 13 05	8 23.3	10 58.2	20 22.2	10 26.5	9 03.9	15 57.0	1 20.6	19 06.1	9 44.7	15 10.4
28 Th	16 20 53	6 22 39	1♎08 08	7♎04 33	8R 24.2	10 27.6	21 23.6	11 08.2	9 06.2	16 04.9	1 16.2	19 08.7	9 45.2	15 09.4
29 F	16 24 50	7 20 13	13 02 54	19 03 46	8 24.3	9 55.4	22 24.7	11 49.8	9 08.2	16 12.8	1 11.7	19 11.2	9 45.7	15 08.3
30 Sa	16 28 46	8 17 46	25 07 37	1♏14 55	8 22.8	9 22.1	23 25.5	12 31.4	9 09.8	16 20.9	1 07.3	19 13.8	9 46.1	15 07.2
31 Su	16 32 43	9 15 17	7♏26 03	13 41 20	8 19.2	8 48.4	24 25.9	13 13.0	9 11.1	16 29.2	1 02.9	19 16.2	9 46.5	15 06.0

LONGITUDE — June 2015

Day	Sid.Time	☉	0 hr ☽	Noon ☽	True ☊	☿	♀	♂	⚳	♃	♄	♅	♆	♇
1 M	16 36 39	10♊12 48	20♏00 57	26♏25 04	8♎13.1	8♊14.7	25♋26.0	13♊54.5	9♒12.0	16♌37.5	0♐58.5	19♈18.7	9♓46.9	15♑04.9
2 Tu	16 40 36	11 10 17	2♐53 43	9♐26 52	8R 04.8	7R 41.7	26 25.7	14 35.9	9 12.6	16 45.9	0R 54.1	19 21.1	9 47.3	15R 03.7
3 W	16 44 32	12 07 45	16 04 21	22 46 00	7 54.9	7 10.0	27 25.0	15 17.3	9R 12.9	16 54.5	0 49.8	19 23.5	9 47.6	15 02.6
4 Th	16 48 29	13 05 13	29 31 29	6♑20 28	7 44.3	6 40.0	28 23.9	15 58.7	9 12.8	17 03.2	0 45.5	19 25.9	9 47.9	15 01.4
5 F	16 52 25	14 02 39	13♑12 36	20 07 25	7 34.1	6 12.3	29 22.3	16 40.0	9 12.3	17 11.9	0 41.2	19 28.2	9 48.1	15 00.2
6 Sa	16 56 22	15 00 04	27 04 33	4♒03 35	7 25.3	5 47.3	0♌20.4	17 21.3	9 11.5	17 20.8	0 36.9	19 30.5	9 48.4	14 58.9
7 Su	17 00 19	15 57 29	11♒04 07	18 05 50	7 18.8	5 25.5	1 18.0	18 02.6	9 10.3	17 29.8	0 32.7	19 32.7	9 48.6	14 57.7
8 M	17 04 15	16 54 53	25 08 26	2♓11 40	7 14.8	5 07.1	2 15.2	18 43.8	9 08.7	17 38.9	0 28.5	19 34.9	9 48.7	14 56.4
9 Tu	17 08 12	17 52 17	9♓15 19	16 19 14	7D 13.1	4 52.6	3 11.9	19 24.9	9 06.8	17 48.1	0 24.3	19 37.1	9 48.9	14 55.1
10 W	17 12 08	18 49 40	23 23 15	0♈27 15	7R 12.9	4 42.0	4 08.2	20 06.0	9 04.5	17 57.4	0 20.2	19 39.2	9 48.9	14 53.8
11 Th	17 16 05	19 47 02	7♈31 07	14 34 41	7 13.1	4D 35.7	5 03.9	20 47.1	9 01.9	18 06.8	0 16.1	19 41.3	9 49.0	14 52.5
12 F	17 20 01	20 44 24	21 37 48	28 40 16	7 12.5	4 33.8	5 59.2	21 28.1	8 58.9	18 16.3	0 12.0	19 43.3	9R 49.0	14 51.2
13 Sa	17 23 58	21 41 46	5♉41 48	12♉42 08	7 09.9	4 36.3	6 53.9	22 09.1	8 55.6	18 25.9	0 08.0	19 45.4	9 49.0	14 49.9
14 Su	17 27 54	22 39 07	19 40 55	26 37 45	7 04.7	4 43.3	7 48.1	22 50.0	8 51.8	18 35.7	0 04.0	19 47.3	9 49.0	14 48.5
15 M	17 31 51	23 36 28	3♊32 13	10♊23 56	6 56.7	4 55.0	8 41.8	23 30.9	8 47.7	18 45.4	0 00.1	19 49.3	9 48.9	14 47.2
16 Tu	17 35 48	24 33 48	17 12 26	23 57 22	6 46.4	5 11.1	9 34.9	24 11.8	8 43.3	18 55.3	29♏56.2	19 51.2	9 48.8	14 45.8
17 W	17 39 44	25 31 07	0♋38 21	7♋15 07	6 34.5	5 31.8	10 27.3	24 52.6	8 38.5	19 05.3	29 52.4	19 53.0	9 48.7	14 44.4
18 Th	17 43 41	26 28 26	13 47 26	20 15 10	6 22.3	5 57.0	11 19.2	25 33.4	8 33.3	19 15.4	29 48.6	19 54.8	9 48.5	14 43.0
19 F	17 47 37	27 25 44	26 38 19	2♌56 55	6 10.9	6 26.7	12 10.4	26 14.1	8 27.8	19 25.6	29 44.9	19 56.6	9 48.3	14 41.6
20 Sa	17 51 34	28 23 02	9♌11 07	15 21 11	6 01.3	7 00.8	13 00.9	26 54.8	8 22.0	19 35.8	29 41.3	19 58.3	9 48.1	14 40.2
21 Su	17 55 30	29 20 19	21 27 27	27 30 19	5 54.1	7 39.2	13 50.8	27 35.5	8 15.8	19 46.2	29 37.7	20 00.0	9 47.8	14 38.8
22 M	17 59 27	0♋17 35	3♍30 16	9♍27 51	5 49.5	8 21.9	14 39.9	28 16.1	8 09.2	19 56.6	29 34.2	20 01.7	9 47.6	14 37.4
23 Tu	18 03 23	1 14 50	15 23 38	21 18 16	5 47.2	9 08.8	15 28.2	28 56.6	8 02.4	20 07.1	29 30.7	20 03.3	9 47.2	14 35.9
24 W	18 07 20	2 12 05	27 12 24	3♎06 44	5 46.6	9 59.8	16 15.8	29 37.1	7 55.2	20 17.7	29 27.3	20 04.8	9 46.9	14 34.5
25 Th	18 11 17	3 09 19	9♎01 55	14 58 40	5 46.5	10 54.9	17 02.6	0♋17.6	7 47.6	20 28.3	29 23.9	20 06.3	9 46.5	14 33.0
26 F	18 15 13	4 06 33	20 57 38	26 59 30	5 46.0	11 54.0	17 48.5	0 58.1	7 39.8	20 39.1	29 20.6	20 07.8	9 46.1	14 31.6
27 Sa	18 19 10	5 03 46	3♏04 51	9♏14 17	5 44.1	12 57.0	18 33.5	1 38.4	7 31.6	20 49.9	29 17.4	20 09.2	9 45.6	14 30.1
28 Su	18 23 06	6 00 58	15 28 18	21 47 18	5 40.0	14 03.9	19 17.7	2 18.8	7 23.1	21 00.8	29 14.3	20 10.6	9 45.1	14 28.6
29 M	18 27 03	6 58 10	28 11 39	4♐41 34	5 33.3	15 14.7	20 00.9	2 59.1	7 14.4	21 11.7	29 11.2	20 11.9	9 44.6	14 27.1
30 Tu	18 30 59	7 55 22	11♐17 09	17 58 25	5 24.2	16 29.3	20 43.1	3 39.4	7 05.3	21 22.8	29 08.2	20 13.2	9 44.1	14 25.7

Astro Data

	Dy	Hr Mn
♄⚼♅	4	6:12
☽0N	14	1:11
☿R	19	1:48
♃⚻♇	21	11:39
☽0S	27	17:17
⚳R	3	4:20
☽0N	10	8:05
☿D	11	22:34
♆R	12	9:08
♄∠♇	20	11:45
♃△♅	22	13:46
☽0S	24	2:41

Planet Ingress

	Dy	Hr Mn
☿ ♊	1	2:00
♀ ♋	7	22:52
♂ ♊	12	2:40
☉ ♊	21	8:45
♀ ♌	5	15:33
♄ ♏R	15	0:36
☉ ♋	21	16:38
♂ ♋	24	13:33

Last Aspect / ☽ Ingress (May)

Last Aspect Dy Hr Mn		☽ Ingress	Dy Hr Mn
2 14:03	♀ △	♏	3 1:47
5 1:49	♂ ☍	♐	5 11:13
7 17:51	♀ ☍	♑	7 18:16
9 20:35	♂ △	♒	9 23:22
11 10:36	☉ □	♓	12 2:53
13 16:55	☉ ⚹	♈	14 5:13
15 12:03	♅ ☌	♉	16 7:02
18 4:13	☉ ☌	♊	18 9:27
19 17:57	♅ ⚹	♋	20 13:56
22 0:36	♅ □	♌	22 21:42
24 10:50	♅ △	♍	25 8:52
27 2:21	♀ ⚹	♎	27 21:42
29 20:20	♀ □	♏	30 9:34

Last Aspect / ☽ Ingress (June)

Last Aspect Dy Hr Mn		☽ Ingress	Dy Hr Mn
1 11:01	♀ △	♐	1 18:39
3 5:59	♅ △	♑	4 0:50
5 10:54	♅ □	♒	6 5:02
7 14:30	♅ ⚹	♓	8 8:16
9 18:08	♂ □	♈	10 11:14
11 23:43	♂ ⚹	♉	12 14:16
13 22:06	♃ □	♊	14 17:51
16 14:05	☉ ☌	♋	16 22:51
19 5:52	♄ △	♌	19 6:22
21 16:09	♄ □	♍	21 16:59
24 5:12	♂ □	♎	24 5:41
25 23:22	♃ ⚹	♏	26 17:57
29 1:50	♄ ☌	♐	29 3:21

☽ Phases & Eclipses

Dy Hr Mn	
4 3:42	○ 13♏23
11 10:36	☾ 20♒26
18 4:13	● 26♉56
25 17:19	☽ 4♍11
2 16:19	○ 11♐49
9 15:42	☾ 18♓30
16 14:05	● 25♊07
24 11:03	☽ 2♎38

Astro Data

1 May 2015
Julian Day # 42124
SVP 5♓02'43"
GC 27♐03.2 ⚴ 29♐58.8R
Eris 22♈55.3 ⚵ 10♌15.4
⚷ 20♓16.8 ⚶ 15♓21.5
☽ Mean ☊ 8♎34.9

1 June 2015
Julian Day # 42155
SVP 5♓02'39"
GC 27♐03.3 ⚴ 23♐59.4R
Eris 23♈12.7 ⚵ 19♌29.5
⚷ 21♓18.4 ⚶ 27♓53.5
☽ Mean ☊ 6♎56.4

July 2015 LONGITUDE

Day	Sid.Time	☉	0 hr ☽	Noon ☽	True ☊	☿	♀	♂	⚳	♃	♄	♅	♆	♇
1 W	18 34 56	8♋52 34	24♐45 11	1♑37 10	5♎13.2	17♊47.6	21♌24.3	4♋19.6	6♒55.9	21♌33.9	29♏05.3	20♈14.5	9♓43.5	14♑24.2
2 Th	18 38 52	9 49 45	8♑33 59	15 35 05	5R 01.5	19 09.6	22 04.4	4 59.8	6R 46.3	21 45.0	29R 02.5	20 15.7	9R 42.9	14R 22.7
3 F	18 42 49	10 46 56	22 39 52	29 47 38	4 50.1	20 35.3	22 43.4	5 40.0	6 36.4	21 56.3	28 59.7	20 16.8	9 42.3	14 21.2
4 Sa	18 46 46	11 44 07	6♒57 40	14♒09 14	4 40.3	22 04.6	23 21.3	6 20.1	6 26.2	22 07.6	28 57.0	20 17.9	9 41.6	14 19.7
5 Su	18 50 42	12 41 18	21 21 37	28 34 11	4 32.8	23 37.5	23 58.0	7 00.2	6 15.8	22 18.9	28 54.4	20 19.0	9 40.9	14 18.2
6 M	18 54 39	13 38 30	5♓46 19	12♓57 30	4 28.1	25 13.8	24 33.5	7 40.2	6 05.1	22 30.4	28 51.9	20 20.0	9 40.2	14 16.7
7 Tu	18 58 35	14 35 41	20 07 21	27 15 31	4 25.9	26 53.6	25 07.7	8 20.2	5 54.2	22 41.9	28 49.4	20 21.0	9 39.5	14 15.2
8 W	19 02 32	15 32 53	4♈21 46	11♈25 56	4 25.4	28 36.7	25 40.6	9 00.2	5 43.0	22 53.4	28 47.1	20 21.9	9 38.7	14 13.7
9 Th	19 06 28	16 30 05	18 27 54	25 27 36	4 25.5	0♋23.0	26 12.2	9 40.1	5 31.6	23 05.1	28 44.8	20 22.8	9 37.9	14 12.2
10 F	19 10 25	17 27 18	2♉25 00	9♉20 05	4 24.8	2 12.5	26 42.3	10 20.0	5 20.0	23 16.7	28 42.6	20 23.6	9 37.1	14 10.8
11 Sa	19 14 21	18 24 31	16 12 47	23 03 05	4 22.3	4 04.8	27 10.9	10 59.9	5 08.2	23 28.5	28 40.4	20 24.4	9 36.2	14 09.3
12 Su	19 18 18	19 21 44	29 50 53	6♊36 08	4 17.4	6 00.0	27 38.1	11 39.7	4 56.3	23 40.3	28 38.4	20 25.1	9 35.3	14 07.8
13 M	19 22 15	20 18 58	13♊18 41	19 58 24	4 09.7	7 57.7	28 03.7	12 19.5	4 44.1	23 52.1	28 36.5	20 25.8	9 34.4	14 06.3
14 Tu	19 26 11	21 16 13	26 35 08	3♋08 45	3 59.7	9 57.7	28 27.6	12 59.2	4 31.8	24 04.0	28 34.6	20 26.4	9 33.5	14 04.8
15 W	19 30 08	22 13 28	9♋39 05	16 06 00	3 48.2	11 59.8	28 49.9	13 39.0	4 19.3	24 16.0	28 32.8	20 27.0	9 32.5	14 03.3
16 Th	19 34 04	23 10 43	22 29 24	28 49 14	3 36.3	14 03.6	29 10.4	14 18.7	4 06.7	24 28.0	28 31.2	20 27.5	9 31.5	14 01.9
17 F	19 38 01	24 07 59	5♌05 29	11♌18 12	3 25.1	16 09.0	29 29.1	14 58.3	3 54.0	24 40.0	28 29.6	20 28.0	9 30.5	14 00.4
18 Sa	19 41 57	25 05 15	17 27 29	23 33 31	3 15.6	18 15.5	29 45.9	15 37.9	3 41.2	24 52.2	28 28.1	20 28.4	9 29.5	13 58.9
19 Su	19 45 54	26 02 31	29 36 32	5♍36 52	3 08.5	20 22.9	0♍00.8	16 17.5	3 28.2	25 04.3	28 26.7	20 28.8	9 28.4	13 57.5
20 M	19 49 50	26 59 47	11♍34 51	17 30 56	3 03.9	22 30.8	0 13.7	16 57.0	3 15.2	25 16.5	28 25.4	20 29.2	9 27.3	13 56.0
21 Tu	19 53 47	27 57 04	23 25 36	29 19 24	3D 01.6	24 39.0	0 24.5	17 36.6	3 02.1	25 28.8	28 24.1	20 29.4	9 26.2	13 54.6
22 W	19 57 44	28 54 21	5♎12 53	11♎06 41	3 01.2	26 47.1	0 33.3	18 16.0	2 49.0	25 41.0	28 23.0	20 29.7	9 25.1	13 53.1
23 Th	20 01 40	29 51 38	17 01 26	22 57 48	3 01.7	28 55.0	0 39.8	18 55.5	2 35.8	25 53.4	28 22.0	20 29.9	9 23.9	13 51.7
24 F	20 05 37	0♌48 55	28 56 28	4♏58 05	3R 02.2	1♌02.3	0 44.1	19 34.9	2 22.6	26 05.7	28 21.0	20 30.0	9 22.7	13 50.3
25 Sa	20 09 33	1 46 13	11♏03 21	17 12 52	3 01.8	3 08.9	0R 46.2	20 14.2	2 09.3	26 18.1	28 20.2	20 30.1	9 21.5	13 48.9
26 Su	20 13 30	2 43 31	23 27 15	29 47 03	2 59.6	5 14.5	0 46.0	20 53.6	1 56.1	26 30.6	28 19.5	20R 30.2	9 20.3	13 47.5
27 M	20 17 26	3 40 50	6♐12 42	12♐44 35	2 55.4	7 19.1	0 43.4	21 32.8	1 42.9	26 43.1	28 18.8	20 30.2	9 19.1	13 46.1
28 Tu	20 21 23	4 38 09	19 22 59	26 07 55	2 49.1	9 22.5	0 38.4	22 12.1	1 29.8	26 55.6	28 18.3	20 30.1	9 17.8	13 44.7
29 W	20 25 19	5 35 29	2♑59 27	9♑57 20	2 41.2	11 24.5	0 31.0	22 51.3	1 16.6	27 08.2	28 17.8	20 30.0	9 16.5	13 43.4
30 Th	20 29 16	6 32 49	17 01 14	24 10 35	2 32.4	13 25.1	0 21.3	23 30.5	1 03.6	27 20.7	28 17.5	20 29.9	9 15.2	13 42.0
31 F	20 33 13	7 30 10	1♒24 44	8♒42 52	2 23.8	15 24.2	0 09.1	24 09.7	0 50.6	27 33.4	28 17.2	20 29.7	9 13.9	13 40.7

August 2015 LONGITUDE

Day	Sid.Time	☉	0 hr ☽	Noon ☽	True ☊	☿	♀	♂	⚳	♃	♄	♅	♆	♇
1 Sa	20 37 09	8♌27 31	16♒04 04	23♒27 22	2♎16.5	17♌21.9	29♌54.5	24♋48.8	0♒37.7	27♌46.0	28♏17.0	20♈29.4	9♓12.5	13♑39.4
2 Su	20 41 06	9 24 54	0♓51 46	8♓16 19	2R 11.0	19 17.9	29R 37.7	25 27.9	0R 24.8	27 58.7	28D 17.0	20R 29.1	9R 11.2	13R 38.0
3 M	20 45 02	10 22 17	15 40 04	23 02 11	2 07.8	21 12.4	29 18.5	26 07.0	0 12.1	28 11.4	28 17.0	20 28.8	9 09.8	13 36.7
4 Tu	20 48 59	11 19 42	0♈21 58	7♈38 49	2D 06.8	23 05.3	28 57.0	26 46.0	29♑59.5	28 24.1	28 17.1	20 28.4	9 08.4	13 35.5
5 W	20 52 55	12 17 07	14 52 13	22 01 52	2 07.2	24 56.6	28 33.4	27 25.0	29 47.1	28 36.9	28 17.3	20 28.0	9 07.0	13 34.2
6 Th	20 56 52	13 14 34	29 07 29	6♉08 58	2 08.2	26 46.3	28 07.8	28 04.0	29 34.8	28 49.7	28 17.6	20 27.5	9 05.6	13 32.9
7 F	21 00 48	14 12 02	13♉06 15	19 59 21	2R 08.9	28 34.4	27 40.2	28 42.9	29 22.6	29 02.5	28 18.0	20 26.9	9 04.1	13 31.7
8 Sa	21 04 45	15 09 32	26 48 21	3♊33 19	2 08.2	0♍21.0	27 10.8	29 21.9	29 10.6	29 15.3	28 18.6	20 26.4	9 02.7	13 30.5
9 Su	21 08 42	16 07 03	10♊14 23	16 51 42	2 05.8	2 05.9	26 39.8	0♌00.8	28 58.8	29 28.2	28 19.2	20 25.7	9 01.2	13 29.3
10 M	21 12 38	17 04 35	23 25 22	29 55 31	2 01.4	3 49.3	26 07.3	0 39.6	28 47.2	29 41.1	28 19.9	20 25.1	8 59.7	13 28.1
11 Tu	21 16 35	18 02 08	6♋22 16	12♋45 44	1 55.3	5 31.2	25 33.5	1 18.4	28 35.8	29 54.0	28 20.7	20 24.3	8 58.2	13 26.9
12 W	21 20 31	18 59 43	19 06 00	25 23 11	1 48.1	7 11.5	24 58.5	1 57.3	28 24.7	0♍06.9	28 21.6	20 23.6	8 56.7	13 25.7
13 Th	21 24 28	19 57 19	1♌37 21	7♌48 38	1 40.6	8 50.2	24 22.7	2 36.0	28 13.7	0 19.8	28 22.6	20 22.8	8 55.2	13 24.6
14 F	21 28 24	20 54 57	13 57 08	20 02 59	1 33.5	10 27.5	23 46.1	3 14.8	28 03.0	0 32.8	28 23.7	20 21.9	8 53.6	13 23.5
15 Sa	21 32 21	21 52 35	26 06 20	2♍07 22	1 27.6	12 03.2	23 09.1	3 53.5	27 52.5	0 45.8	28 24.8	20 21.0	8 52.1	13 22.4
16 Su	21 36 17	22 50 15	8♍06 19	14 03 24	1 23.3	13 37.4	22 31.9	4 32.2	27 42.3	0 58.8	28 26.1	20 20.1	8 50.5	13 21.3
17 M	21 40 14	23 47 56	19 58 57	25 53 16	1D 20.9	15 10.1	21 54.7	5 10.8	27 32.4	1 11.7	28 27.5	20 19.1	8 48.9	13 20.3
18 Tu	21 44 11	24 45 38	1♎46 44	7♎39 46	1 20.1	16 41.2	21 17.7	5 49.4	27 22.7	1 24.8	28 29.0	20 18.0	8 47.3	13 19.2
19 W	21 48 07	25 43 21	13 32 50	19 26 25	1 20.8	18 10.9	20 41.2	6 28.0	27 13.4	1 37.8	28 30.6	20 16.9	8 45.8	13 18.2
20 Th	21 52 04	26 41 05	25 21 03	1♏17 18	1 22.3	19 39.0	20 05.4	7 06.6	27 04.3	1 50.8	28 32.2	20 15.8	8 44.2	13 17.2
21 F	21 56 00	27 38 51	7♏15 45	13 17 00	1 24.0	21 05.5	19 30.5	7 45.1	26 55.5	2 03.8	28 34.0	20 14.6	8 42.6	13 16.3
22 Sa	21 59 57	28 36 37	19 21 40	25 30 21	1R 25.3	22 30.5	18 56.8	8 23.6	26 47.0	2 16.9	28 35.9	20 13.4	8 40.9	13 15.3
23 Su	22 03 53	29 34 25	1♐43 41	8♐02 13	1 25.7	23 53.9	18 24.4	9 02.1	26 38.9	2 29.9	28 37.8	20 12.2	8 39.3	13 14.4
24 M	22 07 50	0♍32 14	14 26 28	20 56 55	1 24.8	25 15.6	17 53.5	9 40.5	26 31.0	2 43.0	28 39.8	20 10.9	8 37.7	13 13.5
25 Tu	22 11 46	1 30 04	27 33 57	4♑17 49	1 22.6	26 35.7	17 24.4	10 18.9	26 23.5	2 56.0	28 42.0	20 09.6	8 36.1	13 12.6
26 W	22 15 43	2 27 56	11♑08 41	18 06 32	1 19.4	27 54.1	16 57.0	10 57.3	26 16.4	3 09.1	28 44.2	20 08.2	8 34.4	13 11.7
27 Th	22 19 40	3 25 48	25 11 12	2♒22 20	1 15.5	29 10.7	16 31.6	11 35.7	26 09.5	3 22.1	28 46.5	20 06.8	8 32.8	13 10.9
28 F	22 23 36	4 23 42	9♒39 24	17 01 43	1 11.7	0♎25.5	16 08.3	12 14.0	26 03.0	3 35.2	28 49.0	20 05.3	8 31.2	13 10.1
29 Sa	22 27 33	5 21 37	24 28 23	1♓58 26	1 08.3	1 38.5	15 47.2	12 52.3	25 56.8	3 48.2	28 51.5	20 03.8	8 29.5	13 09.3
30 Su	22 31 29	6 19 34	9♓30 46	17 04 14	1 06.0	2 49.5	15 28.4	13 30.6	25 51.0	4 01.3	28 54.0	20 02.3	8 27.9	13 08.6
31 M	22 35 26	7 17 32	24 37 39	2♈09 55	1D 04.9	3 58.5	15 11.9	14 08.8	25 45.5	4 14.3	28 56.7	20 00.7	8 26.2	13 07.8

Astro Data Dy Hr Mn	Planet Ingress Dy Hr Mn	Last Aspect Dy Hr Mn	☽ Ingress Dy Hr Mn	Last Aspect Dy Hr Mn	☽ Ingress Dy Hr Mn	☽ Phases & Eclipses Dy Hr Mn	Astro Data
☽0N 7 14:43	☿ ♋ 8 18:52	30 18:18 ♃ △	♑ 1 9:11	1 22:02 ♀ ☍	♓ 1 22:36	2 2:20 ○ 9♑55	1 July 2015
☽0S 21 11:47	♀ ♍ 18 22:38	3 10:38 ♄ ⚹	♒ 3 12:21	3 20:35 ♄ △	♈ 3 23:24	8 20:24 ☾ 16♈22	Julian Day # 42185
♀R 25 9:29	☉ ♌ 23 3:30	5 12:32 ♄ □	♓ 5 14:23	5 23:29 ♃ △	♉ 6 1:29	16 1:24 ● 23♋14	SVP 5♓02'34"
♅R 26 10:38	☿ ♌ 23 12:14	7 14:36 ♄ △	♈ 7 16:37	8 4:46 ♂ ⚹	♊ 8 5:40	24 4:04 ☽ 0♏59	GC 27♐03.3 ⚴ 15♐38.2R
	♀ ♌R 31 15:27	9 13:47 ♀ △	♉ 9 19:49	10 11:45 ♃ ⚹	♋ 10 12:08	31 10:43 ○ 7♒56	Eris 23♈22.9 ⚵ 0♍00.9
♄D 2 5:53		11 21:52 ♄ ☍	♊ 12 0:16	12 17:44 ♄ △	♌ 12 20:52		⚷ 21♓32.2R ⚶ 7♈25.4
♃□♄ 3 10:36	⚳ ♑R 3 23:08	14 3:31 ♀ ⚹	♋ 14 6:14	15 4:36 ♄ □	♍ 15 7:45	7 2:03 ☾ 14♉17	☽ Mean ☊ 5♎21.1
☽0N 3 22:29	☿ ♍ 7 19:15	16 11:24 ♄ △	♌ 16 14:15	17 17:16 ♄ ⚹	♎ 17 20:22	14 14:53 ● 21♌31	
♃⚼♇ 4 19:22	♂ ♌ 8 23:32	18 21:41 ♄ □	♍ 19 0:47	20 2:56 ☉ ⚹	♏ 20 9:24	22 19:31 ☽ 29♏24	1 August 2015
♄∠♇ 13 22:17	♃ ♍ 11 11:11	21 10:07 ♄ ⚹	♎ 21 13:23	22 19:31 ☉ □	♐ 22 20:41	29 18:35 ○ 6♓06	Julian Day # 42216
☽0S 17 19:39	☉ ♍ 23 10:37	23 18:12 ♃ ⚹	♏ 24 2:07	24 22:04 ☿ □	♑ 25 4:22		SVP 5♓02'29"
☿0S 25 22:03	☿ ♎ 27 15:44	26 9:14 ♄ ☌	♐ 26 12:24	27 7:20 ☿ △	♒ 27 8:03		GC 27♐03.4 ⚴ 11♐40.2R
☽0N 31 8:05		28 13:36 ♃ △	♑ 28 18:47	29 7:03 ♄ □	♓ 29 8:51		Eris 23♈24.1R ⚵ 11♍41.0
		30 18:50 ♄ ⚹	♒ 30 21:40	31 6:53 ♄ △	♈ 31 8:33		⚷ 20♓57.0R ⚶ 12♈56.1
							☽ Mean ☊ 3♎42.6

Ephemeris pages reproduced by permission of the publisher: Starcrafts, LLC, 334-A Calef Hwy., Epping, NH 03042. astrocom.com & starcraftspublishing.com

© 2014 Janet Booth | 1-877-293-1607 | JanetsPlan-its.com

LONGITUDE — September 2015

Day	Sid.Time	☉	0 hr ☽	Noon ☽	True ☊	☿	♀	♂	⚳	♃	♄	♅	♆	♇
1 Tu	22 39 22	8♍15 32	9♈39 59	17♈06 53	1♎05.0	5♎05.3	14♌57.8	14♌47.0	25♑40.4	4♍27.4	28♏59.5	19♈59.1	8♓24.6	13♑07.1
2 W	22 43 19	9 13 34	24 29 48	1♉48 06	1 05.9	6 09.9	14R46.0	15 25.2	25R35.6	4 40.4	29 02.3	19R57.5	8R22.9	13R06.5
3 Th	22 47 15	10 11 38	9♉01 16	16 08 56	1 07.2	7 12.2	14 36.8	16 03.4	25 31.2	4 53.4	29 05.3	19 55.8	8 21.3	13 05.8
4 F	22 51 12	11 09 44	23 10 54	0♊07 05	1 08.4	8 12.0	14 29.9	16 41.5	25 27.1	5 06.5	29 08.3	19 54.1	8 19.6	13 05.2
5 Sa	22 55 08	12 07 51	6♊57 30	13 42 16	1R09.1	9 09.2	14 25.5	17 19.6	25 23.4	5 19.5	29 11.4	19 52.3	8 18.0	13 04.6
6 Su	22 59 05	13 06 01	20 21 37	26 55 46	1 09.1	10 03.6	14D23.5	17 57.7	25 20.0	5 32.5	29 14.6	19 50.6	8 16.3	13 04.0
7 M	23 03 02	14 04 13	3♋25 01	9♋49 43	1 08.2	10 55.1	14 23.8	18 35.8	25 17.0	5 45.5	29 17.9	19 48.7	8 14.7	13 03.4
8 Tu	23 06 58	15 02 27	16 10 10	22 26 43	1 06.6	11 43.4	14 26.5	19 13.8	25 14.4	5 58.4	29 21.3	19 46.9	8 13.1	13 02.9
9 W	23 10 55	16 00 43	28 39 43	4♌49 29	1 04.5	12 28.3	14 31.4	19 51.9	25 12.1	6 11.4	29 24.8	19 45.0	8 11.4	13 02.4
10 Th	23 14 51	16 59 00	10♌56 20	17 00 35	1 02.4	13 09.6	14 38.6	20 29.8	25 10.2	6 24.4	29 28.3	19 43.1	8 09.8	13 02.0
11 F	23 18 48	17 57 20	23 02 32	29 02 27	1 00.4	13 47.0	14 48.0	21 07.8	25 08.6	6 37.3	29 31.9	19 41.2	8 08.2	13 01.5
12 Sa	23 22 44	18 55 41	5♍00 36	10♍57 16	0 58.8	14 20.3	14 59.6	21 45.7	25 07.4	6 50.2	29 35.6	19 39.2	8 06.6	13 01.1
13 Su	23 26 41	19 54 05	16 52 42	22 47 11	0 57.9	14 49.1	15 13.2	22 23.7	25 06.6	7 03.1	29 39.4	19 37.2	8 05.0	13 00.7
14 M	23 30 37	20 52 30	28 40 59	4♎34 21	0D57.5	15 13.2	15 28.8	23 01.5	25D06.1	7 16.0	29 43.3	19 35.2	8 03.3	13 00.4
15 Tu	23 34 34	21 50 57	10♎27 38	16 21 06	0 57.6	15 32.2	15 46.3	23 39.4	25 06.0	7 28.8	29 47.2	19 33.1	8 01.8	13 00.1
16 W	23 38 31	22 49 26	22 15 06	28 09 59	0 58.1	15 45.7	16 05.8	24 17.2	25 06.3	7 41.7	29 51.2	19 31.0	8 00.2	12 59.8
17 Th	23 42 27	23 47 56	4♏06 09	10♏03 59	0 58.8	15R53.5	16 27.1	24 55.0	25 06.9	7 54.5	29 55.3	19 28.9	7 58.6	12 59.5
18 F	23 46 24	24 46 29	16 03 56	22 06 26	0 59.6	15 55.1	16 50.2	25 32.8	25 07.8	8 07.2	29 59.5	19 26.8	7 57.0	12 59.3
19 Sa	23 50 20	25 45 03	28 11 58	4♐21 02	1 00.2	15 50.2	17 14.9	26 10.5	25 09.2	8 20.0	0♐03.8	19 24.6	7 55.5	12 59.1
20 Su	23 54 17	26 43 38	10♐34 06	16 51 41	1 00.6	15 38.7	17 41.4	26 48.2	25 10.8	8 32.7	0 08.1	19 22.5	7 53.9	12 58.9
21 M	23 58 13	27 42 16	23 14 15	29 42 16	1R00.7	15 20.1	18 09.4	27 25.9	25 12.9	8 45.4	0 12.5	19 20.3	7 52.4	12 58.8
22 Tu	0 02 10	28 40 55	6♑16 09	12♑56 15	1 00.7	14 54.4	18 39.0	28 03.6	25 15.2	8 58.1	0 17.0	19 18.0	7 50.9	12 58.7
23 W	0 06 06	29 39 36	19 42 50	26 36 05	1 00.6	14 21.6	19 10.1	28 41.2	25 17.9	9 10.7	0 21.5	19 15.8	7 49.4	12 58.6
24 Th	0 10 03	0♎38 18	3♒36 03	10♒42 38	1D00.6	13 41.8	19 42.6	29 18.8	25 21.0	9 23.3	0 26.1	19 13.5	7 47.9	12 58.5
25 F	0 14 00	1 37 02	17 55 37	25 14 33	1 00.6	12 55.3	20 16.5	29 56.4	25 24.4	9 35.9	0 30.8	19 11.3	7 46.4	12D58.5
26 Sa	0 17 56	2 35 48	2♓38 51	10♓07 45	1 00.7	12 02.5	20 51.8	0♍34.0	25 28.1	9 48.4	0 35.6	19 09.0	7 44.9	12 58.5
27 Su	0 21 53	3 34 36	17 40 19	25 15 31	1R00.8	11 04.3	21 28.4	1 11.5	25 32.2	10 00.9	0 40.4	19 06.7	7 43.5	12 58.5
28 M	0 25 49	4 33 25	2♈52 11	10♈29 05	1 00.9	10 01.7	22 06.2	1 49.0	25 36.6	10 13.3	0 45.3	19 04.3	7 42.1	12 58.6
29 Tu	0 29 46	5 32 17	18 05 00	25 38 43	1 00.7	8 55.9	22 45.2	2 26.4	25 41.3	10 25.7	0 50.3	19 02.0	7 40.6	12 58.7
30 W	0 33 42	6 31 10	3♉09 09	10♉35 17	1 00.3	7 48.4	23 25.4	3 03.9	25 46.3	10 38.1	0 55.3	18 59.6	7 39.2	12 58.8

LONGITUDE — October 2015

Day	Sid.Time	☉	0 hr ☽	Noon ☽	True ☊	☿	♀	♂	⚳	♃	♄	♅	♆	♇
1 Th	0 37 39	7♎30 06	17♉56 15	25♉11 23	0♎59.7	6♎40.9	24♌06.8	3♍41.3	25♑51.6	10♍50.4	1♐00.4	18♈57.3	7♓37.8	12♑59.0
2 F	0 41 35	8 29 04	2♊20 11	9♊22 20	0R58.9	5R35.1	24 49.2	4 18.7	25 57.3	11 02.7	1 05.5	18R54.9	7R36.5	12 59.2
3 Sa	0 45 32	9 28 05	16 17 39	23 06 08	0 58.1	4 32.8	25 32.7	4 56.1	26 03.3	11 14.9	1 10.8	18 52.5	7 35.1	12 59.4
4 Su	0 49 28	10 27 08	29 47 56	6♋23 19	0D57.5	3 35.8	26 17.1	5 33.4	26 09.5	11 27.1	1 16.0	18 50.1	7 33.8	12 59.6
5 M	0 53 25	11 26 13	12♋52 35	19 16 10	0 57.4	2 45.6	27 02.6	6 10.8	26 16.1	11 39.3	1 21.4	18 47.7	7 32.5	12 59.9
6 Tu	0 57 22	12 25 20	25 34 33	1♌48 12	0 57.7	2 03.5	27 49.0	6 48.1	26 23.0	11 51.4	1 26.8	18 45.3	7 31.2	13 00.2
7 W	1 01 18	13 24 30	7♌57 40	14 03 26	0 58.5	1 30.8	28 36.2	7 25.3	26 30.2	12 03.4	1 32.3	18 42.9	7 30.0	13 00.6
8 Th	1 05 15	14 23 41	20 06 04	26 06 02	0 59.7	1 08.2	29 24.4	8 02.6	26 37.7	12 15.4	1 37.8	18 40.4	7 28.7	13 00.9
9 F	1 09 11	15 22 56	2♍03 50	7♍59 55	1 01.0	0D56.1	0♍13.4	8 39.8	26 45.5	12 27.3	1 43.4	18 38.0	7 27.5	13 01.3
10 Sa	1 13 08	16 22 12	13 54 44	19 48 41	1 02.1	0 54.7	1 03.2	9 17.0	26 53.5	12 39.2	1 49.0	18 35.6	7 26.3	13 01.8
11 Su	1 17 04	17 21 30	25 42 09	1♎35 28	1R02.8	1 04.1	1 53.7	9 54.2	27 01.9	12 51.0	1 54.7	18 33.1	7 25.1	13 02.2
12 M	1 21 01	18 20 51	7♎28 58	13 22 56	1 02.8	1 23.9	2 45.0	10 31.3	27 10.5	13 02.8	2 00.4	18 30.7	7 23.9	13 02.7
13 Tu	1 24 57	19 20 14	19 17 39	25 13 24	1 01.8	1 53.6	3 37.0	11 08.4	27 19.4	13 14.5	2 06.2	18 28.3	7 22.8	13 03.3
14 W	1 28 54	20 19 38	1♏10 23	7♏08 54	0 59.9	2 32.7	4 29.8	11 45.5	27 28.6	13 26.2	2 12.1	18 25.8	7 21.7	13 03.8
15 Th	1 32 51	21 19 05	13 09 08	19 11 22	0 57.0	3 20.4	5 23.1	12 22.5	27 38.1	13 37.7	2 18.0	18 23.4	7 20.6	13 04.4
16 F	1 36 47	22 18 34	25 15 49	1♐22 45	0 53.6	4 15.9	6 17.2	12 59.6	27 47.8	13 49.3	2 24.0	18 20.9	7 19.6	13 05.0
17 Sa	1 40 44	23 18 05	7♐32 27	13 45 10	0 49.9	5 18.5	7 11.8	13 36.6	27 57.8	14 00.7	2 30.0	18 18.5	7 18.5	13 05.7
18 Su	1 44 40	24 17 37	20 01 13	26 20 54	0 46.6	6 27.3	8 07.1	14 13.5	28 08.1	14 12.1	2 36.0	18 16.1	7 17.5	13 06.3
19 M	1 48 37	25 17 12	2♑44 33	9♑12 29	0 43.9	7 41.6	9 02.9	14 50.4	28 18.6	14 23.4	2 42.1	18 13.7	7 16.6	13 07.0
20 Tu	1 52 33	26 16 48	15 45 00	22 22 25	0D42.3	9 00.7	9 59.3	15 27.3	28 29.4	14 34.6	2 48.3	18 11.3	7 15.6	13 07.8
21 W	1 56 30	27 16 26	29 05 01	5♒53 01	0 41.9	10 23.9	10 56.2	16 04.2	28 40.4	14 45.8	2 54.5	18 08.9	7 14.7	13 08.5
22 Th	2 00 26	28 16 05	12♒46 36	19 45 52	0 42.5	11 50.5	11 53.7	16 41.0	28 51.7	14 56.9	3 00.7	18 06.5	7 13.8	13 09.3
23 F	2 04 23	29 15 46	26 50 48	4♓01 18	0 43.9	13 20.0	12 51.7	17 17.8	29 03.2	15 07.9	3 07.0	18 04.1	7 12.9	13 10.1
24 Sa	2 08 20	0♏15 29	11♓17 04	18 37 43	0 45.4	14 51.9	13 50.2	17 54.6	29 15.0	15 18.9	3 13.3	18 01.7	7 12.1	13 11.0
25 Su	2 12 16	1 15 13	26 02 41	3♈31 13	0R46.3	16 25.8	14 49.1	18 31.4	29 27.0	15 29.7	3 19.7	17 59.4	7 11.3	13 11.9
26 M	2 16 13	2 15 00	11♈02 27	18 35 22	0 46.0	18 01.2	15 48.5	19 08.1	29 39.2	15 40.5	3 26.1	17 57.0	7 10.5	13 12.8
27 Tu	2 20 09	3 14 48	26 08 51	3♉41 43	0 44.2	19 37.8	16 48.4	19 44.7	29 51.6	15 51.2	3 32.5	17 54.7	7 09.7	13 13.7
28 W	2 24 06	4 14 38	11♉12 48	18 40 56	0 40.7	21 15.4	17 48.8	20 21.4	0♒04.3	16 01.8	3 39.0	17 52.4	7 09.0	13 14.7
29 Th	2 28 02	5 14 30	26 05 01	3♊24 07	0 35.9	22 53.8	18 49.5	20 58.0	0 17.2	16 12.3	3 45.5	17 50.1	7 08.3	13 15.7
30 F	2 31 59	6 14 24	10♊37 26	17 44 20	0 30.4	24 32.6	19 50.7	21 34.6	0 30.3	16 22.8	3 52.1	17 47.8	7 07.6	13 16.7
31 Sa	2 35 55	7 14 21	24 44 24	1♋37 22	0 24.9	26 11.8	20 52.3	22 11.2	0 43.6	16 33.2	3 58.7	17 45.5	7 07.0	13 17.7

Astro Data

	Dy Hr Mn
♃⚼♅	3 3:52
♀ D	6 8:29
☽0S	14 2:09
⚳ D	14 19:14
♃☍♆	17 6:54
☿ R	17 18:10
☉0S	23 8:21
♇ D	25 6:58
☽0N	27 19:02
☿0N	9 10:23
☿ D	9 14:58
☽0S	11 8:11
♃△♇	11 23:51
☿0S	15 12:31
♄⚼♅	22 15:59

Planet Ingress

	Dy Hr Mn
♄ ♐	18 2:49
☉ ♎	23 8:21
♂ ♍	25 2:18
♀ ♍	8 17:29
☉ ♏	23 17:47
⚳ ♒	27 15:56
☽0N25	6:02

Last Aspect / ☽ Ingress (September)

Last Aspect Dy Hr Mn		☽ Ingress Dy Hr Mn
1 16:37	♅ ☌	♉ 2 9:02
4 10:20	♄ ☍	♊ 4 11:48
5 23:04	♅ ✶	♋ 6 17:40
9 1:28	♄ △	♌ 9 2:36
11 13:03	♄ □	♍ 11 13:55
14 2:08	♄ ✶	♎ 14 2:41
16 4:22	♂ ✶	♏ 16 15:43
18 19:49	♂ □	♐ 19 3:32
21 8:59	☉ □	♑ 21 12:33
22 23:13	♅ □	♒ 23 17:51
25 4:02	♀ ☍	♓ 25 19:44
26 16:32	♇ ✶	♈ 27 19:29
29 7:45	♀ △	♉ 29 18:57

Last Aspect / ☽ Ingress (October)

Last Aspect Dy Hr Mn		☽ Ingress Dy Hr Mn
1 10:44	♀ □	♊ 1 20:03
3 17:18	♀ ✶	♋ 4 0:22
5 11:04	♅ □	♌ 6 8:31
7 21:10	♅ △	♍ 8 19:50
9 22:12	♇ △	♎ 11 8:45
13 0:06	☉ ☌	♏ 13 21:38
15 0:58	♃ ✶	♐ 16 9:18
18 8:48	☉ ✶	♑ 18 18:52
20 20:31	☉ □	♒ 21 1:38
23 4:22	☉ △	♓ 23 5:18
24 11:18	♂ ☍	♈ 25 6:22
26 12:25	☿ ☍	♉ 27 6:07
28 15:20	♂ △	♊ 29 6:24
31 2:52	☿ △	♋ 31 9:09

☽ Phases & Eclipses

Dy Hr Mn	
5 9:54	☾ 12♊32
13 6:41	● 20♍10
13 6:54:09	P 0.788
21 8:59	☽ 28♐04
28 2:50	○ 4♈40
28 2:47	T 1.276
4 21:06	☾ 11♋19
13 0:06	● 19♎20
20 20:31	☽ 27♑08
27 12:05	○ 3♉45

Astro Data

1 September 2015
Julian Day # 42247
SVP 5♓02'26"
GC 27♐03.5 ⚴ 14♐08.3
Eris 23♈15.7R ⚵ 23♍39.5
⚷ 19♓43.9R ⚶ 11♈54.5R
☽ Mean ☊ 2♎04.1

1 October 2015
Julian Day # 42277
SVP 5♓02'24"
GC 27♐03.6 ⚴ 20♐46.5
Eris 23♈00.5R ⚵ 5♎11.9
⚷ 18♓21.9R ⚶ 5♈12.1R
☽ Mean ☊ 0♎28.8

November 2015 LONGITUDE

Day	Sid.Time	☉	0 hr ☽	Noon ☽	True ☊	☿	♀	♂	⚳	♃	♄	♅	♆	♇
1 Su	2 39 52	8♏14 19	8♋23 11	15♋01 57	0♎20.3	27♎51.1	21♍54.3	22♍47.7	0♒57.1	16♍43.4	4♐05.3	17♈43.3	7♓06.4	13♑18.8
2 M	2 43 49	9 14 20	21 33 55	27 59 26	0R17.0	29 30.6	22 56.6	23 24.2	1 10.9	16 53.6	4 11.9	17R41.1	7R05.8	13 19.9
3 Tu	2 47 45	10 14 22	4♌18 59	10♌33 06	0D15.4	1♏10.0	23 59.4	24 00.7	1 24.8	17 03.7	4 18.6	17 38.9	7 05.3	13 21.0
4 W	2 51 42	11 14 27	16 42 22	22 47 25	0 15.4	2 49.3	25 02.5	24 37.1	1 39.0	17 13.7	4 25.3	17 36.7	7 04.8	13 22.2
5 Th	2 55 38	12 14 34	28 48 54	4♍47 27	0 16.5	4 28.5	26 05.9	25 13.5	1 53.3	17 23.6	4 32.1	17 34.5	7 04.3	13 23.4
6 F	2 59 35	13 14 43	10♍43 42	16 38 18	0 18.1	6 07.5	27 09.7	25 49.9	2 07.9	17 33.4	4 38.8	17 32.4	7 03.9	13 24.6
7 Sa	3 03 31	14 14 54	22 31 50	28 24 51	0R19.4	7 46.2	28 13.8	26 26.2	2 22.6	17 43.1	4 45.6	17 30.3	7 03.5	13 25.8
8 Su	3 07 28	15 15 07	4♎17 54	10♎11 27	0 19.6	9 24.6	29 18.2	27 02.5	2 37.5	17 52.7	4 52.5	17 28.2	7 03.1	13 27.1
9 M	3 11 24	16 15 22	16 05 55	22 01 44	0 18.1	11 02.8	0♎22.9	27 38.8	2 52.7	18 02.2	4 59.3	17 26.2	7 02.7	13 28.4
10 Tu	3 15 21	17 15 39	27 59 12	3♏58 38	0 14.3	12 40.6	1 27.9	28 15.0	3 08.0	18 11.5	5 06.2	17 24.1	7 02.4	13 29.7
11 W	3 19 17	18 15 57	10♏00 15	16 04 16	0 08.4	14 18.1	2 33.2	28 51.2	3 23.4	18 20.8	5 13.1	17 22.1	7 02.1	13 31.0
12 Th	3 23 14	19 16 18	22 10 50	28 20 05	0 00.3	15 55.3	3 38.8	29 27.4	3 39.1	18 30.0	5 20.0	17 20.2	7 01.9	13 32.3
13 F	3 27 11	20 16 40	4♐32 04	10♐46 53	29♍50.9	17 32.2	4 44.6	0♎03.5	3 55.0	18 39.0	5 27.0	17 18.2	7 01.7	13 33.7
14 Sa	3 31 07	21 17 04	17 04 35	23 25 11	29 41.0	19 08.8	5 50.7	0 39.6	4 11.0	18 48.0	5 33.9	17 16.3	7 01.5	13 35.1
15 Su	3 35 04	22 17 29	29 48 46	6♑15 20	29 31.5	20 45.1	6 57.1	1 15.6	4 27.2	18 56.8	5 40.9	17 14.4	7 01.4	13 36.6
16 M	3 39 00	23 17 56	12♑45 00	19 17 49	29 23.5	22 21.0	8 03.7	1 51.6	4 43.6	19 05.5	5 47.9	17 12.6	7 01.3	13 38.0
17 Tu	3 42 57	24 18 24	25 53 54	2♒33 21	29 17.5	23 56.7	9 10.5	2 27.6	5 00.1	19 14.1	5 54.9	17 10.8	7 01.2	13 39.5
18 W	3 46 53	25 18 54	9♒16 19	16 02 55	29 14.0	25 32.1	10 17.5	3 03.5	5 16.8	19 22.6	6 02.0	17 09.0	7D01.2	13 41.0
19 Th	3 50 50	26 19 25	22 53 18	29 47 36	29D12.7	27 07.3	11 24.8	3 39.3	5 33.6	19 30.9	6 09.0	17 07.3	7 01.1	13 42.5
20 F	3 54 47	27 19 57	6♓45 52	13♓48 09	29 12.9	28 42.2	12 32.3	4 15.2	5 50.6	19 39.1	6 16.1	17 05.6	7 01.2	13 44.1
21 Sa	3 58 43	28 20 30	20 54 24	28 04 30	29R13.7	0♐16.9	13 40.0	4 51.0	6 07.8	19 47.2	6 23.1	17 03.9	7 01.2	13 45.6
22 Su	4 02 40	29 21 04	5♈18 12	12♈35 07	29 13.8	1 51.3	14 47.9	5 26.7	6 25.1	19 55.2	6 30.2	17 02.3	7 01.3	13 47.2
23 M	4 06 36	0♐21 40	19 54 45	27 16 29	29 12.0	3 25.6	15 56.0	6 02.4	6 42.6	20 03.0	6 37.3	17 00.7	7 01.5	13 48.8
24 Tu	4 10 33	1 22 16	4♉39 33	12♉03 02	29 07.8	4 59.7	17 04.3	6 38.0	7 00.2	20 10.7	6 44.4	16 59.2	7 01.6	13 50.4
25 W	4 14 29	2 22 55	19 26 01	26 47 29	29 00.8	6 33.6	18 12.9	7 13.7	7 17.9	20 18.3	6 51.5	16 57.7	7 01.8	13 52.1
26 Th	4 18 26	3 23 34	4♊06 25	11♊21 51	28 51.5	8 07.3	19 21.5	7 49.2	7 35.8	20 25.8	6 58.6	16 56.2	7 02.1	13 53.7
27 F	4 22 22	4 24 15	18 32 53	25 38 45	28 40.9	9 41.0	20 30.4	8 24.8	7 53.8	20 33.1	7 05.7	16 54.8	7 02.3	13 55.4
28 Sa	4 26 19	5 24 57	2♋38 49	9♋32 38	28 29.9	11 14.5	21 39.5	9 00.2	8 12.0	20 40.2	7 12.8	16 53.4	7 02.6	13 57.1
29 Su	4 30 16	6 25 41	16 19 54	23 00 30	28 20.0	12 47.9	22 48.7	9 35.7	8 30.3	20 47.3	7 19.9	16 52.0	7 03.0	13 58.8
30 M	4 34 12	7 26 26	29 34 28	6♌02 02	28 11.9	14 21.2	23 58.1	10 11.1	8 48.7	20 54.1	7 27.0	16 50.7	7 03.3	14 00.6

December 2015 LONGITUDE

Day	Sid.Time	☉	0 hr ☽	Noon ☽	True ☊	☿	♀	♂	⚳	♃	♄	♅	♆	♇
1 Tu	4 38 09	8♐27 13	12♌23 30	18♌39 18	28♍06.4	15♐54.4	25♎07.7	10♎46.4	9♒07.3	21♍00.9	7♐34.1	16♈49.5	7♓03.8	14♑02.3
2 W	4 42 05	9 28 01	24 49 59	0♍56 08	28R03.3	17 27.6	26 17.4	11 21.7	9 26.0	21 07.5	7 41.3	16R48.3	7 04.2	14 04.1
3 Th	4 46 02	10 28 50	6♍58 24	12 57 27	28D02.2	19 00.7	27 27.3	11 57.0	9 44.8	21 13.9	7 48.4	16 47.1	7 04.7	14 05.9
4 F	4 49 58	11 29 41	18 54 01	24 48 47	28R02.3	20 33.7	28 37.4	12 32.2	10 03.7	21 20.2	7 55.5	16 46.0	7 05.2	14 07.7
5 Sa	4 53 55	12 30 33	0♎42 27	6♎35 42	28 02.5	22 06.6	29 47.6	13 07.4	10 22.8	21 26.4	8 02.6	16 44.9	7 05.7	14 09.5
6 Su	4 57 51	13 31 27	12 29 12	18 23 34	28 01.5	23 39.5	0♏57.9	13 42.5	10 41.9	21 32.4	8 09.7	16 43.9	7 06.3	14 11.3
7 M	5 01 48	14 32 21	24 19 23	0♏17 09	27 58.5	25 12.3	2 08.3	14 17.5	11 01.2	21 38.2	8 16.8	16 42.9	7 06.9	14 13.2
8 Tu	5 05 44	15 33 18	6♏17 21	12 20 23	27 52.9	26 45.0	3 18.9	14 52.5	11 20.7	21 43.9	8 23.9	16 41.9	7 07.6	14 15.0
9 W	5 09 41	16 34 15	18 26 35	24 36 13	27 44.2	28 17.6	4 29.7	15 27.4	11 40.2	21 49.4	8 30.9	16 41.0	7 08.2	14 16.9
10 Th	5 13 38	17 35 13	0♐49 27	7♐06 23	27 33.0	29 50.1	5 40.5	16 02.3	11 59.8	21 54.8	8 38.0	16 40.2	7 08.9	14 18.8
11 F	5 17 34	18 36 13	13 27 04	19 51 27	27 19.8	1♑22.4	6 51.5	16 37.2	12 19.6	22 00.0	8 45.1	16 39.4	7 09.7	14 20.7
12 Sa	5 21 31	19 37 13	26 19 26	2♑50 52	27 05.8	2 54.6	8 02.6	17 11.9	12 39.4	22 05.1	8 52.1	16 38.7	7 10.5	14 22.6
13 Su	5 25 27	20 38 14	9♑25 34	16 03 18	26 52.4	4 26.5	9 13.7	17 46.6	12 59.4	22 09.9	8 59.2	16 38.0	7 11.3	14 24.6
14 M	5 29 24	21 39 16	22 43 52	29 27 02	26 40.6	5 58.1	10 25.0	18 21.3	13 19.5	22 14.6	9 06.2	16 37.3	7 12.1	14 26.5
15 Tu	5 33 20	22 40 19	6♒12 37	13♒00 25	26 31.6	7 29.3	11 36.4	18 55.9	13 39.6	22 19.2	9 13.2	16 36.7	7 13.0	14 28.5
16 W	5 37 17	23 41 22	19 50 19	26 42 12	26 25.6	9 00.1	12 47.9	19 30.4	13 59.9	22 23.6	9 20.2	16 36.2	7 13.9	14 30.4
17 Th	5 41 14	24 42 25	3♓36 00	10♓31 42	26 22.5	10 30.3	13 59.5	20 04.8	14 20.3	22 27.7	9 27.1	16 35.7	7 14.9	14 32.4
18 F	5 45 10	25 43 29	17 29 17	24 28 45	26 21.5	11 59.9	15 11.2	20 39.2	14 40.7	22 31.8	9 34.1	16 35.2	7 15.9	14 34.4
19 Sa	5 49 07	26 44 33	1♈30 04	8♈33 13	26 21.5	13 28.6	16 23.0	21 13.5	15 01.3	22 35.6	9 41.0	16 34.8	7 16.9	14 36.4
20 Su	5 53 03	27 45 38	15 38 06	22 44 36	26 20.9	14 56.4	17 34.8	21 47.8	15 21.9	22 39.3	9 47.9	16 34.5	7 17.9	14 38.4
21 M	5 57 00	28 46 42	29 52 27	7♉01 24	26 18.4	16 23.0	18 46.8	22 22.0	15 42.7	22 42.8	9 54.8	16 34.2	7 19.0	14 40.4
22 Tu	6 00 56	29 47 47	14♉11 00	21 20 46	26 13.3	17 48.2	19 58.8	22 56.1	16 03.5	22 46.1	10 01.6	16 34.0	7 20.1	14 42.4
23 W	6 04 53	0♑48 53	28 30 09	5♊38 29	26 05.2	19 11.7	21 10.9	23 30.2	16 24.4	22 49.2	10 08.4	16 33.8	7 21.2	14 44.4
24 Th	6 08 49	1 49 58	12♊45 06	19 49 16	25 54.5	20 33.2	22 23.1	24 04.1	16 45.4	22 52.2	10 15.2	16 33.6	7 22.4	14 46.5
25 F	6 12 46	2 51 04	26 50 18	3♋47 34	25 42.0	21 52.4	23 35.4	24 38.0	17 06.5	22 55.0	10 22.0	16 33.5	7 23.6	14 48.5
26 Sa	6 16 43	3 52 10	10♋40 28	17 28 33	25 29.1	23 08.7	24 47.8	25 11.9	17 27.6	22 57.6	10 28.8	16D33.5	7 24.8	14 50.5
27 Su	6 20 39	4 53 17	24 11 25	0♌48 51	25 17.1	24 21.9	26 00.2	25 45.7	17 48.9	23 00.0	10 35.5	16 33.5	7 26.0	14 52.6
28 M	6 24 36	5 54 24	7♌20 44	13 47 05	25 07.1	25 31.2	27 12.7	26 19.4	18 10.2	23 02.2	10 42.2	16 33.6	7 27.3	14 54.7
29 Tu	6 28 32	6 55 32	20 08 04	26 23 55	24 59.7	26 36.1	28 25.3	26 53.0	18 31.6	23 04.3	10 48.8	16 33.7	7 28.6	14 56.7
30 W	6 32 29	7 56 39	2♍35 02	8♍41 50	24 55.2	27 35.9	29 38.0	27 26.5	18 53.0	23 06.1	10 55.4	16 33.9	7 30.0	14 58.8
31 Th	6 36 25	8 57 48	14 44 53	20 44 44	24D53.1	28 29.8	0♐50.7	28 00.0	19 14.6	23 07.8	11 02.0	16 34.1	7 31.4	15 00.8

Astro Data

	Dy Hr Mn
♃⚻♅	5 22:01
☽0S	7 15:03
♀0S	11 10:39
♂0S	18 9:58
♆ D	18 16:31
☽0N	21 15:32
♄□♆	26 12:15
☽0S	4 23:35
☽0N	18 23:01
♅ D	26 3:53

Planet Ingress

	Dy Hr Mn
☿ ♏	2 7:06
♀ ♎	8 15:31
☊ ♍R	12 0:57
♂ ♎	12 21:41
☿ ♐	20 19:43
☉ ♐	22 15:25
♀ ♏	5 4:15
☿ ♑	10 2:34
☉ ♑	22 4:48
♀ ♐	30 7:16

Last Aspect / ☽ Ingress (November)

Last Aspect Dy Hr Mn		☽ Ingress Dy Hr Mn
2 3:35	♂ ⚹	♌ 2 15:48
4 1:46	♅ △	♍ 5 2:22
7 12:47	♀ ☌	♎ 7 15:14
9 2:42	♅ ☍	♏ 10 4:02
12 14:54	♂ ⚹	♐ 12 15:14
14 3:18	♃ □	♑ 15 0:21
16 20:53	☉ ⚹	♒ 17 7:24
19 8:19	☿ □	♓ 19 12:21
21 13:23	☉ △	♈ 21 15:12
22 19:16	♅ ☌	♉ 23 16:26
25 1:26	♃ △	♊ 25 17:15
27 3:35	♀ △	♋ 27 19:27
29 12:46	♀ □	♌ 30 0:47

Last Aspect / ☽ Ingress (December)

Last Aspect Dy Hr Mn		☽ Ingress Dy Hr Mn
2 3:09	♀ ⚹	♍ 2 10:09
4 4:59	♃ ☌	♎ 4 22:34
7 2:03	☿ ⚹	♏ 7 11:26
9 6:39	♃ ⚹	♐ 9 22:25
11 16:06	♃ □	♑ 12 6:46
13 23:07	♃ △	♒ 14 12:59
16 7:17	☉ ⚹	♓ 16 17:45
18 15:14	☉ □	♈ 18 21:26
20 22:01	☉ △	♉ 21 0:13
22 14:26	♃ △	♊ 23 2:31
24 20:04	♂ △	♋ 25 5:26
27 3:36	♀ △	♌ 27 10:31
29 17:38	♀ □	♍ 29 18:58

☽ Phases & Eclipses

Dy Hr Mn	
3 12:24	☾ 10♌45
11 17:47	● 19♏01
19 6:27	☽ 26♒36
25 22:44	○ 3♊20
3 7:40	☾ 10♍48
11 10:29	● 19♐03
18 15:14	☽ 26♓22
25 11:12	○ 3♋20

Astro Data

1 November 2015
Julian Day # 42308
SVP 5♓02'21"
GC 27♐03.6 ⚴ 0♑10.6
Eris 22♈42.2R ⚵ 16♎43.3
⚷ 17♓16.9R ⚶ 29♓12.0R
☽ Mean ☊ 28♍50.2

1 December 2015
Julian Day # 42338
SVP 5♓02'16"
GC 27♐03.7 ⚴ 10♑36.2
Eris 22♈27.0R ⚵ 27♎02.8
⚷ 16♓56.5 ⚶ 29♓38.8
☽ Mean ☊ 27♍14.9

Moon Family Table

by Dietrech Pessin

Take the guess work out of forecasting for yourself, clients, business matters and more.
The unique patterns of this powerful predictive tool unlock the mystery of the timing of events.

New Moon				First Quarter Moon				Full Moon				Third Quarter Moon			
15/Oct/2012	22°	♎	32	16/Jul/2013	23°	♎	46	**15/Apr/2014**	**25°**	♎	**15**	13/Jan/2015	22°	♎	52
13/Nov/2012	**21°**	♏	**56**	14/Aug/2013	21°	♏	49	14/May/2014	23°	♏	54	12/Feb/2015	23°	♏	5
13/Dec/2012	21°	♐	45	12/Sep/2013	20°	♐	5	13/Jun/2014	22°	♐	5	13/Mar/2015	22°	♐	49
11/Jan/2013	21°	♑	45	11/Oct/2013	18°	♑	47	12/Jul/2014	20°	♑	3	12/Apr/2015	21°	♑	55
10/Feb/2013	21°	♒	43	10/Nov/2013	18°	♒	0	10/Aug/2014	18°	♒	2	11/May/2015	20°	♒	25
11/Mar/2013	21°	♓	24	9/Dec/2013	17°	♓	42	9/Sep/2014	16°	♓	19	9/Jun/2015	18°	♓	29
10/Apr/2013	20°	♈	40	8/Jan/2014	17°	♈	46	**8/Oct/2014**	**15°**	♈	**5**	8/Jul/2015	16°	♈	21
10/May/2013	**19°**	♉	**31**	6/Feb/2014	17°	♉	55	6/Nov/2014	14°	♉	25	7/Aug/2015	14°	♉	16
8/Jun/2013	18°	♊	0	8/Mar/2014	17°	♊	53	6/Dec/2014	14°	♊	17	5/Sep/2015	12°	♊	31
8/Jul/2013	16°	♋	17	7/Apr/2014	17°	♋	27	5/Jan/2015	14°	♋	30	4/Oct/2015	11°	♋	19
6/Aug/2013	14°	♌	34	7/May/2014	16°	♌	30	3/Feb/2015	14°	♌	47	3/Nov/2015	10°	♌	45
5/Sep/2013	13°	♍	4	5/Jun/2014	15°	♍	6	5/Mar/2015	14°	♍	50	3/Dec/2015	10°	♍	48
5/Oct/2013	11°	♎	56	5/Jul/2014	13°	♎	24	**4/Apr/2015**	**14°**	♎	**24**	2/Jan/2016	11°	♎	14
3/Nov/2013	**11°**	♏	**15**	4/Aug/2014	11°	♏	35	4/May/2015	13°	♏	22	1/Feb/2016	11°	♏	41
3/Dec/2013	10°	♐	59	2/Sep/2014	09°	♐	55	2/Jun/2015	11°	♐	49	1/Mar/2016	11°	♐	48
1/Jan/2014	10°	♑	57	1/Oct/2014	08°	♑	32	2/Jul/2015	09°	♑	55	31/Mar/2016	11°	♑	20
30/Jan/2014	10°	♒	55	31/Oct/2014	07°	♒	36	31/Jul/2015	07°	♒	55	30/Apr/2016	10°	♒	13
1/Mar/2014	10°	♓	39	29/Nov/2014	07°	♓	6	29/Aug/2015	06°	♓	6	29/May/2016	08°	♓	32
30/Mar/2014	09°	♈	58	28/Dec/2014	06°	♈	56	**28/Sep/2015**	**04°**	♈	**40**	27/Jun/2016	06°	♈	30
29/Apr/2014	**08°**	♉	**51**	27/Jan/2015	06°	♉	54	27/Oct/2015	03°	♉	44	26/Jul/2016	04°	♉	21
28/May/2014	07°	♊	21	25/Feb/2015	06°	♊	46	25/Nov/2015	03°	♊	20	25/Aug/2016	02°	♊	22
27/Jun/2014	05°	♋	37	27/Mar/2015	06°	♋	19	25/Dec/2015	03°	♋	19	23/Sep/2016	00°	♋	47
26/Jul/2014	03°	♌	51	25/Apr/2015	05°	♌	27	24/Jan/2016	03°	♌	29	22/Oct/2016	29°	♋	48
25/Aug/2014	02°	♍	18	25/May/2015	04°	♍	11	22/Feb/2016	03°	♍	33	21/Nov/2016	29°	♌	27
24/Sep/2014	01°	♎	7	24/Jun/2015	02°	♎	38	**23/Mar/2016**	**03°**	♎	**17**	21/Dec/2016	29°	♍	37
23/Oct/2014	**00°**	♏	**24**	24/Jul/2015	00°	♏	58	22/Apr/2016	02°	♏	30	19/Jan/2017	00°	♏	2
22/Nov/2014	00°	♐	7	22/Aug/2015	29°	♏	23	21/May/2016	01°	♐	13	18/Feb/2017	00°	♐	20
22/Dec/2014	00°	♑	6	21/Sep/2015	28°	♐	4	20/Jun/2016	29°	♐	32	20/Mar/2017	00°	♑	13
20/Jan/2015	00°	♒	8	20/Oct/2015	27°	♑	7	19/Jul/2016	27°	♑	40	19/Apr/2017	29°	♑	31
18/Feb/2015	29°	♒	59	19/Nov/2015	26°	♒	35	**18/Aug/2016**	**25°**	♒	**51**	19/May/2017	28°	♒	14
20/Mar/2015	**29°**	♓	**27**	18/Dec/2015	26°	♓	22	**16/Sep/2016**	**24°**	♓	**19**	17/Jun/2017	26°	♓	27
18/Apr/2015	28°	♈	25	16/Jan/2016	26°	♈	16	16/Oct/2016	23°	♈	14	16/Jul/2017	24°	♈	26
18/May/2015	26°	♉	55	15/Feb/2016	26°	♉	3	14/Nov/2016	22°	♉	37	15/Aug/2017	22°	♉	25
16/Jun/2015	25°	♊	7	15/Mar/2016	25°	♊	32	14/Dec/2016	22°	♊	25	13/Sep/2017	20°	♊	39
16/Jul/2015	23°	♋	14	14/Apr/2016	24°	♋	38	12/Jan/2017	22°	♋	27	12/Oct/2017	19°	♋	22
14/Aug/2015	21°	♌	30	13/May/2016	23°	♌	21	**11/Feb/2017**	**22°**	♌	**28**	10/Nov/2017	18°	♌	38
13/Sep/2015	**20°**	♍	**10**	12/Jun/2016	21°	♍	47	12/Mar/2017	22°	♍	13	10/Dec/2017	18°	♍	26
13/Oct/2015	19°	♎	20	12/Jul/2016	20°	♎	7	11/Apr/2017	21°	♎	32	8/Jan/2018	18°	♎	35
11/Nov/2015	19°	♏	0	10/Aug/2016	18°	♏	32	10/May/2017	20°	♏	24	7/Feb/2018	18°	♏	49
11/Dec/2015	19°	♐	2	9/Sep/2016	17°	♐	13	9/Jun/2017	18°	♐	53	9/Mar/2018	18°	♐	49

How to Use: Read Moon Family table left to right. Notice how each phase occurs nine months beyond the one before it. The symbolism of a New Moon relates to new developments, the budding growth of an issue is apparent at the First Quarter, the complete awareness is openly charged at the Full Moon, and the pay-off is gained at the Third Quarter phase. The Moon Families with solar or lunar eclipses (in bold print) are bursting with even more activity. Compare the zodiacal degrees of Moon Families to a natal chart to note what's impacted. See if you can make a connection to current events and developments. **Bold dates are eclipses. Bold lines demarcate phases occurring in 2015.**

The table begins on October 15, 2012 to show the initial Third Quarter Moon of 2015 on January 13. The last line shows the Moon Family of 2015's last New Moon on December 11, which lasts until March of 2018.

ALL STAR LIST

Dates are based on Eastern time zone.

This table shows the year's major astrological phenomena by zodiac position. After the sign abbreviation are the degree, a period, and the minutes of arc (60ths of a degree). Find the parts of your chart contacted by this phenomena. Look by sign to locate events at the degree of each chart point (+/- 2°). Read about them in the Star Pages (pp. 76–86). Your chart points are also influenced by phenomena at degrees of signs in the same Mode (see p. 99) if the event is a conjunction, semisquare, square, opposition or sesquiquadrate—the aspects that bring the most action into our lives. When a planet in your chart is affected, the impact extends to any house (see p. 5) that starts with a sign ruled by that planet (see p. 98).

Sign	Degree	Date	Phenomenon/Aspect	Sign	Degree	Date	Phenomenon/Aspect
AR	0.41	9/26/15	South Node trine Saturn	GE	4.38	6/10/15	Mercury sextile Venus
AR	1.41	2/22/15	Venus conjunct Mars	GE	6.07	5/27/15	Sun semisquare Venus
AR	**4.40**	**9/27/15**	**Lunar Eclipse Full Moon**	GE	13.09	5/18/15	Mercury turns Retrograde
AR	13.17	1/31/15	South Node conjunct Uranus	GE	14.58	6/5/15	Sun quincunx Pluto
AR	13.17	1/31/15	Uranus opposite North Node	GE	15.02	6/2/15	Mars quincunx Pluto
AR	13.51	1/21/15	South Node square Pluto	GE	17.20	6/5/15	Mars sextile Jupiter
AR	14.35	3/3/15	Uranus trine Jupiter	GE	17.47	6/8/15	Sun sextile Jupiter
AR	15.18	3/16/15	Uranus square Pluto	GE	26.46	6/16/15	Sun semisquare Venus
AR	16.33	12/25/15	Uranus turns Direct				
AR	16.39	12/10/15	Uranus opposite Mars	CA	0.11	5/7/15	Venus quintile Uranus
AR	16.56	11/25/15	Uranus semisextile Chiron	CA	1.28	5/9/15	Venus biquintile Ceres
AR	17.09	11/17/15	Uranus quintile Ceres	CA	1.32	6/26/15	Mars biquintile Ceres
AR	17.11	11/16/15	Uranus biquintile Mercury	CA	1.57	6/23/15	Sun biquintile Ceres
AR	17.12	11/15/15	Uranus biquintile Sun	CA	2.04	6/23/15	Sun quintile Uranus
AR	17.18	11/12/15	Uranus quincunx Mercury	CA	2.10	6/27/15	Mars quintile Uranus
AR	17.23	11/9/15	Uranus quincunx Sun	CA	21.07	5/27/15	Venus semisquare Sun
AR	17.32	11/5/15	Uranus quincunx Jupiter				
AR	17.39	4/27/15	Uranus quintile Ceres	LE	4.38	6/10/15	Venus sextile Mercury
AR	17.59	5/4/15	Uranus sesquiquadrate Saturn	LE	9.46	6/16/15	Venus semisquare Sun
AR	18.04	10/22/15	Uranus sesquiquadrate Saturn	LE	12.35	4/8/15	Jupiter turns Direct
AR	18.11	5/7/15	Uranus quintile Venus	LE	12.36	4/11/15	Jupiter quintile Venus
AR	18.36	10/9/15	Uranus biquintile Jupiter	LE	12.41	3/31/15	Jupiter biquintile Chiron
AR	19.55	9/2/15	Uranus sesquiquadrate Jupiter	LE	14.23	9/6/15	Venus turns Direct
AR	20.02	6/22/15	Uranus trine Jupiter	LE	14.35	3/3/15	Jupiter trine Uranus
AR	20.03	6/22/15	Uranus quintile Ceres	LE	14.38	5/15/15	Jupiter quintile Mars
AR	20.04	6/23/15	Uranus quintile Sun	LE	14.55	9/1/15	Venus conjunct Mars
AR	20.10	6/27/15	Uranus quintile Mars	LE	14.57	5/18/15	Jupiter biquintile Chiron
AR	20.16	8/19/15	Uranus semisextile Chiron	LE	14.58	2/27/15	Jupiter quincunx Pluto
AR	20.30	7/26/15	Uranus turns Retrograde	LE	15.15	5/21/15	Jupiter quincunx Pluto
AR	22.05	1/9/15	Eris turns Direct	LE	16.01	2/18/15	Jupiter quincunx Ceres
AR	22.16	2/26/15	Eris semisquare Neptune	LE	16.09	2/17/15	Jupiter quincunx Chiron
AR	22.20	12/22/15	Eris semisquare Neptune	LE	17.20	6/5/15	Jupiter sextile Mars
AR	22.21	12/15/15	Eris quincunx Jupiter	LE	17.47	6/8/15	Jupiter sextile Sun
AR	22.27	11/29/15	Eris sesquiquadrate Saturn	LE	20.02	6/22/15	Jupiter trine Uranus
AR	23.07	9/17/15	Eris sesquiquadrate Jupiter	LE	20.32	6/25/15	Jupiter biquintile Pluto
AR	23.12	9/8/15	Eris semisquare Neptune	LE	21.32	6/30/15	Jupiter quincunx Chiron
AR	23.13	9/5/15	Eris biquintile Saturn	LE	21.37	7/1/15	Venus conjunct Jupiter
AR	23.20	8/18/15	Eris biquintile Mercury	LE	22.39	8/15/15	Venus conjunct Sun
AR	23.21	6/25/15	Eris biquintile Saturn	LE	23.24	7/10/15	Jupiter trine Eris
AR	23.24	7/10/15	Eris trine Jupiter	LE	28.17	8/3/15	Jupiter square Saturn
AR	23.25	7/19/15	Eris turns Retrograde	LE	28.34	8/4/15	Jupiter sesquiquadrate Pluto
				LE	28.35	8/4/15	Venus conjunct Jupiter
GE	0.36	4/11/15	Venus quintile Jupiter	LE	29.27	10/7/15	Venus semisquare Sun
GE	1.23	4/12/15	Venus quintile Chiron				
GE	2.38	5/15/15	Mars quintile Jupiter	VI	0.46	7/25/15	Venus turns Retrograde
GE	2.52	5/16/15	Mars quintile Chiron	VI	4.55	9/2/15	Jupiter sesquiquadrate Uranus
GE	4.34	6/11/15	Mercury turns Direct	VI	7.58	9/17/15	Jupiter opposite Neptune

Sign	Degree	Date	Phenomenon/Aspect
VI	8.07	9/17/15	Jupiter sesquiquadrate Eris
VI	10.52	10/1/15	Jupiter sesquiquadrate Ceres
VI	12.36	10/9/15	Jupiter biquintile Uranus
VI	13.02	10/11/15	Jupiter trine Pluto
VI	15.38	10/25/15	Venus conjunct Jupiter
VI	16.28	8/17/15	Mercury quintile Saturn
VI	17.12	11/3/15	Jupiter opposite Chiron
VI	17.20	8/18/15	Mercury biquintile Eris
VI	17.32	11/5/15	Jupiter quincunx Uranus
VI	18.16	11/10/15	Jupiter sesquiquadrate Ceres
VI	18.21	11/10/15	Jupiter sextile Sun
VI	18.45	11/13/15	Jupiter sextile Mercury
VI	**20.10**	**9/13/15**	**Solar Eclipse New Moon**
VI	22.21	12/15/15	Jupiter quincunx Eris
VI	24.02	11/2/14	Venus conjunct Mars
LI	0.41	9/26/15	North Node sextile Saturn
LI	0.54	10/9/15	Mercury turns Direct
LI	10.31	11/17/15	Venus semisquare Sun
LI	13.17	1/31/15	North Node opposite Uranus
LI	13.51	1/21/15	North Node square Pluto
LI	14.12	12/6/15	Mars square Pluto
LI	**14.24**	**4/4/15**	**Lunar Eclipse Full Moon**
LI	14.27	10/7/15	Sun semisquare Venus
LI	15.55	9/17/15	Mercury turns Retrograde
LI	16.39	12/10/15	Mars opposite Uranus
SC	17.18	11/12/15	Mercury quincunx Uranus
SC	17.23	11/9/15	Sun quincunx Uranus
SC	18.21	11/10/15	Sun sextile Jupiter
SC	18.45	11/13/15	Mercury sextile Jupiter
SC	22.30	11/15/15	Sun quintile Ceres
SC	22.48	11/16/15	Mercury quintile Ceres
SC	23.11	11/16/15	Mercury biquintile Uranus
SC	23.12	11/15/15	Sun biquintile Uranus
SC	25.31	11/17/15	Sun semisquare Venus
SC	28.17	8/2/15	Saturn turns Direct
SC	28.17	8/3/15	Saturn square Jupiter
SC	28.21	8/12/15	Saturn sextile Ceres
SC	28.23	8/13/15	Saturn semisquare Pluto
SC	28.28	8/17/15	Saturn quintile Mercury
SC	29.13	9/5/15	Saturn biquintile Eris
SC	29.21	6/25/15	Saturn biquintile Eris
SC	29.39	6/20/15	Saturn semisquare Pluto
SG	0.41	9/26/15	Saturn sextile N. Node/trine S. Node
SG	2.59	5/4/15	Saturn sesquiquadrate Uranus
SG	3.04	10/22/15	Saturn sesquiquadrate Uranus
SG	3.54	4/19/15	Saturn sextile Ceres
SG	4.56	3/14/15	Saturn turns Retrograde
SG	6.33	11/22/15	Saturn sextile Ceres
SG	7.02	11/26/15	Saturn square Neptune
SG	7.27	11/29/15	Saturn sesquiquadrate Eris
CP	12.58	9/25/15	Pluto turns Direct
CP	13.02	10/11/15	Pluto trine Jupiter
CP	13.23	8/13/15	Pluto semisquare Saturn
CP	13.34	8/4/15	Pluto sesquiquadrate Jupiter
CP	13.51	1/21/15	Pluto square North & South Node

Sign	Degree	Date	Phenomenon/Aspect
CP	14.12	12/6/15	Pluto square Mars
CP	14.32	6/25/15	Pluto biquintile Jupiter
CP	14.38	2/15/15	Ceres conjunct Pluto
CP	14.39	6/20/15	Pluto semisquare Saturn
CP	14.58	2/27/15	Pluto quincunx Jupiter
CP	14.58	6/5/15	Pluto quincunx Sun
CP	15.02	6/2/15	Pluto quincunx Mars
CP	15.15	5/21/15	Pluto quincunx Jupiter
CP	15.18	3/16/15	Pluto square Uranus
CP	15.33	4/16/15	Pluto turns Retrograde
CP	16.01	2/18/15	Ceres quincunx Jupiter
CP	16.15	2/19/15	Ceres sextile Chiron
CP	25.06	9/14/15	Ceres turns Direct
CP	25.52	10/1/15	Ceres sesquiquadrate Jupiter
CP	28.21	8/12/15	Ceres sextile Saturn
AQ	1.18	2/11/15	Mercury turns Direct
AQ	2.10	11/5/15	Ceres semisquare Chiron
AQ	3.16	11/10/15	Ceres sesquiquadrate Jupiter
AQ	3.54	4/19/15	Ceres sextile Saturn
AQ	4.30	11/15/15	Ceres quintile Sun
AQ	4.48	11/16/15	Ceres quintile Mercury
AQ	4.58	4/24/15	Ceres semisquare Chiron
AQ	5.09	11/17/15	Ceres quintile Uranus
AQ	5.39	4/27/15	Ceres quintile Uranus
AQ	6.31	7/3/15	Ceres semisquare Chiron
AQ	6.33	11/22/15	Ceres sextile Saturn
AQ	7.28	5/9/15	Ceres biquintile Ceres
AQ	7.32	6/26/15	Ceres biquintile Mars
AQ	7.57	6/23/15	Ceres biquintile Sun
AQ	8.03	6/22/15	Ceres quintile Uranus
AQ	9.13	6/3/15	Ceres turns Retrograde
AQ	17.05	1/21/15	Mercury turns Retrograde
PI	7.01	11/18/15	Neptune turns Direct
PI	7.02	11/26/15	Neptune square Saturn
PI	7.16	2/26/15	Neptune semisquare Eris
PI	7.20	12/22/15	Neptune semisquare Eris
PI	7.58	9/17/15	Neptune opposite Jupiter
PI	8.12	9/8/15	Neptune semisquare Eris
PI	9.49	6/12/15	Neptune turns Retrograde
PI	16.09	2/17/15	Chiron quincunx Jupiter
PI	16.15	2/19/15	Chiron sextile Ceres
PI	16.56	11/25/15	Chiron semisextile Uranus
PI	16.56	11/28/15	Chiron turns Direct
PI	17.10	11/5/15	Chiron semisquare Ceres
PI	17.12	11/3/15	Chiron opposite Jupiter
PI	18.41	3/31/15	Chiron biquintile Jupiter
PI	19.23	4/12/15	Chiron quintile Venus
PI	19.58	4/24/15	Chiron semisquare Ceres
PI	20.16	8/19/15	Chiron semisextile Uranus
PI	20.52	5/16/15	Chiron quintile Mars
PI	20.57	5/18/15	Chiron biquintile Jupiter
PI	21.31	7/3/15	Chiron semisquare Ceres
PI	21.32	6/30/15	Chiron quincunx Jupiter
PI	21.33	6/24/15	Chiron turns Retrograde
PI	**29.27**	**3/20/15**	**Solar Eclipse New Moon**

See p. 60 for the key to sign abbreviations.
Check the degrees and dates of 2015's New and Full Moons on p. 61. Eclipses are shown above.

Janet's Plan-its™ STAR PAGES

The Star Pages will fill you in on some important astrological details, month by month.

Check the Keywords (pp. 98–99) for more about planets, signs and aspects.

NOTE: The abbreviations for signs used here are the same as for 2015 On a Page (p. 60).

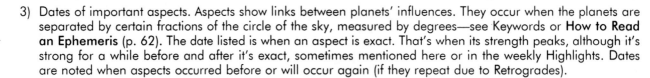

★ ★ ★ ★ ★ TYPES OF DATA LISTED IN STAR PAGES ★ ★ ★ ★ ★

1) Time frames when a planet (other than the Moon) is traveling through a sign and its effects there.

2) Beginning and end of Retrograde and Direct motion—see 2015 On a Page for further explanation.

3) Dates of important aspects. Aspects show links between planets' influences. They occur when the planets are separated by certain fractions of the circle of the sky, measured by degrees—see Keywords or **How to Read an Ephemeris** (p. 62). The date listed is when an aspect is exact. That's when its strength peaks, although it's strong for a while before and after it's exact, sometimes mentioned here or in the weekly Highlights. Dates are noted when aspects occurred before or will occur again (if they repeat due to Retrogrades).

After each star is the number of the day of the month. Sometimes the same moment is on adjacent calendar days, late night in Pacific time (P) and after midnight Eastern (E). In that case, both the (P) and (E) dates are listed. NOTE: There may be more than one entry for a particular day.

While anyone can utilize these recommendations to advantage, the impact from a particular planet is felt most personally when a part of your chart is touched by a degree discussed (within 2° of the same sign or any sign of the same Mode—see Keywords). Read **Making It Personal** (p. 5), see the **2015 All Star List** (pp. 70–71) and you may want to learn how to use the ephemeris.

Things are always on the move in astrology, so keep abreast of the planets' zodiac positions. The slow-moving outer planets (from Saturn out to Eris) don't change signs often. In 2015, Saturn settles into a different sign. As usually occurs, Jupiter passes through parts of two signs this year. Ceres visits three. The quicker planets – Mercury, Venus and Mars – shift signs frequently (except when Retrograde). The Sun's sign changes once a month, like clockwork.

The Moon circles the zodiac in 27 days, changing signs every 2–3 days (see the weekly calendar pages). Just as the Moon reflects the Sun's light, people's emotions and responses are reflected by the Moon's sign.

SIGN	Typical behavior when the Moon travels through this sign:
Aries	fast to react (sometimes in an angry way but this passes quickly), focused on oneself, desiring personal attention
Taurus	security-oriented, calm (slow to enrage), self-indulgent (fond of sweets), craving affection
Gemini	distrustful of emotions (more thought-oriented), talkative especially about feelings, flexible, changeable
Cancer	more attuned to a sixth sense, moody, attached to family, safety conscious and security-oriented, interested in food
Leo	brave, dramatic, creative, stubborn, strong-willed, seeking the spotlight
Virgo	nervous, health conscious, practical, helpful, communicative, critical, analytical
Libra	diplomatic, just, conflict-averse, rational, indecisive, hungry for companionship
Scorpio	extreme, reactionary, determined, harsh, in need of an emotional outlet, interested in intimacy and sex, acting on survival instincts
Sagittarius	easy-going, restless, drifting, inconsistent, optimistic, philosophical, bookish, adventurous
Capricorn	rather unemotional, thick-skinned, playing things safe, matter-of-fact, requiring respect
Aquarius	unpredictable, humanitarian, usually friendly but possibly cool and aloof, filtering feelings through intellect, wanting space
Pisces	easily moved, empathetic, charitable, escapist, yearning to believe in something or someone

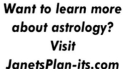

Want to learn more about astrology? Visit JanetsPlan-its.com

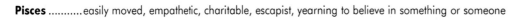

AS WE BEGIN 2015...

Here are the positions of the planets (and the Moon's Nodes), noted from the farthest out to the innermost.

Eris in Aries [1926–2048] With an orbit three times farther out than Pluto, taking 556.7 years to circle the Sun and the zodiac, chances are almost everyone you know has Eris (named for Mars' bitchy sister) in Aries. This is the period of history of the rise of women's power. We could speculate a culture-wide effect for generations in which the Aries traits of aggression, self-centeredness and haste add to Eris' attributes of disorder and discord. We might all try slowing down and becoming more conscious of others. The positive side of Eris in Aries is strength, confidence and independence. In 2015, Eris is at 22–23° of Aries. If it connects to something in your chart, perhaps you'll have an especially stressful year in which you must learn to accept and adapt to some level of chaos in your life.

Pluto in Capricorn [2008–2024] It's likely entire systems will be discarded and slowly rebuilt on new ground. Pluto's extremes impact Capricorn's arena of conformity and may lead to authoritarianism. Personally, we'll feel the weight of responsibilities and obligations more than ever. Pluto can help us let go of a need to be in control or act maturely. Using keywords, you could translate this as death (Pluto) of the boss/father/old man (Saturn, ruler of Capricorn). Expect a big transition in how the elderly are treated.

Neptune in Pisces [2011–12 until 2025–26] Many people have a greater sixth sense and more respect for psychics, including medical intuitives. Art, music, film, theater, and dance develop in extremely imaginative ways. What we glamorize as a culture shifts to being emotion-based rather than intelligence-based, as was the case during Neptune's visit to Aquarius. The techno geek held sway; the next hero may be the psychic or healer. We pay more attention to our oceans and sea-life, as well as the seafood supply.

Uranus in Aries [2010–11 until 2018–19] The planet of unpredictability and technology in the sign of conflict and armaments may bring surprise attacks and inventions of high-tech weaponry. Aries is also the sign for sports and competition, so expect new types of exercise equipment or computer games. Unrest or anxiety is likely on a group or individual level. You might reinvent yourself or become more your true self. Spontaneous outbursts are possible, especially if you have chronic anger issues or a strong temper.

Chiron in Pisces [2010–11 until 2018–19] This indicator of repair or healing is powerful in the sign of health, spirituality and charity. All these arenas are slated for attention and improvement now. The down side: sometimes difficulties have to be painfully experienced before solutions are sought. Look for significant medical discoveries and increased sympathy for people on the lowest rungs of society's ladder. More focus will be on water quality and availability, as well as the condition of the world's oceans, especially since Neptune (ruler of the seas) will be in Pisces even longer than Chiron.

Saturn in Sagittarius [12/23/14–6/14/15; again 9/17/15–12/19/17] The planet of organization and structure visits the sign associated with higher education, law-making and courts, foreign travel and interactions, and widespread information sharing. Saturn's sobering and mature influence may calm the divisiveness and antagonism in government. Expect consolidation in international businesses, more regulation of internet commerce and increased standardization of educational methods and materials. Individuals may be more flexible about interpersonal boundaries and obeying laws.

Jupiter in Leo [7/16/14–8/11/15] Everyone wants to be like a kid again when the planet of expansiveness moves through the sign of children. We embrace life as an adventure. Creativity increases and wanderlust spurs us to hit the road and experience places we've never been before. Education incorporates fun or entertainment. People may be more dramatic about their philosophies or legal matters. We have extra willpower and stubbornness.

Ceres in Sagittarius [10/27/14–1/8/15] The dwarf planet of abundance in a sign of largess is perfect for the Thanksgiving cornucopia season. This also tantalizes our taste buds for foreign fare and fans the flames of our intellect and wanderlust.

Mars in Aquarius [12/4/14–1/12/15] (See Mutual Receptions.) You're likely to act on what you "know" to be true (even if it's just your own opinion). Take a stand for a friend or for humanity's sake, or serve in a leadership position in a group to which you belong.

North Node in Libra, South Node in Aries [3/22/14–10/9/15] These two signs are the ones most concerned with how personal needs can conflict with those of a significant other or someone who acts as one's representative. When the Nodes move through this pair of signs, we're supposed to develop the Libran qualities of the North Node and move away from the Aries traits of the South Node. We will learn how to simultaneously consider the situation of a partner or teammate, balancing it against our own desires. It is a time to get over anger and develop cooperation and diplomacy.

Sun in Capricorn [12/21/14–1/20/15] The bottom line is at the top of our list and we value efficient means to our intended ends. We're willing to do our duty, whatever form it takes, especially if it helps us up the ladder toward success. Hard work seems worth the effort.

Venus in Capricorn [12/10/14–1/3/15] This is a time to clarify what our most important values are, as well as organize finances and straighten out any kinks in our social lives. We're more likely to be practical than sentimental and consider the result of decisions in the long-run.

Mercury in Capricorn [12/16/14–1/4/15] Part of the time Mercury is in Capricorn, Venus is also there (see above), doubling our penchant to be unemotional in decision-making. We're drawn to science and facts, being assured by their reliability and solidity. This is a good time to get paperwork and files organized and systems streamlined as we close out the old year and prepare for the next one.

LONG-TERM INFLUENCES:

Uranus square Pluto These two slow planets related to change and evolution have been roughly 90° apart since 2011, wreaking havoc on financial markets and prompting many uprisings. They make seven exact squares from 2012–15 (see March 16). The rollercoaster ride continues as people buck the system. The status quo has got to go! Quick-moving planets often amplify its effects. This year, a slower planet (Saturn) exacerbates this square's power (see below). Like a saving grace, Chiron intercedes (see below) to ensure that even the most turbulent clouds have silver linings.

Chiron semisextile Uranus Traveling about one sign apart for more than a decade, Chiron (an asteroid nicknamed the "wounded healer") is in this mildly positive link to Uranus. Chiron in Pisces wants to gently nudge us toward gradual modifications whereas Uranus in Aries prefers to shock us into awareness. Together they bring improvements (Chiron's forte) for the populace as a whole (Uranus's purview). They are in an exact semisextile 26 times between 2009 and 2021. By the time this link is over, each planet will have changed its sign. (See Aug. 19.)

Chiron sextile Pluto Chiron is two signs ahead of Pluto from 2011 to 2015, often within one degree of a sextile, though sometimes not forming the aspect exactly (see Feb. 2). Pluto specializes in transformation; Chiron, in repairs. Frequently Pluto brings destruction ahead of reconstruction. Chiron points to hurts we need to process. Operating in concert, they build anew on what's outworn or injurious. This sextile serves as a base for Finger of God triangles (see Keywords, p. 99), providing chances for this benign restorative factor to operate. Twice in 2015, Jupiter makes such a Finger of God. (See Feb. 2–8 Astro-Overview and Feb. 2, below.)

Saturn sesquiquadrate Uranus and semisquare Pluto (See May 3–4 and June 20.) Saturn first bumped into the Uranus-Pluto square close to its sixth occurrence in late 2014 (Dec. 15). Now that the square is separating, Saturn's aspects to this pair are not as close in time, yet still represent a potent influence. Saturn's affiliation with rules, systems and structures shows arenas where the force for change will operate strongly. Or will Saturn apply its brakes to slow the run-away train of this crazy square?

Jupiter square Saturn These two medium-speed planets began their current 20-year cycle in 2000. They are three-quarters of the way through at this square, which stimulates adjusting the balance between growth and consolidation. (See Aug. 3.)

Saturn square Neptune Last together in 1989, these two join again in 2026 in their 37-year cycle. The opening square was in 1998; their opposition was in 2006–07. This closing square reoccurs twice in 2016. The late 2015 square is the only time they interact simultaneously with Eris (see Nov. 26). Saturn gives form to Neptune's dreams but manifesting a vision isn't easy during a square; it takes a lot of planning and hard work. Eris interjects chaos into the process.

Neptune semisquare Eris This aspect is within a 1° orb for more than half of 2015, in two periods: 1/25–4/5 (exact 2/26) and 7/22/15–1/27/16 (exact 9/8 & 12/22). Neptune can cause confusion on its own, worse now in its long stay in Pisces (see prior page). When it clashes with the dwarf planet named for the goddess of discord, imagine the difficulty to keep things straight! Neptune represents the down-trodden while Eris incites intimidation. We need to be vigilant about power-tripping and help those who suffer at the hands of abusers.

"OUT OF BOUNDS" PLANETS:

The signs form the circumference of the zodiac belt, which also has a width defined by the earth's 23°27' tilt on its axis relative to the Sun. Planets sometimes ride higher or lower in the sky than the Sun's apparent path. Such an "out of bounds" planet doesn't play by the rules, going too far in whatever it represents.

Mercury [5/3–5/18; 11/27–12/24] We over-think situations or speak too little or too much. Instruments and communication devices may not work correctly.

Venus [4/18–6/1] There's too much love or not enough, or it stems from the wrong reasons. Fiscal matters may be grossly out of balance, such as a decrease in income or increase in expenses.

Mars [6/6–7/16] People are more rash, impatient, selfish or angry than usual. Skirmishes escalate. Energy levels are off the scale.

Ceres [12/27/14–12/25/15, a year out of bounds!] (This is not a typo.) The maternal instinct is weak or applied inappropriately. We try to reap what is not ours or we may miss getting what we deserve.

MUTUAL RECEPTIONS:

This condition blends the effects of two planets that are in the signs ruled by each other.

Mercury and Venus There are two mutual receptions between Mercury and Venus in 2015. In spring [4/14–4/30], Mercury is in Venus-ruled Taurus as Venus visits Mercury-ruled Gemini. In autumn, Mercury is in Libra (another sign ruled by Venus) and Venus is in a second Mercury-ruled sign, Virgo [10/8–11/1 (P), 11/2 (E)]. People are attracted to each other's mind and find ideas appealing, wanting to implement the best and profit from them. This affiliation is good for socializing with or possibly courting co-workers or colleagues.

Mercury and Jupiter [11/20–12/9] During Jupiter's year-plus visit to Mercury-ruled Virgo, for a brief 19 days, Mercury is in Jupiter-ruled Sagittarius.

Mars and Uranus [12/4/14–1/12/15] This is the second of four periods that Mars travels through Uranus-ruled Aquarius during the seven-plus years Uranus is in Mars-ruled Aries. Individuals have a stronger need for freedom. People act quickly without deliberation or hesitation. Intuition and initiative work together to give a positive push to endeavors. Potential drawbacks to this aspect are jumping to conclusions and thinking you know everything.

Saturn and Pluto [10/5/12–12/23/14 & 6/14/15–9/17/15] Saturn is in Pluto-ruled Scorpio for more than two years while Pluto is in Saturn-ruled Capricorn for over a decade. Saturn was in a positive sextile with Pluto in 2012-13. Now that it's further into Scorpio, it's in an abrasive semisquare with Pluto from late 2014 well into 2015. Their interplay promotes regulation and revision of financial systems and creating methods to bring about change in any arena or activity. This is a time to get serious about simplicity and pare down to basics, shedding what no longer works. Both planets and signs have a stark, matter-of-fact approach and lack warmth, imbuing a "grin and bear it" demeanor.

SEASONAL SYNOPSES

Factors present at the start of a season set the pace for the entire three months to follow. These analyses of the inception charts cover challenges and opportunities we may encounter. (Also see the weekly Highlights when seasons begin.)

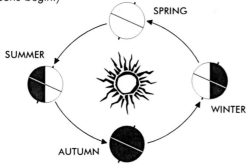

Seasons Change as the Earth Travels Around the Sun

The earth tilts on its axis. This causes a variation in the way the Sun's rays reach us, resulting in the seasons.

WINTER [12/21/14–3/20/15] The beginning of the end is in sight for the madness that's plagued us for years. The Uranus-Pluto square exerts its final major blast this winter. A week before the Solstice, the square was exact for the sixth of seven times, magnified by Uranus's standstill precisely on the Solstice. Their last square is 3/16. As winter begins, Mercury and Venus surround Pluto, marking a time to discuss values, resources and finances. Since they're in Capricorn, talks should be mature and responsible. But Mercury and Venus are also out of bounds. Judgments and a superior attitude can intrude. The Sun and Moon semisquare Mars sets a confrontational tone. Mercury sesquiquadrate Jupiter turns up the volume. With the Moon at the end of its cycle, certain situations are poised for a finale. In broadminded and flexible Sagittarius, it aids legislative and international issues. Saturn at Scorpio's last degree adds another impetus for endings. Venus and Saturn in a semisquare increase pressure to set fiscal matters straight. Both spar with the Nodes, adding incentive to steer in a different direction.

SPRING [3/20–6/21] Unlike 2014, when all seasonal starts had a waning Moon, each of 2015's has a waxing Moon. It will be easier to launch new projects this year. That said, the New Moon just before the equinox is at the very end of Pisces, indicating a strong dose of karma and some degree of suffering or being mired in feelings. Jupiter plays a strong role now. In sunny Leo (ruled by the Sun), we may be more interested in fun and creativity than work. These areas may not bring the desired joy with the Sun sesquiquadrate Jupiter. Whatever we do, we need to be careful not to bite off more than we can chew. Energy may slump due to a Mars-Neptune semisquare, which drains motivation. We may think and talk too much, too little or off topic with Mercury and Jupiter quincunx, part of two Fingers of God (see p. 99). One with Pluto prompts us to change our minds for the better. The other, with the North Node, points us in a positive mental direction and improves relationships. Shortly before the equinox is the final occurrence of the Uranus-Pluto square (see above), which will be great to put in the rear view mirror!

SUMMER [6/21–9/23] As the Uranus-Pluto square fades, we face a different Pluto problem: a semisquare with Saturn, exact a day before the Summer Solstice, for the second of three times (usually the toughest hit). Both planets bring out a bossy side, especially in their mutual reception (see prior page). The Solstice Moon is at the last degree of Leo, introducing paternalism and a haughty sense of entitlement into the mix as it tightly squares Saturn and sesquiquadrates Pluto. The Sun and Venus are semisquare (as they often are). They're at potent degrees of the zodiac (on the "Cardinal axis") that have widespread impact. This will affect the economy adversely and hit individuals in finances and romances. Close to the Sun, in late Gemini, Mars also semisquares Venus. This normally arouses heated arguments but may be counteracted by a Sun-Ceres-Uranus Quintile Triangle, offering friendly, open-hearted support. Another QT between Jupiter, Mercury and Pluto keeps minds open and makes communication productive. A trine from Venus and Jupiter to Uranus bodes good fortune and lucky surprises.

AUTUMN [9/23–12/21] The Moon is Void as the Sun enters Libra to start fall, hindering whatever begins in the next three months. Its last aspect sets the tone: a stifling square to wild Uranus. Will unpredictability be the spoiler or will it be foiled? Libra's ruling planet, Venus, is trine Uranus, portending surprises. Mercury is Retrograde in Libra and semisquare Mars in the final degree of Leo. Communication is jumbled, with chips on shoulders; pride takes a toll. The Sun and North Node, less than a degree apart, both sextile Saturn, advising us to keep our noses clean. Libra asks for fairness and cooperation. Saturn brings maturity, respect and restraint. With Saturn semisquare Pluto, too tight a grip could strangle or unseen forces may upset order. The web of Ceres square Eris and both sesquiquadrate Jupiter throws its weight around, especially since the equinox Moon joins Ceres. Together, they abrogate the ability to give and receive nurturing support. Jupiter in Virgo heightens criticism, Capricorn hardens hearts and Eris expands selfishness. Love is in for a rocky season.

WINTER [12/21/15–3/20/16] Practicality is prominent with pragmatic Earth signs dominating at the Solstice. There's a Grand Trine between the Moon in Taurus (a stabilizing factor), Jupiter in Virgo (beneficial for the work force) and a Mercury-Pluto pairing in Capricorn (boosting commerce). Chiron and Venus in Water signs expand the Grand Trine into Kites, bringing emotions into play in a balanced way and adding a loving, healing touch. Many things fall into place effortlessly. But there are challenges. Finances and relationships suffer from strange conditions and detours due to a Venus-Jupiter-Eris Finger of God. A Venus-Ceres-Moon T-square foments friction in families. Neptune's final semisquare to Eris a day after the Solstice brings another season with discord and mayhem. Mars opposite Eris and sesquiquadrate Neptune contributes an angry edge and fuel the fires of religious zealotry. Uranus, Pluto, Mercury, Mars and Eris in a loose T-square push us into action. The question is whether we'll plan first, taking only calculated risks. Mars in Libra wants us to have a collaborator, rather than go it alone.

MONTHLY STAR PAGES

The planets (and the Moon's Nodes) each represent a number of conditions, modified by their zodiac positions. As they move through the signs, they set the stage for their associated activities and areas of life. Certain angular connections between planets (called aspects) indicate when their energies interact. When an aspect forms between slow planets (Jupiter, Saturn, Chiron, Uranus, Neptune, Pluto and Eris), the link strongly colors the atmosphere for many days (or even weeks) before and after the date it's exact. Interactions involving the Nodes or quick planets (Sun, Mercury, Venus, Mars and Ceres) have a shorter impact, for just a few days. When you see three (or more) dates listed for an influence, this is due to a planet retracing its steps while Retrograde (see p. 60). Check the weekly calendar pages for mention of phenomena in the Star Pages. Also, see the Overview of 2015 (p. 1), 2015 On a Page (pp. 60–61) and the Keywords (see pp. 98–99).

JANUARY 2015

★ **1** Be sure to read As We Begin 2015 (p. 73) and Overview of 2015 (p. 1).

★ **3** *Venus enters Aquarius* [until 1/27] Social contacts increase in importance and add value in some way to our lives. We enjoy group activities or being with friends, although our connection feels more intellectual than emotional now.

★ **4** *Mercury enters Aquarius* [until 3/12, going Retrograde here] New topics of interest arise. People are more curious about metaphysics and anything labeled "New Age." Inventiveness and intuition are strong but so are opinions. We gravitate toward shared learning opportunities and discussions.

★ **4** *Full Moon (14°31' CA)* The Moon and Sun, which are opposite by definition at a Full Moon, are both exactly square the North and South Nodes, which are also opposite by definition, forming a Grand Cross. The Sun is just past Pluto and the South Node is closing in on Uranus, accentuating the Uranus-Pluto square. (See the Astro-Overview and Highlights for the week of Dec. 28, 2014–Jan. 4, 2015.) This Full Moon is within one degree of where a Grand Cross occurred April 20–23, 2014. The Moon now occupies the spot where Jupiter was then. This is the degree of the Sun in the USA's chart. Important occurrences or developments in April will likely have related circumstances or a culmination or conclusion around this Full Moon, for America and for individuals who have planets at 11–16° of Cardinal signs. Mercury's semisquare to Chiron could give rise to some painful discussions or hurtful comments, although the stronger tendency is for people to be supportive of one another, communicating cooperatively, thanks to Mercury and Venus traveling close together in Aquarius.

★ **8** *Ceres enters Capricorn* [until 4/3; again 8/3–10/27; a two-part visit due to going Retrograde here] Buckling down with your nose to the grindstone brings rewards. We enjoy the beauty of order and want to make our nests more organized. We take nurturing seriously.

★ **9** *Eris (22°5' AR) turns Direct* [Retrograde since 7/19/14; Direct until 7/19/15] There's likely to be more disorder and disruption when Eris is at a standstill for a couple weeks on either side of its change of direction. Once it's moving forward again, we're better able to assert our independence, handle disruptions and deal with competition.

★ **12** *Mars enters Pisces* [until 2/19] There's a tendency to sidestep arguments and any appearance of anger is more likely an act of passive aggression than a direct confrontation. Some people may feel like they're swimming against the tide. Put energy into spiritual or artistic pursuits and fight for the underdog.

★ **20** *Sun enters Aquarius* [until 2/18] Humanitarian urges surge and friendships flourish each year when the Sun visits Aquarius. We have a strong need to be part of a group, even if the result is to affirm our individuality and the unique contribution we can make to the whole.

★ **20** *(P),* **21** *(E) North Node (13°51' LI) & South Node (13°51' AR) square Pluto (13°51' CP)* Any planet square the Nodes is said to be at the "bendings," a shifting point. This is a time to move toward the uncertain future (shown by the North Node) and release what needs to be put into the past (spurred by the South Node). This is especially true when Pluto is involved. It's the harbinger of transformation, the "garbage man" of the solar system. With the Nodes in Aries (sign of the self) and Libra (sign of the significant other), it may be necessary to alter one's approach to relationships, particularly handling joint finances (under Pluto's sway).

★ **21** *Mercury (17°5' AQ) turns Retrograde* [Direct since 10/25/14; Retrograde until 2/11] The entire Retrograde is in Aquarius, inclining us to re-examine our friendships and organizational affiliations. As the "Messenger of the Gods" retraces its steps, we review recent conversations, documents or decisions. Revisions may be required. You can voluntarily take a second look or circumstances might force you to. Be careful in current communications not to create problems that necessitate re-work or that later make you ask, "What was I thinking?" Vehicles may need attention.

★ **27** *Venus enters Pisces* [until 2/20] Compassion and artistic sensibilities increase. Fantasies abound and are natural now, but delusions in romance or finances take vigilance to avoid. Some people will be self-indulgent in their addictions, such as gambling, shopping, eating, smoking, drinking or self-medicating. Others will be philanthropic.

★ **31** *South Node (13°17' AR) conjunct Uranus (13°17' AR)* The South Node indicates what comes easily and could hold us back from our growth by providing a cushy comfort zone. Here, that's a facility for going it alone and doing your own thing to the detriment of teamwork or partnership. Impulsive tendencies are not inhibited and risks are taken without much forethought.

FEBRUARY

★ **2** *Chiron (15°16′ PI) leaves 1° range of sextile to Pluto (14°16′ CP)* [since 11/20/14; before 6/18/11–7/22/11, 4/21/12–6/9/12 (exact 5/12/12), 8/8/12–9/28/12 (exact 9/6/12), 3/15/13–4/23/13 (exact 4/4), 10/5/13–11/29/13 (exact 10/28/13) & 1/24–3/20/14 (exact 2/25/14)] See Long-term Influences, p. 74. In a one-degree range seven times (the middle five with exact sextiles), this aspect represents the need and ability for healing to come through regeneration, casting off the outworn and starting anew. Chiron's position in Pisces shows our belief systems are undergoing a renovation and Pluto's transit through Capricorn is expected to transform all kinds of systems, organizations, rules, corporations and governments. For individuals, it's a time to re-write the rules you live by in order to be healthier and more successful. This sextile is close enough to exact to form a Finger of God with Ceres and Jupiter, which is imprecise but still effective due to its length of about two weeks. (See Feb. 15, 17, 18, 19 & 27.)

★ **11** *Mercury (1°18′ AQ) turns Direct* [Retrograde since 1/21; Direct until 5/18] Once Mercury is in forward motion again, mix-ups in communication subside and we clear up confusion or resolve issues that arose during the Retrograde, primarily during the exiting shadow period through 3/8 (see 2015 On a Page, pp. 60–61). It should be easier now to connect with people with whom we've recently played phone or email tag.

★ **13** *Friday the 13th* (We also have a Friday the 13th in March and November of this year.) Friday is named for Freya, the Norse goddess of sex and fertility (somewhat like Venus, whose name you hear in the French name for Friday, Vendredi). Thirteen is a number sacred to goddess worshippers, the number of moon cycles in a year. On Friday the 13th, instead of working, you were supposed to stay home and make love to honor the goddess. You can see how a patriarchal, repressive religion would regard this as bad and cast a pall on the day by vilifying it.

★ **15** *Ceres (14°38′ CP) conjunct Pluto (14°38′ CP)* (Part of a Finger of God with Jupiter and Chiron—see Feb. 2.) Ceres is the dwarf planet of fertility and harvest. Paired with Pluto, ruler of reproduction, they bring forth new conditions and entities. In Capricorn, these are likely to be business-related. Strict or structured nurturance fosters change.

★ **17** *Jupiter (16°9′ LE) quincunx Chiron (16°9′ PI)* [before 9/23/14; again 6/30/15] (Part of a Finger of God—see above. Also see June 30.) In a low expression, this might manifest as a disconnect between cavalier fun and sensitivity to insult, such as teasing. A higher use is to bring creativity to healing. (The Finger of God helps us use this aspect with more compassion.)

★ **18** *New Moon (29°59′54″ AQ)* This border between Aquarius and Pisces is the degree of the switchover from the Age of Pisces to the Age of Aquarius. (An Age is about 2,160 years long and there's no way to know exactly when it occurs.) You can use this as a marker to celebrate the New Age. It's the only New Moon this close to the dividing line. Pisces is associated with beliefs while Aquarius is aligned with objective information. Part of the shift is to gravitate from religion to science as what underlies motivation and action.

★ **18** *Chinese New Year—Year of the Sheep (also called Goat or ram), Wood element, Year 4713* (The Chinese calendar is lunar-based, counting from the New Moon which occurs on the Feb. 18 in the west, on the 19th in China. This is about as late on the western calendar as a Chinese New Year ever begins and consequently, this Year of the Sheep will be a short one.) The Sheep corresponds to Cancer in the western zodiac. Some Chinese couples avoid having a Sheep baby, believing it would lead an unhappy life, suffering heartbreak and business failures. Their virtuous traits of being passive, loyal, kind and generous are under-valued in a competitive world. Perhaps the general populace will be more docile and herd-like in the Year of the Sheep. The Wood element relates to practicality, marking a time when diligence and hard work contribute to prosperity and well-being. Recent Years of the Sheep were 1919, 1931, 1943, 1955, 1967, 1979, 1991 and 2003. If you're turning 60, you are of the Wood element, like this year. Colors associated with the Year of the Sheep are red, green and purple and the stones are jade, moonstone and sapphire. The affiliated directions are East, Southeast and South. It is the eighth sign of the Chinese zodiac, a number the Chinese consider lucky. Sheep attributes we might all try to emulate this year are being nurturing and supportive, calm and peace-loving. Think of this as a Cancer year, appropriate for family activities, attending to domestic matters and housing concerns, and building a nest egg.

★ **18** *Sun enters Pisces* [until 3/20] You're inspired to delve more deeply into your spirituality or the arts. Identify with people in need or who've been mistreated, and take the lead in assisting them. At the Pisces time of year, we tune in to our dreams (both the day and night varieties) and appreciate what's unseen.

★ **18** *Ceres (16°1′ CP) quincunx Jupiter (16°1′ LE)* (Part of a Finger of God—see Feb. 2.) A sincere desire to be supportive and help practical situations move forward clashes with a playful or childlike avoidance of whatever sounds like work. When blended with Chiron (see below) in the Finger of God, Jupiter in Leo contributes novel approaches to solving problems.

★ **19** *Ceres (16°15′ CP) sextile Chiron (16°15′ PI)* (Part of a Finger of God—see above.) Improvements and repairs result from planning and proceeding step-by-step. The collective resources needed are likely to be found, thanks to Pluto's participation in the Finger of God (see Feb. 15, and Feb. 27).

★ **19** *Mars enters Aries* [until 3/31] This is Mars' sign of rulership, where it travels for about a month in its average two-year orbit (unless it hangs out longer when Retrograde). This time around, part of its visit (Feb. 20–March 17), Venus will be in Aries, as well (see next two items) and another part (March 20–31) coincides with the Sun's transit here. Take advantage of these powerful periods! Energy levels and zest for physical activities should soar. The entire time Mars is in Aries, there's a strong impetus to engage in new activities or get projects underway. We are braver than usual and some people take more risks than they normally would.

★ **20** *Venus enters Aries* [until 3/17] Go after your heart's desires, whether in the form of a relationship or a

Continued on next page.

material acquisition, though attractions or flirtations may pass quickly. Be proactive in social matters and fight for fairness, equality and individual rights.

★ **21** *(P)*, **22** *(E)* Venus *(1°41' AR)* conjunct Mars*(1°41' AR)* [again 8/31 (P), 9/1 (E) & 11/2] These two entered Aries less than 24 hours apart (see above). From Feb. 11 through March 2, they are within five degrees of one another for a hot combo that marries action to attraction. New relationships will form and existing ones heat up. People enjoy competition by which to measure themselves and be stimulated to do their best.

★ **26** Neptune *(7°16' PI)* semisquare Eris *(22°16' AR)* [again 9/8 & 12/22] (This aspect is referenced multiple times in Janet's Plan-its 2015. See weekly Astro-Overviews and Highlights, Overview of 2015 (p. 1) and Long-term Influences (p. 74).) Usually the slower planet wields more power. That's Eris, in this case. It operates with better results in difficult aspects, according to astrologer Thomas Canfield, who researched its role in American History. (See his *Yankee Doodle Discord* and his new booklet, *Eris in Signs, Houses, Aspects*.) Positive actions inspired by Eris are standing up for independence and personal strength, and fighting for women's rights and equality. When embroiled with Neptune, strong beliefs and feelings come to the fore and people (especially women) who have been bullied or mistreated are likely to raise a ruckus or provoke push-back.

★ **27** Jupiter *(14°58' LE)* quincunx Pluto *(14°58' CP)* [before 9/5/14; again 5/21/15] (Part of a Finger of God—see Feb. 2, 15, 17, 18 & 19.) A jovial side is at odds with a serious bent. This would work nicely if we could incorporate creativity into our work but stodginess may try to squelch originality.

MARCH

★ **3** Jupiter *(14°35' LE)* trine Uranus *(14°35' AR)* [before 9/25/14; again 6/2/15] What a difference from early 2014, when Jupiter was square Uranus! Good fortune results when the planet of luck blends nicely with the planet of surprises. Enthusiasm and persistence boost the already positive tendencies. Some people will travel suddenly or have a fortuitous turn of events in legal or educational matters.

★ **8** Daylight Saving Time begins at 2:00 am local time.

★ **12** Mercury enters Pisces [until 3/30] Our sympathy and understanding increase and we're more amenable to benefiting others in charitable and humanitarian ways. Imagination is strong as are the tendencies for projection and worry.

★ **14** Saturn *(4°56' SG)* turns Retrograde [Direct since 7/20/14; Retrograde until 8/2] Over the coming four months, we backtrack to address obligations we've overlooked or avoided. We look to ourselves for the standards to apply to our lives, rather than accepting other people's notions of right and wrong.

★ **16** Uranus *(15°18' AR)* square Pluto *(15°18' CP)* [before 6/24/12, 9/19/12, 5/20/13, 11/1/13, 4/21/14, 12/15/14—a total of 7 times!] This final occurrence will likely seem milder than prior instances. It's not part of a T-square nor a Grand Cross. No other planets make a difficult aspect with it at all. Yet whatever work it has left to do, this is the chance. (See Long-term Influences, p. 74.) The economy (under Pluto's purview) has been shaken by Uranus's turbulence. Energy production (primarily linked to Uranus) is undergoing an evolution. Individuals need to learn to be more self-reliant (a feature of both Uranus and Aries) and work in groups (another Uranus association) instead of counting on support from collective coffers (Pluto's arena). Whatever is entrenched in our lives (our Capricorn foundation) is subject to a shake-up, forcing us to embody the Aries qualities of courage and forging a new path. If you used keywords for these two daunting planets, you might say people (Uranus) versus Plutocrats (Pluto) or a revolution (Uranus) in how resources are distributed (Pluto). On the downside, it can even equate to sudden or mass (Uranus) death (Pluto). We could see damage to power-generating capabilities or a radically new energy delivery system. The square is cushioned to an extent by Chiron sextile Pluto and semisextile Uranus, and this time around, some of the venom is removed from its bite by Jupiter's trine to Uranus (see March 3) and quincunx to Pluto (see Feb. 27).

★ **17** Venus enters Taurus [until 4/11] Venus' love of beauty and desire for material security are strongest when she sashays through this sign that she rules. Attend to accounts, add to possessions, spruce up your home or garden, and enjoy all the good things in life, especially physical expressions of love. Taurus likes to get to the finish line.

★ **20** Solar Eclipse New Moon *(29°27' PI)* So close to the equinox but not quite on the Aries side of the line, this powerful stimulus is instead in the final degree of the zodiac, a degree that is considered precarious and karmic. It signals that certain situations which no longer serve us will unravel or evaporate. This is a degree of suffering in the sign of those underfoot, so attention may turn to people who need help the most. This Eclipse takes place in the vicinity of the South Node, signaling a tendency to take the easy way out or pointing out what needs to be released. Uranus and the South Node are less than five degrees apart after their union Jan. 31 in Aries. Unpredictable actions and sudden bursts of anger are possible; the results are apt to be negative. This is exacerbated by Mars and Eris closely conjunct in Aries, a formula for ugly selfishness, disruption and reckless impulses. This is the tail end of a 0° "Moon Groove" (see p. 60) that began at the New Moon on Sept. 24, 2014, near the Autumn Equinox (at degree 29, it's within one degree of zero) and occurs just half a day away from the Spring Equinox. The times of season changes are important "seed" times for new energies to enter collective consciousness, and a Groove of New Moons at zero degrees shows an extended period of fresh approaches that spur growth. The Moon and Sun are sesquiquadrate Jupiter, inciting individuals to shy away from a sense of self-importance and focus more on their place within the whole of society. The month that follows this Eclipse is sure to be intense, particularly around the Full Moon, a Lunar Eclipse April 4 (see below).

★ **20** Spring Equinox—See Seasonal Synopses, p. 75.

★ **20** Sun enters Aries [until 4/20] As nature awakens from winter hibernation, people are motivated to be more physically active and to initiate new projects. The drive to distinguish oneself from the pack heightens. This is a natural time to exhibit leadership tendencies. Impatience also increases and many are in a rush.

★ **24** *Sun (3°38' AR) trine Juno (3°38' LE)*, in a Grand Trine with Saturn (4°49' SG). The Moon in Gemini makes this a Kite from approximately 10:30 am (P)/1:30 pm (E) to 4:30 pm (P)/7:30 pm (E), an acceptable window for a marriage chart. In addition, there is a Finger of God from Venus (8°13' TA) sextile Neptune (8°13' PI), exact in the wee hours that morning), both quincunx the North Node (10°32 LI). For a nice chart, aim to be pronounced a couple just minutes before sunset.

★ **30** *Mercury enters Aries* [until 4/14] This is a time to be forward and forceful in communications, though be aware that you could come on too strong for some people's tastes. Your speech may be quicker than usual and you're more prone to jumping to conclusions or sparking arguments.

★ **31** *Jupiter (12°41' LE) biquintile Chiron (18°41' PI)* [before 8/30/14; again 5/18/15] (Part of a Quintile Triangle with Venus—see April 11 & 12.) Beneficial improvements stem from this connection. It fosters relaxation creativity, spirituality and healing.

★ **31** *Mars enters Taurus* [until 5/11] It's time to slow down our actions and become deliberate and thorough. Though anger doesn't spring up quickly, once aroused it can be quite intense. Inertia is strong; it takes more time and oomph to get going, but after we're in motion, persistence leads to completion.

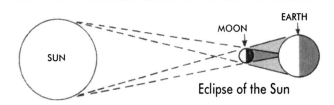

Eclipse of the Sun

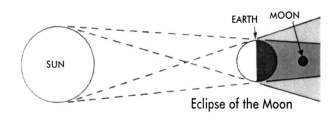

Eclipse of the Moon

APRIL

★ **3** *Ceres enters Aquarius* [until 8/3 (going Retrograde here) & again 1027–1/28/16] We want to nurture our friends and we find our relationship with them is very beneficial for us, too. We grow by involvement with a group or when engaging in humanitarian endeavors.

★ **4** *Lunar Eclipse Full Moon (14°24' LI)* This Lunar Eclipse is practically a twin to the one six months ago, with the Sun and Moon switching positions. Both eclipses are in a T-square with the Uranus-Pluto square and although that aspect is "officially over" now (see March 16), it is still in a tight orb and actually this T-square is tighter than the one at the Oct. 8, 2014 Eclipse. The Moon is near the North Node, which is supposed to help us move forward toward greater Libran harmony. In addition, the Moon is in a Quintile Triangle with Venus and Neptune, blending love and compassion into our relationships. In both 2014 and 2015, lunar eclipses fall on Jewish holidays, in the spring at Passover (4/15/14 and 4/4/15) and in autumn at the Feast of the Tabernacles, also called Sukkot (10/8/14 and 9/28/15). This is extremely rare! Of course, "end-timers" believe this portends the "Last Days" are upon us. In a way, they're right: the end of the Age of Pisces (dominated by Christianity) is here! (See Feb. 18.)

★ **8** *Jupiter (12°35' LE) turns Direct* [Retrograde since 12/8/14; Direct until 1/7/16] It's easier to grow and make progress when Jupiter is Direct. Pursuits are smoother in higher education, legal matters and long distance travel or communication with those at a distance (including the media and the internet).

★ **11** *Venus enters Gemini* [until 5/7] People are youthful, playful and flirtatious, possibly leading on more than one partner. Some may even find both genders attractive. Concepts and words are appealing and tact in conversations should come easily.

Although the Jupiter-Chiron biquintile is not exact now (see March 31), it is just under 1º from exact as Venus connects to them both, forming a fortuitous Quintile Triangle (next two aspects).

★ **11** *Venus (0°36' GE) quintile Jupiter (12°36' LE)* Creative talents are highlighted, especially in a verbal medium because of Venus' position in Gemini. Communications are open-minded and loving. Prospects improve for diplomatic efforts and better international relations (the Chiron component, below, helps in this regard).

★ **12** *Venus (1°23' GE) quintile Chiron (19°23' PI)* The healing power of love applies a salve to all types of relationships, particularly between siblings (a Gemini association) and partners or teammates of all sorts (Venus' territory).

★ **14** *Mercury enters Taurus* [until 4/30] We may absorb information slowly but our retention is greatly enhanced. Pay heed to monetary matters and pragmatic concerns. A good way to ground yourself is to roll up your sleeves in the kitchen, studio, workshop or outdoors.

★ **16** *Pluto (15°33' CP) turns Retrograde* [Direct since 9/22/14; Retrograde until 9/25/15] This shift can be subtle and go unnoticed, showing its effects more in retrospect. It signals a turning point, perhaps on a deep inner level, when we begin to re-assess values and resources, ours and other people's, to determine what's most important. The backward journey of Pluto is a time to be our own force for change in our lives, rather than expecting outside influences to turn our lives in a new direction. Financial matters may be strained around the time of the directional changes. With Pluto Retrograde in Capricorn, we re-examine the power structure of organizations and corporations to see what internal changes are needed. In our personal lives, we re-visit what we need to eliminate or move past, or what we can invest to further our careers.

★ **19** *Ceres (3°54' AQ) sextile Saturn (3°54' SG)* [again 8/11 (P), 8/12 (E) & 11/22] Putting time and effort into prodding projects or people along produces steady growth and plans that have fruitful prospects. A wide-ranging intellectual approach works well when these two planets are in Aquarius and Sagittarius now and at their third sextile. At their second sextile, they've retreated back into Capricorn and Scorpio, respectively (see Aug. 11–12).

★ **20** *Sun enters Taurus* [until 5/21] Our delight in nature and beauty is at its height, and we're creative in a tangible way (arts and crafts, gardening, etc.). Our practical side takes priority, with a focus on finances and possessions. This is a good time to seek and give physical affection.

★ **24** *Ceres (4°58' AQ) semisquare Chiron (19°58' PI)* [again 7/3 & 11/5] An attempt to "mother" humanity (even if you're a male) crashes into the lengthy list of ailments and problems needing attention. If you're dragging any emotional baggage from how you were raised (especially due to an aloof or unavailable parent), that hampers your ability to rescue others now.

★ **27** *Ceres (5°39' AQ) quintile Uranus (17°39' AR)* (Part of a Quintile Triangle with Venus—see May 7–9. Each occurrence of this aspect is part of a QT!) Individuals easily express their unique style and find friends or colleagues to be very supportive. On its own, this aspect is better suited to solo pursuits, but blended with Venus, it brings out a more social side.

★ **30** *Mercury enters Gemini* [until 7/8, going Retrograde here] Curiosity drives us to learn something in every activity. There's a lot more talk than usual, and more traveling in the local area. Increased contact with neighbors or siblings is likely.

MAY

★ **3** *(P),* **4** *(E) Saturn (2°59' SG) sesquiquadrate Uranus (17°59' AR)* [before 12/3/14; again 10/22] Although this is a "minor" aspect, the planets involved are major and the tension generated is significant. There is rebellion against the established stronghold and people in power attempt to repress those who want to alter the status quo. It's not just youth versus age, although there may be some of that perennial conflict, especially in personal lives. With Sagittarius involved, arenas of conflict are likely to include legislatures, institutions of higher learning and international relations. The Fire signs signal hot heads and rash behavior.

★ **7** *Venus enters Cancer* [until 6/5] Love of home, family, tribe and nation are of utmost importance. Nesting instincts are also strong. Attention turns to decorating or increasing the value of properties. It's natural to be emotional about relationships and exhibit a caring, protective side. Be careful how feelings affect monetary matters, though.

The Venus quintile and biquintile on May 7–9 form a Quintile Triangle with the Ceres-Uranus quintile on April 27 (see above).

★ **7** *Venus (0°11' CA) quintile Uranus (18°11' AR)* (Part of a Quintile Triangle—see April 27.) Associates bolster one another with warm affection and encouragement. Group endeavors flourish.

★ **9** *Mercury (9°30' GE) square Neptune (9°30' PI)* [again 5/29 & 6/23] This is the first of three repetitions due to Mercury going Retrograde on May 18. A left brain/right brain battle pits logic against imagination or wishful thinking. Conversations may take on a whiny tone or consist of complaints and requests for assistance.

★ **9** *Venus (1°28' CA) biquintile Ceres (7°28' AQ)* Camaraderie and cooperation team up to benefit any activity. Friends seem like family and family relations are very friendly.

★ **11** *Mars enters Gemini* [until 6/24] The tendency is to think fast, talk fast and drive fast. Minds are quicker than tongues, leading to stumbling speech. Be careful not to be too confrontational when being forward in conversations. A good debate hones mental skills.

Mars forms a Quintile Triangle with the Jupiter-Chiron biquintile (see the next three aspects):

★ **15** *Mars (2°38' GE) quintile Jupiter (14°38' LE)* Fresh ideas infused with enthusiasm and excitement spur creativity. Everyone seems lifted by a dose of youthful energy. Combined with Chiron (see next item), this QT is wonderful for school projects that are health-related or demonstrate problem-solving techniques, as well as educational meetings for health professionals.

★ **15** *(P),* **16** *(E) Mars (2°52' GE) quintile Chiron (20°52' PI)* Cutting edge concepts offer solutions and people take risks to make positive changes. Shy people are more comfortable speaking up and everyone seems to be vocal about their thoughts and feelings.

★ **18** *Jupiter (14°57' LE) biquintile Chiron (20°57' PI)* [before 8/30/14 & 3/31] A broad perspective and the ability to laugh at foibles help people to be nonjudgmental and forgiving. This marks a time of forward leaps in education or medicine.

★ **18** *Mercury (13°9' GE) turns Retrograde* [Direct since 2/11; Retrograde until 6/11] This entire back-up takes place in Gemini, which Mercury rules. Consequently, it's the most difficult sign for a Mercury Retrograde. Even though Mercury also rules Virgo and Retrogrades in that sign are troublesome, too, the Gemini backtracks affect ground transportation more since that is ruled by Gemini. (In both signs, communications suffer more than they do when Mercury is Retrograde in any of the other ten signs.) Compounding the potential for mix-ups and miscommunications in this round are the three squares Mercury makes to Neptune in the zigzag process, on 5/9, 5/29 and 6/23. Just to rub some salt in that wound, right as Mercury turns Retrograde this evening (less than 15 minutes afterward), the Moon squares Neptune, and 6 hours later conjuncts Mercury, in the wee hours of 5/19.

★ **21** *Sun enters Gemini* [until 6/21] Like social butterflies, everyone's flitting from one event or gathering to another, hearing stories and telling their own. Speech is dramatic. Mental or verbal originality is widely evident.

★ **21** *Jupiter (15°15' LE) quincunx Pluto (15°15' CP)* [before 9/5/14 & 2/27/15] (Part of two Fingers of God in June, first with Mars June 2–5 and then with the Sun June 5–8. See below.) See Feb. 27. Each planet is less than half a degree away from their positions at their earlier quincunx. In both instances, Jupiter is at the center of a fixed sign, a degree that operates similarly to 0° of Cardinal signs, having a wide impact.

Thank you for using Janet's Plan-it's Celestial Planner!

★ **27** *Venus (21°7' CA) semisquare Sun (6°7' GE)* [again 6/16, 10/7 & 11/17] This is the first of four semisquares in 2015 between Venus and the Sun. It's part of their regular dance to make two pair of semisquares. The two aspects in each pair are not far apart in time. The two pairs occur on either side of a Retrograde, one with Venus ahead of the Sun (as the Evening Star), the other with Venus behind the Sun (as the Morning Star). This Evening Star semisquare is in place for two New Moons (on May 17–18 and June 16), thus strongly affecting an eight-week period. With any semisquare between these two, love is more challenging, whether that's love between people or of oneself, maybe especially the latter. Financial matters can also be strained or suffer setbacks. This is part of the Grand Cross of April 20-23.

JUNE

From June 2 to 8, Mars and then the Sun form Fingers of God with the May 21 Jupiter-Pluto quincunx.

★ **2** *Mars (15°2' GE) quincunx Pluto (15°2' CP)* (Part of a Finger of God—see May 21, and June 5.) Tough talk to try to hold onto power is likely to have unintended consequences. It's better to take time to plan what to say and how and when to express it.

★ **2** (P), **3** (E) *Ceres (9°13' AQ) turns Retrograde* [Direct since 6/1/14; Retrograde until 9/14/15] Nurture yourself instead of looking to others for your care and emotional support. This is a good time to review your finances or insurance coverage with an eye toward making improvements.

★ **5** *Venus enters Leo* [until 7/18 & again 7/31 until 10/8, a two-part visit due to Venus' Retrograde] We're generous and dramatic in our affections, as well as loyal and steadfast. All forms of entertainment delight us and some people will yearn for the spotlight and benefit by being in it. The Retrograde portion (see p. 61) may bring problems from self-aggrandizement.

★ **5** *Sun (14°58' GE) quincunx Pluto (14°58' CP)* (Part of a Finger of God—see May 21.) Talk is cheap; results are what matters. Adaptability is an asset as long as it doesn't mutate into drifting off-course. Strong leadership and/or will power can keep things on track.

★ **5** *Mars (17°20' GE) sextile Jupiter (17°20' LE)* Part of a Finger of God—see May 21.) There's plenty of energy and determination to undertake large projects and push them toward completion. But be careful of unrealistic expectations and taking on more than is feasible. (Just by starting now brings this influence to an endeavor; it's not necessary for it be finished soon.)

★ **8** *Sun (17°47' GE) sextile Jupiter (17°47' LE)* (Part of a Finger of God—see May 21.) Utilizing an optimal level of confidence is the key to getting the most from this aspect and the opportunities it brings. Bright ideas abound and creative activities prosper.

★ **10** *Mercury (4°38' GE) sextile Venus (4°38' LE)* [again 7/5] Mercury has slowed to a stop (see June 11) and once it resumes forward motion, it will travel sextile Venus (with an orb of less than 5°) until July 10. By then, Venus is slowing down for its Retrograde and Mercury is getting up to full speed. This should be a period of harmonious communication and prosperous commerce.

★ **11** *Mercury (4°34' GE) turns Direct* [Retrograde since 5/18; Direct until 9/17] It will be a great relief to have Mercury moving forward again after this very trying backtrack (see May 18). We're not out of the woods until the shadow ends June 26 (see p. 61).

★ **12** *Neptune (9°49' PI) turns Retrograde* [Direct since 11/16/14; Retrograde until 11/18/15] Our personal connection to the Divine is more important to us than what others believe. Some may question their faith (or even their belief in themselves) but this is part of the process of re-affirming it. Now is a time when our busy lives remind us of the need for downtime.

★ **14** *Saturn re-enters Scorpio* [until 9/17/15; here before 10/5/12–12/23/14] Bring hard work and discipline to bear in areas needing major transformation. Perseverance and a "do or die" attitude ensure seeing things through to conclusion, even if it takes a long time. Undertake monumental projects, especially if these require the efforts and resources of many people. Economically, we may have a protracted period of slow growth (though it should be a steady trend). However, the opposite was the case when Saturn was in Scorpio in the Roaring 20s, mid-50s and mid-80s. The regulatory climate (under Saturn's bailiwick as ruler of laws) is an important factor. [See Mutual Receptions, p. 74.]

★ **16** *Venus (9°46' LE) semisquare Sun (26°46' GE)* [before 5/27; again 10/7 & 11/17] See May 27.

★ **20** *Saturn (29°39' SC) semisquare Pluto (14°39' CP)* [before 11/27/14; again 8/13/15] This is the second of three occurrences of the only difficult aspect these two planets make during their mutual reception of 2+ years. Last year, they were sextile and helped improve the running of organizations. Now, we assess if there are additional measures needed to get everything squared away and working right. Probably something needs to be eradicated and there is resistance to removing it until a replacement is available. Financial impediments hinder progress on individual and collective levels.

★ **21** *Summer Solstice*—See Seasonal Synopses, p. 75.

★ **21** *Sun enters Cancer* [until 7/22] People are more sensitive and emotional when the Sun is in Cancer. It's natural to put feelings into action, conveying lots of care. Our attention is on nutrition and enjoying culinary originality. People get into being homebodies and may have a greater interest in heritage and nationality.

★ **22** *Jupiter (20°2' LE) trine Uranus (20°2' AR)* [before 9/25/14 & 3/3/15] See March 3. This occurrence is especially beneficial for people or entities with something around 20° of a Fire sign in their birth chart.

★ **22** *Ceres (8°3' AQ) quintile Uranus (20°3' AR)* [before 4/27; again 11/17] (Part of a Quintile Triangle with the Sun June 23 and with Mars June 26–27.) See April 27. Something new comes out of the blue. Be careful if you don't want an unintended pregnancy—this afternoon is ripe for reproduction. (June 23 is not as conducive.)

★ **23** *Sun (1°57' CA) biquintile Ceres (7°57' AQ)* [Part of a Quintile Triangle—see June 22.] This fertile and creative combination is favorable for inventions and can be used well in group situations. It's great for brainstorming meetings.

★ **23** *Sun (2°4' CA) quintile Uranus (20°4' AR)* [Part of a Quintile Triangle—see June 22.] Occurring about three hours after the aspect directly above, the QT blends amplifies ingenuity. With the Sun in Cancer, activities at home or involving families would be fitting.

★ **24** *Chiron (21°33' PI) turns Retrograde* [Direct since 11/23/14; Retrograde until 11/28/15] It's time to address old hurts and put them in a current context to see the lessons learned. Look inward for healing and wisdom rather than receiving these from external sources.

★ **24** *Mars enters Cancer* [until 8/8] The tendency is to act on emotions, often impulsively. We're security-oriented, focused primarily on protecting home, family, tribe and nation.

★ **25** *Saturn (29°21' SC) biquintile Eris (23°21' AR)* [before 12/7/14; again 9/5] (Part of a Quintile Triangle with the Sun at 5° CA overnight June 26–27) Saturn quells some of the brashness and rashness that Eris in Aries generates. In both the 2015 occurrences, Saturn is at the last degree of Scorpio as it makes this aspect. Eris is famous for chaos. This aspect may open the door for volatility in financial markets (ruled by Scorpio) unless regulations (associated with Saturn) are in place to keep situations from spiraling out of control. The QT with the Sun in Cancer brings the public's emotions and worries into play: confidence drives markets up sharply; alarm prompts a downturn.

★ **25** *Jupiter (20°32' LE) biquintile Pluto (14°32' CP)* [before 10/7/14 & 1/20/15 (not in the Star Pages because there was no QT then)] The ability to make positive changes is enhanced, especially when creativity and the needed resources are applied. The Moon turns this into a brief Quintile Triangle on June 26 as it passes through 2° VI, providing an opportunity to use this beneficial transformative force on the job, in service to others or for health matters. The peak time is around 4:00 pm (P), 7:00 pm (E).

★ **26** *Mars (1°32' CA) biquintile Ceres (7°32' AQ)* (Part of a Quintile Triangle—see June 22.) When Mars is in Cancer, we don't usually approach a situation head-on, rather we come at it sideways. Here, a nurturing instinct pushes gently to bring out uniqueness or support group efforts.

★ **27** *Mars (2°10' CA) quintile Uranus (20°10' AR)* (Part of a Quintile Triangle—see June 22 and 26.) Confidence is strong enough to overcome shyness or insecurity and people take risks they might not otherwise try. This combo boosts a talent for starting something new.

In its Retrograde cycle, Venus makes the next aspects three times. This is the only instance in which they occur nearly simultaneously (magnified by the proximity to Jupiter—see July 1), creating challenging conditions in relationships.

★ **29** *Venus (20°12' LE) trine Uranus (20°12' AR)* [again 8/19 & 9/22] People are more free-wheeling in relationships and financial matters than they usually are, possibly ignoring future consequences and bordering on reckless

behavior. Self-concern is a stronger motivator than caring for others. Favorable lunar aspects the afternoon of June 30 offer the best opportunity for using this energy advantageously.

★ **29** *Venus (20°25' LE) semisquare North Node (5°25' LI) & sesquiquadrate South Node (5°25' AR)* [again 8/24 & 9/16] A hard choice between pleasing oneself and accommodating a partner or teammate must be made. The scales tip toward the selfish side of the equation.

★ **30** *Jupiter (21°32' LE) quincunx Chiron (21°32' PI)* [before 9/23/14 & 2/17/15] See Feb. 17. Your shine is enveloped in fog. You might trip up putting your best foot forward or get lost in the crowd when you're trying to stand out. Efforts for the benefit of a greater whole can be subverted by a single individual, especially if ego is out of proportion.

JULY

★ **1** *Venus (21°37' LE) conjunct Jupiter (21°37' LE)* [again 8/4 & 10/25] (The first two instances of this aspect are part of Venus' Retrograde cycle, now in the lead up to the actual backtrack and again while retracing its steps. Jupiter moves out of the Retrograde degree range before their third conjunction.) Normally, a Venus-Jupiter conjunction is very positive for love, but coming near the tough links to the Nodes (see June 29), it may have less of a boosting effect. Financially, it will likely be favorable, as long as investments or expenditures are not hasty or ill-conceived (see Venus trine Uranus, also on June 29). One thing for sure: this conjunction will be magnificent to behold in the western night sky after sunset for days before and after its exact, as it will be again in late July/early August.

★ **3** *Ceres (6°31' AQ) semisquare Chiron (21°31 PI)* [before 4/24; again 11/5] See April 24.

★ **3** *Venus (23°23' LE) trine Eris (23°23' AR)* [again 8/14 & 9/29] (Another triple aspect due to Venus' Retrogradation.) Being in a hurry rushes the development of relationships or consideration of expenditures. People tend to pay more attention to what they want than what is best for all concerned.

★ **8** *Mercury enters Cancer* [until 7/23] Feelings intrude into our thinking and logic may elude us at times. Discussing or journaling about emotions brings insight. Our minds are on home or family issues and there could be news on this front. ESP is enhanced. In a few days (7/10–12), Mercury will pass the USA's natal Venus and Jupiter, which may bring announcements about financial or international issues.

★ **10** *Jupiter (23°24' LE) trine Eris (23°24' AR)* [before 11/23/14 & 12/26/14] International relations suffer if leaders are unreasonably stubborn and selfish or egotistical. In families or companies, similar overbearing dictatorial practices could cause problems. This high-energy aspect can be used in a positive way in sports or competitions.

Want to learn more about astrology? Visit JanetsPlan-its.com

★ **18** *Venus enters Virgo* [until 7/31, going Retrograde here; returning 10/8–11/8] Social niceties and etiquette are important. Appreciate refinement and when care is given to details. Try to avoid being critical in relationships. Be selective in accepting social invitations, choosy about partners or friends, and careful in finances.

★ **19** *Eris (23°25' AR) turns Retrograde* [Direct since 1/9/15; Retrograde until 1/10/16] When Eris is Retrograde, we can benefit by examining how we undermine our own efforts or bring disorder into our lives. When it's Direct, we're more likely to notice how disruption comes from sources beyond ourselves.

★ **22** *Sun enters Leo* [until 8/23] Fun and innovation take center stage, whether with children or by letting our inner child out to play. Romance and risk-taking are appealing. Go after your heart's desires with unwavering determination.

★ **23** *Mercury enters Leo* [until 8/7] Our playful side emerges, along with lots of creativity. It's easy to communicate with children and to express joy. People speak dramatically and might be stubborn or self-concerned in their thinking.

★ **25** *Venus (0°46' VI) turns Retrograde*, marked on Janet's Plan-its daily lines by **VR** [Direct since 1/31/14; Retrograde until 9/6/15] Venus goes Retrograde five times in eight earth years, like clockwork. If you plot the degrees of the Retrograde stations on the zodiac circle, they create a five-pointed star (related to using pentagrams in magic). During a Venus Retrograde, some people may re-connect with a former lover or person of significance in their lives, or a current relationship may repeat a pattern of a prior one or involve a new partner reminiscent of an old one. This is a time to re-affirm your love for yourself or work on issues of self-acceptance. This is always true of a Venus Retrograde, but especially so this time as Venus backtracks from self-critical Virgo into egocentric Leo.

★ **26** *Uranus (20°30' AR) turns Retrograde* [Direct since 12/21/14; Retrograde until 12/25/15] Benefits come from re-assessing friendships and group affiliations to see whether they promote or hinder one's individuality. There is an increased need to be more authentic or to develop uniqueness. We re-examine ways to do this.

★ **31** *Venus re-enters Leo* [until 10/8; before 6/5–7/18] See June 5.

AUGUST

★ **2** *Saturn (28°17' SC) turns Direct* [Retrograde since 3/14/15; Direct until 3/25/16] Putting things into clear form and understanding the rules of the game are easier when Saturn is Direct. People are better at responding to external authority and conforming to objective standards, relying less on personal judgments.

★ **3** *Jupiter (28°17' LE) square Saturn (28°17' SC)* [again 3/23/16 & 5/26/16—these repetitions are after Jupiter enters Virgo and Saturn returns to Sagittarius] This is by far the hardest occurrence of the three, coming with nearly concurrent difficult aspects from Jupiter and Saturn to Pluto (see Aug. 4 & 13), exacerbated by the involvement of Mercury and Venus (see Highlights and Astro-Overview

for August 3–9). As the sole Jupiter-Saturn square from Leo to Saturn, it prods us to pierce pride and step up to the plate of responsibilities, probably to an extreme measure because of their interaction now with Pluto. The party's over, if there even was one. These are Fixed signs, focusing us on maintaining what's in motion. However, a square calls for a modification. We drag our feet toward change. It will be easier to adapt with the next two squares in Mutable signs.

★ **3** *Ceres re-enters Capricorn* [until 10/27; here before 1/8–4/3] See Jan. 8.

★ **4** *Jupiter (28°34' LE) sesquiquadrate Pluto (13°34' CP)* [There are no repetitions of this aspect. One and done. They are in the second half of their current cycle, Jupiter having opposed Pluto in April 2014 for the midway point. The cycle began when Jupiter passed Pluto (once) on 12/11/07 and lasts until they meet again three times in 2020.] If there's a situation that should have been over, more than a year ago, now is the time to give up the ghost. It's impossible to move forward without leaving something behind. If it's slow-going, go slowly, but go.

★ **4** *Venus (28°35' LE) conjunct Jupiter (28°35' LE)* [before 7/1; again 10/25] See July 1. This occurrence isn't an easy time for finances (though the prior instance wasn't so bad for them), nor for romance and relationships. This is not only because Venus is now Retrograde, but also due to the current Jupiter- Saturn-Pluto tangle (see Aug. 3). Venus is also sesquiquadrate Pluto today! The usual glory of a Venus-Jupiter conjunction is dimmed, other than the stunning beauty of these two bright planets in the twilight sky. The self-love that ordinarily comes with this team-up may be twisted into sickeningly sweet manipulation by Pluto's power-driven agenda. At best, joy comes from beautification via taking out the trash, or generosity of spirit or funds contributes to making a difference in some way, but it comes at a price.

★ **7** *Mercury enters Virgo* [until 8/27] As you pay close attention to your work, don't get lost in details. Those who tend to be conscientious about serving others might put themselves on the back burner. Health is on our minds.

★ **8** *Mars enters Leo* [until 9/24] Our actions are dramatic and we bring a creative flair to all we do. We have a high level of vitality. Our "inner child" wants to come out to play. This is a good time to get in touch with masculine power, the hero archetype, of which everyone regardless of gender is capable. Sports and competitions offer a joyful respite from our labors.

★ **11** *Jupiter enters Virgo* [until 9/9/16] After a year when play and creativity dominated the landscape, we turn to the mound of work that always awaits us. We are up to the task and can handle a plethora of details well. Benefits follow where Jupiter moves. Virgo represents labor conditions and the work force. Expect an increase in union participation, bargaining and lobbying. Virgo is an earth sign and related to health, so we'll turn our attention to the health of the earth and its inhabitants. Virgo is also a sign of service and assistance, while Jupiter is a planet indicating international affairs. NGOs will play a greater role in improving the lot of people in underprivileged countries.

★ **11** *(P)*, **12** *(E)* *Ceres (28°21' CP) sextile Saturn (28°21' SC)* [before 4/19; again 11/22] At their other sextiles, these two are in different signs (see April 19). Now the emphasis is on sharing and strategic use of resources. The tendency is to be more practical (probably even downright frugal) rather than free-wheeling and uninhibited, as at the other occurrences.

★ **13** *Saturn (28°23' SC) semisquare Pluto (13°23' CP)* [before 11/27/14 & 6/20/15] This is the third of three occurrences of this aspect (see June 20) and apt to be the most difficult since Jupiter is still in proximity of grating against these two planets (see August 3).

★ **15** *Venus (22°39' LE) conjunct Sun (22°39' LE)* This is a very quick conjunction, within a 1° orb for only about 30 hours. Venus and the Sun whip past each other and flee off in opposite directions, unlike their conjunction when Venus is Direct. Then they travel together at about the same speed, within 1° for eight days. Their meeting in the sign the Sun rules highlights the joie de vivre, passion, creativity and fashionable flair of Leo.

The next two aspects form a Quintile Triangle with the Saturn-Eris biquintile—see Sept. 5.

★ **17** *Mercury (16°28' VI) quintile Saturn (28°28' SC)* People notice those who are intelligent and know what they're talking about. Words, chosen carefully, garner respect and turn opinions, helping bring about smart changes.

★ **18** *Mercury (17°20' VI) biquintile Eris (23°20' AR)* Open mouth, insert foot, beat yourself up after. OR out of a sense of duty, say the hard things that need to be said, even if you come under attack for it.

★ **19** *Chiron (20°16' PI) semisextile Uranus (20°16' AR)* [before 13 times 2009–14; again 11/25/15, 8/9/16, 12/10/16 & 9 more times 2017–2021] Letting your uniqueness shine is very healing. It should be a source of satisfaction rather than shame. If you've felt you had to hide in the shadows because of some flaw, you will have many chances over the coming years to make improvements. Treat yourself gently regarding your imperfections rather than berating yourself. (See Long-term Influences, p. 74.)

★ **23** *Sun enters Virgo* [until 9/23] We're patient, polite and humble (except when taking pride in a job well done). Helping comes naturally and great care can be given to all the little things. Most of us shy away from big risks. Watch out for Virgo's down side: analysis leads to paralysis.

★ **24** *Venus (17°26' LE) semisquare North Node (2°26' LI) & sesquiquadrate South Node (2°26' AR)* [before 6/29; again 9/16] See June 29.

★ **27** *Mercury enters Libra* [until 11/1 (P), 11/2 (E), going Retrograde in this sign—see Sept. 17] Fairness is on our minds. Social conversation is easy, aimed at keeping the peace by using negotiating skills. We're easily able to conceptualize and understand abstractions and we enjoy a lively debate.

★ **31** *(P)* See September 1.

To get Janet's free e-newsletters, sign-up at JanetsPlan-its.com.

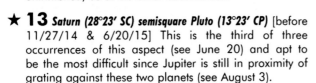

SEPTEMBER

★ **1** *(E)* *Venus (14°55' LE) conjunct Mars (14°55' LE)* [before 2/22; again 11/2—neither time is part of the current Retrograde cycle] This occurs at the degree of the Feb. 3 Full Moon. Current developments may connect to what was happening then; issues or events from around that time may spiral to a new level now. Passions are dramatic when these two meet in Leo. We're impatient to fulfill fervent desires. Our fires can burn resolutely.

★ **2** *Jupiter (4°55' VI) sesquiquadrate Uranus (19°55' AR)* (Just to show how far past its square to Pluto that Uranus has traveled, it's been a month since Jupiter was sesquiquadrate Pluto. With a tight square, only a few days would elapse between the two aspects.) The atmosphere now may be reminiscent of April 20–23, 2014, when Jupiter, Uranus and Pluto last had a run-in. The luck of the Jupiter-Uranus trine (see June 22) has faded, replaced by sudden weird occurrences and unusual difficulties. Impetus to move forward is dragged down by the weight of details and duties, the trappings of Virgo.

★ **5** *Saturn (29°13' SC) biquintile Eris (23°13' AR)* [before 12/7/14 & 6/25/15] (Part of a Quintile Triangle with Mercury on Aug. 17–18.) See June 25. The QT with Mercury presents an opportunity to be a spokesperson for change by shaking trees. This aspect certainly doesn't let established ways continue without a hitch. Something goes awry to expose the weak spots in a process or system so they may be addressed.

★ **6** *Venus (14°23' LE) turns Direct* [Retrograde since 7/25; Direct until 3/4/17] After 40 days of relationship and/or financial matters seeming to slip backwards, we can turn them around and apply the lessons learned to achieve momentum for a new way ahead. Even as progress resumes, there are situations to clear up related to the aspects that have already occurred twice, first in the lead-up to the Retrograde and then during the back-up itself. An important trait to carry forward is the self-approval from Leo to counteract the self-criticism from Virgo as Venus enters that sign again on Oct. 8.

★ **8** *Neptune (8°12' PI) semisquare Eris (23° 12' AR)* [before 2/26; again 12/22] (The Aug. 29 Full Moon in Pisces conjunct Neptune put this aspect in the spotlight—see Highlights for August 24–30). See Feb. 26. This is a heavier influence than the prior instance due to Jupiter's magnifying aspects to these two (see Sept. 16–17) and the Solar Eclipse Sept. 13.

★ **9** *Mercury (13°2' LI) square Pluto (13°2' CP)* [again 9/24 & 10/22] This is the only aspect Mercury makes three times in its fall Retrograde cycle. It does make semisquares to Venus and Saturn, but only twice since they move out of Mercury's Retrograde range. A drive to uncover motives, secrets or foundations spurs us to dig below surfaces and research. Discussions are probing and likely to be uncomfortable. Everybody seems to be an armchair psychologist now.

★ **12** *(P)*, **13** *(E)* *Solar Eclipse New Moon* This is a tame eclipse by recent standards. It's rather weak: the Moon and Sun are as far from a Node as is possible to produce an eclipse. (In this case, it's the Node they're near, pulling us in the direction of more equitable relations.) They only make two tight aspects, an opposition to Chiron and a quincunx to Uranus, amplifying the Chiron-Uranus semisextile (exact 8/19 & 11/25). The focus is on helpfulness in general and aiding the masses, especially workers who have suffered discrimination. Individuals may be motivated to exercise more for the sake of their health. There are no major aspect patterns present. The Nodes' interaction with Saturn (see Sept. 26) is fairly strong at this eclipse and even stronger at the next one, the Full Moon on Sept. 27.

★ **14** *Ceres (25°6' CP) turns Direct* [Retrograde since 6/3; Direct until 8/31/16] We have a better chance of receiving abundance during Ceres' Direct times. When we feel that our "cup runneth over," we share more and are rewarded with additional bounty. We're also able to express our nurturing side more easily when Ceres is Direct. Having backtracked into Capricorn from Aquarius, we gained a better appreciation for the rules that permit society to function. When Ceres re-enters Aquarius, we bring that understanding into our group interactions. In our personal lives, we've drawn lines that soon we'll find enable us to be a better friend.

★ **16** *Venus (16°15' LE) semisquare North Node (1°15' LI) & sesquiquadrate South Node (1°15' AR)* [before 6/29 & 8/24] See June 29.

★ **16** *(P)*, **17** *(E) Jupiter (7°58' VI) opposite Neptune (7°58' PI)* [Another one-hit wonder, this aspect does not repeat.] Trust issues mar operations in service situations. People either expect too much or have a misguided notion of what is realistic. Health conditions are magnified. The tendency for projection is high.

★ **17** *Mercury (15°55' LI) turns Retrograde* [Direct since 6/11; Retrograde until 10/9] Another backtrack for the planet of communication and ground transportation, this time entirely in the sign of Libra. Relationships undergo review, re-thinking, re-discussing, and after running everything through the mill, hopefully come out better balanced and more harmonious.

★ **17** *Jupiter (8°7' VI) sesquiquadrate Eris (23°7' AR)* Disruptions interrupt our work and progress, agitating impatient people. Criticism causes discord. We get wrapped up in our own concerns and don't stop to help others.

★ **17** *Saturn enters re-Sagittarius* [until 12/19/17; here before 12/23/14–6/14/15] See As We Begin 2015, p. 73.

★ **23** *Autumn Equinox*—See Seasonal Synopses, p. 75. Pluto's nearby station (see Sept. 24–25) means there is inertia to overcome before we can make much progress.

★ **23** *Sun enters Libra* [until 10/23] Relationships are foremost on our radar screen. Social obligations keep us busy, to the detriment of personal objectives. Seek balance in your life and harmony in your soul.

★ **24** *Mars enters Virgo* [until 11/12] We're more fastidious and precise in our actions and prefer not to do dirty work, unless it's cleaning up. Arguments are laced with judgments. The pen is mightier than the sword. Time to work out and shape up.

★ **24** *(P)*, **25** *(E) Pluto (12°58' CP) turns Direct* [Retrograde since 4/16/15; Direct until 4/18/16] Financial matters involving more than one person's money (banking, investments, insurance, inheritance, grants, etc.) function

more smoothly when Pluto is Direct. Examine motives in order to better understand the foundation of situations. It should be easier to proceed with letting go of what's outworn in our lives.

★ **26** *North Node (0°41' LI) sextile & South Node (0°41' AR) trine Saturn (0°41' SG)* These directional indicators for forward progress (North Node) and what needs to be released or left behind to move ahead (South Node) are at the end of their passage through Libra and Aries, the sign of significant other and self, respectively. They're at the important 0° of Cardinal signs, heralding the widespread effects of the positive shifts promoted by the good boundaries, respect, maturity and hard work that Saturn inspires us to achieve. Since the position of the Nodes is always in range of eclipse degrees and this aspect occurs the day before an eclipse, the effects are all the more potent and far-ranging.

★ **27** *Lunar Eclipse Full Moon (4°40' AR)* No aspect patterns are precise at this Full Moon, so even though any eclipse packs more of a punch than a vanilla new or full moon, this one is tame for the most part (hence the 4 day rating). The tightest aspects present (all less than a degree from exact) are some that many astrologers ignore either because the aspect is minor, as with Mercury semisextile Jupiter, or planets involved are dwarfs: Ceres sesquiquadrate and Neptune semisquare Eris. The Venus-Sun semisquare is 2-1/2° from being precise and is another minor aspect (still, the toughest connection possible between these two heavenly bodies). The outstanding aspect award goes to Mars square Saturn, just over a degree in orb. While a hard link between two malefics is no picnic, when it's not aggravated by other planets, it's not so bad. It signifies an uphill struggle but not an impossible aim. We'll feel it more on the 25th when the Moon makes a brief T-square with them. As a South Node eclipse, it heralds a time for release. Its sign, Aries, shows what to discard: anger.

★ **30** *(P)* See Oct. 1.

OCTOBER

★ **1** *(E) Ceres (25°52' CP) sesquiquadrate Jupiter (10°52' VI)* [again 11/10 & 3/13/16] Ceres is named for the harvest goddess and relates to the cornucopia as a symbol. Jupiter is a planet of growth and expansion. Both are associated with abundance. So when they clash, there may be difficulties with crops (Virgo rules grains), fertility or returns on investments.

★ **7** *Venus (29°27' LE) semisquare Sun (14°27' LI)* [before 5/27 & 6/16; again 11/17] See May 27. This semisquare is within a 1° orb from Oct. 3 to Oct. 15, including at the New Moon on Oct. 12. Venus and the Sun are also in a mutual reception (see p. 74). Venus is traveling behind the Sun now, visible in the morning sky. Generally, this is considered the time of Venus in her warrior guise rather than the archetype of the lover. The fight could be for fairness.

★ **8** *Venus re-enters Virgo* [until 11/8; here before 7/18–7/31 See July 18.

★ **9** *Mercury (0°54' LI) turns Direct* [Retrograde since 9/17; Direct until 1/5/16] It's time to get communication within relationships back on track.

★ **9** *Jupiter (12°36' VI) biquintile Uranus (18°36' AR)* [again 4/10/16 & 7/9/16] (not part of a Quintile Triangle) Benefits spout from this positive connection from the planet of increase and good fortune to the planet that acts suddenly and out of the blue.

★ **9** *North Node (29°59' VI) enters Virgo & South Node (29°59' PI) enters Pisces* [until 4/28/17] The Nodes spend about 18 months in a pair of opposite signs, stimulating us to aspire toward the best qualities of the North Node's sign and move past the most challenging traits of the South Node's sign. Eclipses occur in the signs where the Nodes travel, emphasizing this journey of growth. Both Virgo and Pisces are service-oriented, making that a key theme in the coming year-and-a-half. Virgo entreats us to be grounded, efficient, useful, conscientious and self-perfecting. Piscean characteristics to consider eliminating are spacing out, drifting, letting things slide, laziness or laissez-faire-ness.

★ **11** *Jupiter (13°2' VI) trine Pluto (13°2' CP)* [again 3/16/16 & 6/26/16] Motivation is heightened to excel in our work, succeed in business or career endeavors, and make a difference in some area. There's a greater tendency to go overboard or to extremes when either of these planets is active; when combined, double that.

★ **22** *Saturn (3°4' SG) sesquiquadrate Uranus (18°4' AR)* [before 12/3/14 & 5/3 (P), 5/4 (E)] See May 3–4.

★ **23** *Sun enters Scorpio* [until 11/22] For the next four weeks, try to change your life in some way, applying will power and intention to move past blocks and obstacles. Begin a new chapter with a greater sense of control. Tenacity won't let anything get the better of you.

★ **25** *Venus (15°38' VI) conjunct Jupiter (15°38' VI)* [before 7/1 & 8/4] See July 1. Both these bright celestial objects are Morning Stars now, so to see their meet-up, you'll have to get up before dawn. The aspects they share around this conjunction (near to Mars and trine to Pluto) are much nicer than in the prior two occurrences. Hence, finances and relationships should fare better now.

★ **27** *Ceres enters Aquarius* [until 1/28/16] This period is the time to increase your group affiliations and add to your circle of friends and acquaintances. You'll find encouragement and support is a two-way street with them. Applying an intelligent approach to any situation helps it flourish.

NOVEMBER

★ **1** *Daylight Saving Time* ends at 2:00 am local time. Re-set time devices to an hour earlier.

★ **1** *(P),* **2** *(E) Mercury enters Scorpio* [until 11/20] Our minds may be on survival matters, finances, sex or reproduction, and our thinking is affected by deep feelings. We have a sharp understanding of motives (including our own) and what makes people tick.

★ **2** *Venus (24°2' VI) conjunct Mars (24°2' VI)* [before 2/21–22 & 8/31–9/1] The two prior conjunctions were in Fire signs, sparking us into action. Now, we deliberate and assess. What we choose to do will be based on core values.

★ **3** *Jupiter (17°12' VI) opposite Chiron (17°12' PI)* [again 2/23/16 & 8/12/16] This aspect weaves a harsh knot with Ceres (see Nov. 5 & 10). At worst, there is increased pain in care-taking situations. At best, healing comes through more or better nurturing, but this isn't easy to achieve.

★ **5** *Jupiter (17°32' VI) quincunx Uranus (17°32' AR)* [again 3/6/16 & 8/13/16] (This aspect forms a Finger of God with the Sun (Nov. 9–19) and Mercury Nov. 12–13—see below.) An overload of details could slow us down. People have a hard time balancing their personal agenda with what they need to do for others or for their work. The best this duo can offer us is brainy ingenuity. The upcoming Fingers of God just might bring that out.

★ **5** *Ceres (2°10' AQ) semisquare Chiron (17°10 PI)* [before 4/24 & 7/3] See April 24.

★ **8** *Venus enters Libra* [until 12/4] Fairness and equality are top values now, and we want relationships to be on an even keel. People act with more gentility and diplomacy. Romance flourishes.

★ **9** *Sun (17°23' SC) quincunx Uranus (17°23' AR)* We want to rebel against "the boss" in whatever form that takes: a father, an authority figure, even one's own self-imposed rules. However, the situation is not clear-cut and we may hold back.

★ **10** *Ceres (3°16 AQ) sesquiquadrate Jupiter (18°16' VI)* [before 9/30 (P), 10/1 (E); again 3/13/16] See Sept. 30–Oct. 1. Midway between then and now, Mars joins Jupiter and echoes the sesquiquadrate with Ceres (see Astro-Overview for the week of Oct. 12–18).

★ **10** *Sun (18°21' SC) sextile Jupiter (18°21' VI)* This beneficial aspect improves the expression of the two quincunxes it joins into a Finger of God (see Nov. 5 & 9). In this combination, wisdom and leadership have a moderating effect on impatience and agitation. The creative traits of the Sun blend with Uranus's inventiveness, while Jupiter in Virgo steers the results into a useful outcome.

★ **12** *Mercury (17°18' SC) quincunx Uranus (17°18' AR)* (in a Finger of God with the Jupiter-Uranus quincunx Uranus of Nov. 5) Following on the heels of the Sun's Finger of God (Nov. 10), this configuration spreads the news and puts flesh on the bones of what was envisioned then.

★ **12** *Mars enters Libra* [until 1/3/16] Libra is opposite Aries, the sign Mars rules, and Mars doesn't get to be its usual independent and assertive self now. We offer cooperation instead of being defensive. Physical vitality might be low and we accept aid more readily.

★ **13** *Mercury (18°45' SC) sextile Jupiter (18°45' VI)* Research and hard work go hand-in-hand to promote the smart ideas generated with the other two components of this Finger of God triangle (see Nov. 5).

The next five aspects are part of a very precise Quintile Triangle Nov. 15–17. Mercury and the Sun were just quincunx Uranus in Fingers of God (see Nov. 9–13). Since a biquintile (144º) and a quincunx (150º) are only 4 degrees apart, speedy heavenly bodies like Mercury and the Sun easily shift to a QT from a Finger of God or vice versa. This pattern involves Ceres instead of Jupiter; both indicate growth and prosperity.

★ **15** *Sun (22°30' SC) quintile Ceres (4°30' AQ)* Originality and inspiration contribute to the success of individual or group undertakings. When values or resources are shared, everybody benefits.

★ **15** *Sun (23°12' SC) biquintile Uranus (17°12' AR)* Bravery and confidence propel us forward to the cutting edge.

★ **16** *Mercury (22°48' SC) quintile Ceres (4°48' AQ)* We find the right words to make a difference, with a wide impact.

★ **16** *Mercury (23°11' SC) biquintile Uranus (17°11' AR)* Deep insights flash like lightening: quick, sudden, brightening.

★ **17** *Ceres (5°9' AQ) quintile Uranus (17°9' AR)* Unusual ways of showing support work to advantage. Intelligence combines with bravado to help us take smart risks.

★ **17** *Venus (10°31' LI) semisquare Sun (25°31' SC)* [before 5/27, 6/16 & 10/7) See May 27 and Oct. 7. This semisquare is within a 1° orb from Nov. 7 through Nov. 25, including at the New Moon on Nov. 11.) Relationships may have a better time now since Venus is in Libra and together both rule partnering.

★ **18** *Neptune (7°1' PI) turns Direct* [Retrograde since 6/12; Direct until 6/13/16] After months of turning to ourselves for spiritual guidance, we incorporate input from others in matters of faith. We find it easier to trust people.

★ **20** *Mercury enters Sagittarius* [until 12/9] Minds are quick and intuition is strong, though our attention span may be shorter than usual. Reading and learning (perhaps a new language) are appealing. This doesn't have to mean books and the library; the internet is a rich source of information. (See Mutual Receptions, p. 74.)

★ **22** *Ceres (6°33 AQ) sextile Saturn (6°33' SG)* [before 4/19 & 8/11 (P), 8/12 (E)] See April 19.

★ **22** *Sun enters Sagittarius* [until 12/21] The sky's the limit! Stretch yourself upward and onward. It's a good time for travel, study, law, journalism and contact with those at a distance – anything that increases our knowledge and understanding.

★ **25** *Chiron (16°56' PI) semisextile Uranus (16°56' AR)* [before 13 times 2009–2014 & 8/19/15; again 8/9/16, 12/10/16 & 9 more times through 2021] See Aug. 19. Occurring close to the Chiron Direct station Nov. 28 makes this instance likely to be more long-lasting in the assistance it provides.

★ **26** *Saturn (7°2' SG) square Neptune (7°2' PI)* [again 6/17/16 & 9/10/16] (This occurrence doesn't happen as a singular event. It comes encumbered in a tangle of tough aspects with other planets, most notably Eris. See Highlights and Astro-Overview for Nov. 23–29, Nov. 29, below and Feb. 26.) Like a heavy-weight prize fight, this powerful aspect will go many rounds before it's done with knocking some sense into our belief systems.

★ **28** *Chiron (16°56' PI) turns Direct* [Retrograde since 6/24; Direct until 6/27/16] The past five months were a time to address our internal wounds and be our own inspiration for improvement. Going forward, we can seek such support externally and more easily provide it to others, as well. As both Neptune and Chiron advance rather than retreat, health matters are more likely to improve.

★ **29** *Saturn (7°27' SG) sesquiquadrate Eris (22°27' AR)* [This doesn't repeat by Retrograde.] Saturn's confining rings cannot corral Eris' unruly character entirely, but we do try to keep a lid on disruptive influences. The attempt to stick to principles may fly out the window when faced with urgent expediencies.

DECEMBER

★ **4** *Mars (13°5' LI) biquintile Neptune (7°5' PI)* (Part of a Quintile Triangle with Mercury Dec. 6–7, below.) Compassion and a belief in equality move us to come to the aid of people who are being mistreated.

★ **4** *Venus enters Scorpio* [until 12/29 (P), 12/30 (E)] Your level of passion increases for people and things you desire. Any insecurity you might have about love or money is more likely to surface now. Extremes are possible in fashion or spending; this is not when you stick to the middle road.

★ **6** *Mars (14°12' LI) square Pluto (14°12' CP)* The last time Mars was in Libra (in the first half of 2014), it was Retrograde there, forming T-squares with Uranus and Pluto three times. The second time, on one intense day (April 23), occurred right as Jupiter in Cancer made a Grand Cross with them. Mars is opposite Uranus Dec. 10 (see below). This T-square, occurring over four days, is not as short nor as sharp as last year's but will likely still sting and perhaps bring our attention back to issues that were prominent then. Mars' simultaneous involvement in a QT (see below) will take the edge off.

The next two aspects are in a Quintile Triangle with the Mars-Neptune biquintile on Dec. 4 (see above).

★ **6** *Mercury (25°6' SG) quintile Neptune (7°6' PI)* Far-sighted vision mixes with imagination to cook up creative ideas. Sympathy is strong, especially for students and foreigners.

★ **7** *Mercury (26°57' SG) quintile Mars (14°57' LI)* Thoughts and words are easily translated into action, though not in a pushy way. Consideration for others is an important ingredient.

★ **9** *Mercury enters Capricorn* [until 1/1/16; again 1/8/16–2/13/16] Mental acuity results from concentrating on one item at a time. Focus is easy to achieve, but at the cost of tenderness. Some turn a cold shoulder toward weakness, in themselves or others. Get organized in your communications and say things simply.

★ **10** *Mars (16°39' LI) opposite Uranus (16°39' AR)* See Dec. 6. A clash between these two is volatile and accident-prone. The prospects for a fight are reduced because of Mars' position in conflict-averse Libra.

★ **15** *Jupiter (22°21' VI) quincunx Eris (22°21' AR)* [again 1/31/16 (when Ceres creates a Finger of God with them) & 8/8/16 (P), 8/9/16 (E)] The Virgo tendency for analysis to lead to paralysis may slow Eris in Aries' impulsiveness down enough to prevent reckless errors. Jupiter contributes a big heart to counteract Aries' selfishness.

★ **21** *Winter Solstice*—See Seasonal Synopses, p. 75.

Do you have your 2016 Janet's Plan-its Celestial Planner?

★ **21** *Sun enters Capricorn* [until 1/20/16] A focus on work and career, coupled with conscientious effort, helps us achieve goals and win appreciation on the job. We care what people think about us and strive to maintain a good reputation.

★ **21** *(P),* **22** *(E) Neptune (7°20' Pl) semisquare Eris (22°20' AR)* [before 2/26 & 9/8] See Feb. 26. By the third instance of an aspect, the hard part is usually over. This occurrence comes without additional difficulty of simultaneous harsh aspects, as was the case in Sept.

★ **25** *Uranus (16°33' AR) turns Direct* [Retrograde since 7/26; Direct until 7/29/16] The past five months, we've turned inward to seek a spark for self-development. While

Uranus is Direct, our individuality is recognized and promoted by others. When Uranus is Retrograde, we sometimes rebel against our own advice to ourselves. When it's in forward motion, we're more likely to revolt against other people's orders.

★ **29** *(P),* **30** *(E) Venus enters Sagittarius* [until 1/23/16] Optimism in romance is much easier than earlier this month. Significant others are supportive and beneficial. Better possibilities are ours for the taking in social and/or financial matters. Connect with people far and wide, whether in person or via mail, phone or the internet. This is a sweet note upon which to bring the year to a close!

JANUARY 2016

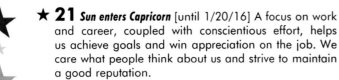

The Sun, South Node and Mars form a Quintile Triangle from Jan. 1–2 to Jan. 5 (see below). While this configuration is in process, Mars changes sign, shifting us from being highly concerned about what others think of us to being on a mission for change no matter the cost.

★ **1** *Mercury enters Aquarius* [until 1/8; again 2/13–3/5; a two-part visit due to going Retrograde] (Mercury barely steps into Aquarius before it turns tail and heads back to Capricorn, going Retrograde 1/5—see below). New topics of interest arise. People are more curious about metaphysics and anything labeled "New Age." Inventiveness and intuition are strong but so are opinions. We gravitate toward group learning opportunities and discussions.

★ **1** *(P),* **2** *(E) Sun (11°14' CP) quintile Mars (29°14' LI)* It's possible be strong and resolute while also being attentive and caring. This aspect blends both stances nicely.

★ **3** *Mars enters Scorpio* [until 3/5/16; again 5/27–8/2] (Mars moves through Scorpio into Sagittarius, where it goes Retrograde 4/17/16, then backtracks into Scorpio for a second visit. Once it's Direct, it re-enters Sagittarius.) This is the time to make changes and discard what isn't working in your life. With Mars' anger tendency added to Scorpio's explosive side, sensitivities easily escalate into arguments. Physical activities (workouts, sex, etc.) are more intense. Beware of going to extremes.

★ **4** *Sun (13°25' CP) quintile South Node (25°25' Pl)* If there's an area in which you are too lenient for your own good (or someone else's), this aspect will help you nip that tendency without gravitating to an overbearing opposite pole.

★ **5** *Mercury (1°3' AQ) turns Retrograde* [Direct since 10/9/15; Retrograde until 1/25/16] This backtrack asks us to revisit practical concerns after considering non-mainstream views. Ideally, we'll enjoy the best of both once Mercury returns to forward motion.

★ **5** *South Node (25°20' Pl) biquintile Mars (1°20' SC)* The urge to purge from Mars in Scorpio is softened (but not eliminated) by sentimentality, so you'll kiss those mementos goodbye before you throw them away. Mars' intensity in Scorpio could be diluted by the ease with which we drift off-course from the South Node in Pisces. It's more likely that with the Capricorn Sun in this QT, we'll be driven by goals or a sense of duty.

LOOKING AHEAD TO 2016

Be sure to see 2016 On a Page (p. 89).

The Jupiter-Saturn square, which got underway in 2015 (see Aug. 3), heats up for another occurrence on March 23 (at 16°24' VI & SG). It joins in the action at the Solar Eclipse New Moon on March 8. The Moon and Sun then (18°55 Pl) will be tightly opposite Jupiter (18°13 VI) and all three are less than three degrees from a square to Saturn (16°10' SG). Chiron (20°54' Pl) is on the edges of this T-square. Uranus (18°41' AR) is less than two degrees separated from a square to Pluto (17°4' CP) and these two make semisextiles and trines to components of the eclipse T-square. This will usher in a period of major adjustments, probably precipitated by some kind of meltdown. Expect break-ups and breakthroughs, too.

From mid-2016 into 2017, Uranus reaches and eventually passes Eris in a series of three conjunctions around 23° Aries (6/9/16, 9/25/16, 3/17/17). This volatile pairing likely coincides with earthquakes, volcanoes and destructive accidents. Yet it may be an exciting time for women to ascend to more power in society.

Janet Booth is available for readings by phone and Skype. Readings are recorded for your convenience. Visit JanetsPlan-its.com for details.

2016 Janet's Plan-its™ On a Page

	MERCURY	VENUS	MARS	CERES	JUPITER	SATURN	CHIRON	URANUS	NEPTUNE	PLUTO	MOON PHASES
	B 12/19/15, 14°55' CP				**B** 10/12/15, 13°15' VI	**B** 12/19/15, 9°47' SG	**D** 11/28/15, 15°56' PI	**D** 12/25/15, 16°33' AR	**D** 11/18/15, 7°1' PI	**B** 12/28/15, 14°56' CP	**E** = ECLIPSE
JANUARY	**R** 1/5, 1°3' AQ **D** 1/25, 14°55' CP				**R** 1/7, 23°14' VI					(next **R** shadow) **E** 1/15, 15°33' CP (prior **R** shadow)	New 1/9, 19°13' CP ● Full 1/23, 3°29' LE ○
FEBRUARY	**E** 2/14, 1°3' AQ		**B** 2/17, 23°3' SC						**B** 2/21, 9°14' PI (next **R** shadow)		New 2/8, 19°16' AQ ● Full 2/22, 3°34' VI ○
MARCH		V E N U S D O E S N O T G O R E T R O G R A D E I N 2 0 1 6 .			**R** 3/25, 16°24' SG	**B** 3/5, 20°40' PI (next **R** shadow) **E** 3/19, 21°33' PI (prior **R** shadow)		**E** 3/8, 9°49' PI (prior **R** shadow)		New 3/8, 18°56' PI **E** Full 3/23, 3°17' LI **E**
APRIL	**B** 4/14, 14°20' TA		**R** 4/17, 8°54' SG				**E** 4/10, 20°30' AR **B** 4/11, 20°33' AR		**R** 4/18, 17°29' CP	New 4/7, 18°4' AR ● Full 4/22, 2°31' SC ○
MAY	**R** 4/28, 23°36 ' TA **D** 5/22, 14°20' TA				**D** 5/9, 13°15' VI					New 5/6, 16°41' TA ● Full 5/21, 1°14' SG ○
JUNE	**E** 6/7, 23°36' TA		**B** 6/13, 21°8' AR **D** 6/29, 23°3' SC			**R** 6/27, 25°15' PI		**R** 6/13, 12°2' PI		New 6/4, 14°53' GE ● Full 6/20, 29°33' SG ○
JULY								**R** 7/29, 24°30' AR		New 7/4, 12°54' CN ● Full 7/19, 27°40' CP ○
AUGUST	**B** 8/10, 14°49' VI **R** 8/30, 29°5' VI	**E** 8/22, 8°54' SG	**R** 8/31, 5°24' TA	**E** 8/6, 23°14' VI	**D** 8/13, 9°47' SG				New 8/2, 10°58' LE ● Full 8/18, 25°52' AQ ○
SEPTEMBER	**D** 9/22, 14°49' VI								**D** 9/26, 14°56' CP	New 9/1, 9°21' VI **E** Full 9/16, 24°20' PI **E** New 9/30, 8°15' LI ●
OCTOBER	**E** 10/6, 29°5' VI									Full 10/16, 23°14' AR ○ New 10/30, 7°44' SC ●
NOVEMBER					**B** 11/10, 13°13' LI	**E** 11/19, 16°24' SG		**D** 11/19, 9°14' PI		Full 11/14, 22°38' TA ○ New 11/29, 7°43' SG ●
DECEMBER	**B** 12/1, 28°51' SG **R** 12/19, 15°8' CP	**D** 12/9, 21°8' AR **E** 2/24/17, 5°24' TA		**B** 12/30, 21°11' SG **B** 2/6/17, 23°8' LI	**D** 12/1, 20°40' PI **R** 4/6/17, 27°48' SG	**D** 12/29, 20°33' AR **E** 3/24/17, 25°15' PI	**E** 4/14/17, 24°30' AR	**E** 3/10/17, 12°2' PI	**B** 12/29, 16°51' CP (next **R** shadow) **E** 1/16/17, 17°29' CP (prior **R** shadow)	Full 12/13, 22°26' GE ○ New 12/29, 7°59' CP ●

Legend (right margin):
E Shadow ends · **D** Direct · **R** Retrograde · **B** Shadow begins · **(E)** Eclipse · ○ Full Moon · ● New Moon

The shadows of Chiron, Neptune, Pluto and Eris overlap, creating brief double shadows (darker shading). Eris begins 2016 Retrograde, turning Direct 1/10 at 22°18' AR. It has overlapping shadows from 3/1 to 5/28 between 22°32' AR and 23°25' AR. Eris turns Retrograde 7/19 at 23°38' AR. It next turns Direct 1/9/17 at 22°32' AR.

Dates based on Eastern Time Zone.

Cycles of Eight, of Transformation, on Earth and Within Your Life!

Eight Phases of the Sun, defining the seasons of each Solar Year and the stages of plant life.
Eight Phases of the Moon, by month, and by your own lifetime progressed Lunar Phase Cycle.

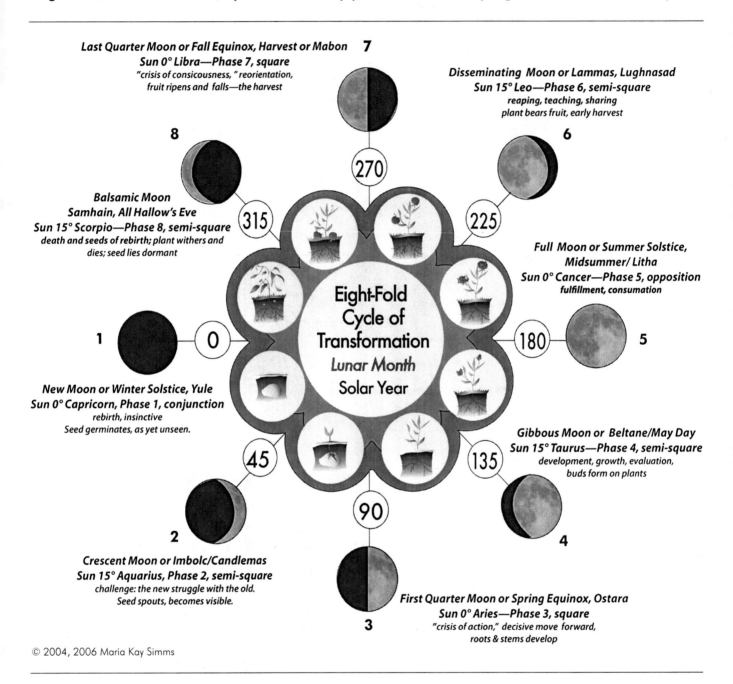

Last Quarter Moon or Fall Equinox, Harvest or Mabon 7
Sun 0° Libra—Phase 7, square
"crisis of consicousness," reorientation,
fruit ripens and falls—the harvest

Disseminating Moon or Lammas, Lughnasad
Sun 15° Leo—Phase 6, semi-square
reaping, teaching, sharing
plant bears fruit, early harvest

8

Balsamic Moon
Samhain, All Hallow's Eve
Sun 15° Scorpio—Phase 8, semi-square
death and seeds of rebirth; plant withers and
dies; seed lies dormant

6

Full Moon or Summer Solstice,
Midsummer/ Litha
Sun 0° Cancer—Phase 5, opposition
fulfillment, consumation

1

**Eight-Fold
Cycle of
Transformation**
Lunar Month
Solar Year

5

New Moon or Winter Solstice, Yule
Sun 0° Capricorn, Phase 1, conjunction
rebirth, insinctive
Seed germinates, as yet unseen.

Gibbous Moon or Beltane/May Day
Sun 15° Taurus—Phase 4, semi-square
development, growth, evaluation,
buds form on plants

2

4

Crescent Moon or Imbolc/Candlemas
Sun 15° Aquarius, Phase 2, semi-square
challenge: the new struggle with the old.
Seed spouts, becomes visible.

First Quarter Moon or Spring Equinox, Ostara
Sun 0° Aries—Phase 3, square
"crisis of action," decisive move forward,
roots & stems develop

3

© 2004, 2006 Maria Kay Simms

This graphic from my book, **Moon tides, Soul Passages**, summarizes the Eight-fold Cycle of Transformation, each lunar phase with its corresponding phase in the solar seasonal cycle. Just as Moon passes through 8 phases each month of about 30 days, the secondary progressed cycle of our natal Moon defines the 8 phases in each 30 years of life. Our life begins with the phase we are born within, and progresses from there. Our birth phase defines an important aspect of who we are, and our progression into each successive phase becomes a powerful method to understand the inner and outer changes we are experiencing, as well as to anticipate what may lie ahead.

– Maria Kay Simms

Moon Tides, Soul Passages
Lunar Phases and the Seasons of Life

Moon, Sun and Earth show us the seasons of life, and the archetypical spirit, soul and body of all three live within. The Moon has 8 distinct phases, as first defined by Dane Rudhyar. By secondary progression, the 8 lunar phases can be defined as a 29-1/2 – 30 year cycle of life experience.

I've been long fascinated with this powerful cycle of 8–especially its progressed phases that I've found to "work" well in my life, as well as in anyone else's I've studied. I'm also intrigued with the correlation of the 8 phases with the themes of the solar-seasonal cycle of 8, basic to ancient pagan sabbats. The core significance of the sabbats (though many are unaware of the origin) lives on in major holidays that fall on or very near the onset of each seasonal phase.

New Moon
New Moon, like the Maiden Goddess dances out of chaos, independent and free. As New Moon born, you project yourself onto your world, acting on instinct. At progressed New Moon, we enter a new major phase of life. Something significant to our past is ending, but we don't analyze; we just act. We make changes, driven by instinct.

Ritual/Action: New Moon is good for brainstorming. Get a pad & pen, dance to drumming or recorded music to raise energy, then chant this rhyme 9 times: *By magic charm, by 3 times 3, new ideas come to me! Jot them down!*

Crescent Moon
The dark is over and there's a sense of anticipation. Born at Crescent phase, you try to pull away from the past to forge something new. You have a vision, but must overcome something from the past to move forward. In progressed Crescent phase, it may feel as though each time you take two steps forward, there's a step back. You may know what you want, but there's resistance. that you must overcome.

Ritual/Action: When you see the waxing Crescent above, lift and cup your hands around her. Draw down her light and say: *Maiden Moon, come to me, Flow of bright new energy. My spirit lifts, my path is clear, my will is charged, my goal is near. Praise to thee and blessed be!*

First Quarter Moon
Now half light, half dark, the challenge is to move forward—act NOW! This is the "crisis of action!" If your birth phase, you like things that way! During progressed First Quarter, you've become very aware of the new direction that has been brewing. Now you make a clean break with what's past and move forward without looking back. Instinct still drives you, but now with a greater sense of direction.

Ritual/Action: Turn to each of the four directions, now with respect, say the appropriate phrase and listen to Spirit: *To the East I turn for clarity. To the South I turn for energy. To the West for intuition true.To the North for strength to see it through.* Then give thanks for insight received.

Gibbous Moon
Almost Full...but not quite...born at Gibbous phase, you constantly strive for an ideal, and your drive to reach it is strong. In progressed Gibbous, your goal is clear, but you're not quite there yet. There are still things to do. Persist — perfect your method.

Ritual/Action: Plant flowers with your pledge to bring your goal to full flower. As you plant say: *Lovely flowers, as you grow, strength and beauty I will see, Inspiring me to grow as well, In Her service, blessed be!*

Full Moon
Born at Full Moon, you have a deep sense of inner purpose, and must weigh opposing forces to balance and fulfill your intent. At progressed Full Moon, you reach a culmination that can be seen. If you remain vested in your purpose, you'll continue. If not, you may move on to create something else.

Ritual/Action: Draw down the Full Moon, a powerful experience. Cup her within your hands and draw her energy down through you, then send energy back to Her. Speak words of thanksgiving for what has been achieved.

Disseminating Moon
This is a phase of sharing, of giving back from what has been learned, achieved. If your natal phase, you are to demonstrate, teach and be a good example. The same theme holds for the 3-1/2 year progressed phase. Show what you can do!

Ritual/Action: Donate your time to a worthy charity to do a talk or demonstrate what you can do well.

Third Quarter Moon
Key phrase for this phase is "crisis of consciousness." If your natal phase, you are an iconoclast that doesn't fit into the mainstream. In the progressed phase, you experience an inner reorientation. Tired of what you've been doing, you begin a process of inner change.

Ritual/Action: Take a symbol of what you feel ready to let go of, and let it go with thanks, into an element of your choice: fire, air, earth or water.

Balsamic Moon
The waning crescent appears, and the lunar cycle draws to a close. The balsamic born are often visionary, and somehow feel different. At the progressed phase, we feel a sense of ending, perhaps a sense of isolation, a need to "be" rather than "do." But seeds of the new are stirring within.

Ritual/Action: Light a candle for guidance. Say: *Lady, guide me through the night, until new light I see. Inspire me toward my highest good. In love and trust, so mote it be!*

Anatomical Man

This famous illustration was painted by the Limbourg brothers for their patron, the Duc de Berry (brother of Charles V of France).
It shows the signs associated with various parts of the body, from the ram on the woman's head to the fish at her feet.
At her back, a man faces the opposite direction. Together they represent the feminine and masculine polarities.
The zodiac signs surround them in typical order from Aries at the top left, circling counterclockwise to Pisces at the top right.

"Anatomical Man" Annotated

by Diane L. Cramer, M.S., NCGR IV

The signs of the zodiac seen on the Anatomical Man are associated with different parts of the body. Each sign also has attributes describing their action and reaction in the body. Various health issues are common to each sign, as well. Due to polarity (see Keywords, p. 98), the signs are subject to ailments affiliated with the opposite sign. A pair of opposite signs may share a connection to a particular function or to related bodily systems. For example, Gemini and Sagittarius might indicate locomotive disorders; Leo and Aquarius can affect the heart and circulation. The following descriptions are applicable to one's Sun sign, rising sign, and in some instances, to the sign of the Moon.

ARIES
The ram on the top of the head represents Aries, a fire sign, which rules the brain, skull, outer ears, eyeball, upper jaw, adrenal medulla and pituitary gland. The head, face and teeth can be areas of distress. Aries shuns limits and needs to conserve energy or have a sound exercise program as an outlet for excess energy. Aries needs iron and may require meat more than other signs. Problems: fever, inflammation. Aries is also linked with renal function due to polarity with its opposite sign, Libra. Helpful herbs: ginseng or bergamot for mental exhaustion, lavender for headaches and borage for depletion of energy.

TAURUS
Taurus, the first of the earth signs, is represented by the bull at the back of the neck. Taurus rules the neck, throat, inner ears, gums, vocal chords and thyroid. Taurus tends to have endurance and a strong constitution but can be inflexible, which leads to a tense or stiff body. Body massages are useful for Taurus. Ruled by Venus, Taurus tends to overindulge in rich food and needs roughage and variety in the diet. Problems: sensitive vocal cords subject to infections, sore throats and hearing disorders. Helpful foods and herbs: black currants, coltsfoot and fenugreek to control sore throats; parsley and oregano to liven up the system; and root vegetables to help clean the digestive tract.

GEMINI
Gemini, the first of the air signs, is represented by the twins peeking around the shoulders. Gemini rules the arms, shoulders, hands, tongue, trachea and bronchi. Gemini rules all tubes in the body. Worry is a negative attribute which Gemini needs to overcome by positive thinking. Problems: nervous or respiratory disorders, allergies and weak lungs. Helpful: deep breathing exercises and aerobics as an outlet for Gemini's nervous energy; vitamins A, B, C and D to aid the lungs; herbs like skullcap for nervous excitability, flaxseed for coughs and bronchial complaints and bergamot for relaxation and sleep.

CANCER
The first of the water signs, Cancer is represented by the crab on the breastbone. Cancer rules all containers and coverings in the body. This includes the breasts, rib cage, sinus cavity, stomach, womb and the pleura of the lungs. Problems: a tendency toward water retention and disorders of the stomach. Helpful: raw enzymes to aid digestion from foods such as pineapple or papaya, and herbs such as bilberry for water retention, cloves for stomach gas, and honeysuckle and arrowroot to calm the stomach. Cancer needs to include fiber like bran and whole fruits in the diet. Lettuce, a Cancer plant, soothes the stomach.

LEO
Leo, the second of the fire signs, represented by the lion at the heart, is a sign of energy and vitality. The constitution is strong and when ill, Leo recovers quickly. Leo rules the heart muscle, spine and middle back. Rich foods tend to increase cholesterol levels so Leo would do well to avoid fatty foods. Problems: heart and muscle strain, backache, sunstroke and high fevers or inflammatory disorders. Helpful: herbs such as angelica for heartburn, dandelion as a tonic and blood purifier, rosemary as a heart tonic and mustard to alleviate back pains. Also beneficial: Vitamin E, magnesium and activities such as yoga that encourage flexibility in the torso and back.

VIRGO
Virgo, the second earth sign, represented by the virgin on the stomach, is a sign of assimilation and utilization. Virgo has a sensitive constitution and needs to keep the bowels and nervous system functioning in good order. Virgo rules the small intestines, pancreas, duodenum, the enzyme action of the liver and peristalsis of the bowels. Virgo has strong preferences and dislikes, and does well on a diet of natural foods, including plenty of fiber and whole grains. Problems: digestive disturbances, weak intestines, nervous complaints and illness due to poor nutrition. Helpful herbs: balm and borage for nervous troubles, angelica to stimulate the digestive tract, fenugreek for inflammation of the intestines, fennel seeds for gas and skullcap to tone the nervous system.

Continued on page 94

Disclaimer: This material is for informational and entertainment purposes only and does not replace nor is it to be used for the purpose of medical diagnosis or treatment. For medical attention, see a licensed medical professional.

LIBRA

Libra, the second of the three air signs, represented by the scales at the midsection, is a sign of balance and harmony. Libra needs to live a balanced and harmonious life and benefits from a balanced diet. Libra rules the kidneys, the lower back and the skin, from a cosmetic standpoint. Libra can be weak in the kidney area and would benefit from drinking lots of water every day to keep the kidneys flushed. Problems: headaches, lower back pains, skin complaints and health disorders due to Libra's love of sweets. Helpful herbs: bilberry and borage to promote kidney action, burdock for kidney weakness, feverfew to strengthen and cleanse the kidneys, and thyme for headaches.

SCORPIO

Scorpio, the second of the water signs, represented by the scorpion at the loins, is a sign of transformation, elimination and regeneration. Scorpio has a strong constitution with much vital force. Scorpio rules the eliminative and procreative organs in the body. As a fixed sign, Scorpio can be tense at times so would benefit from walking to increase flexibility. Scorpio may also be attracted to alternative healing methods, such as acupressure and biofeedback. Problems: bladder or bowel disorders; female complaints; a weak prostate in men; and predisposition to hemorrhoids, constipation and hernia in both genders. Helpful: daily roughage; fruits and vegetables; herbs such as chicory as a laxative, witch hazel for hemorrhoids, lavage as a general tonic and blessed thistle to force out impurities in the body; and a diet containing leeks, prunes, onions, beans and barley for energy.

SAGITTARIUS

Sagittarius, the last of the three fire signs, is represented by the archer at the thighs. Sagittarius can be expansive, optimistic and generous. However Sagittarius tends to excess and may overindulge in sweets, alcoholic beverages and meat. Sagittarius rules the hips, thighs and liver. Problems: gout, sciatica, hip injuries, obesity, rheumatism and diabetes or hypoglycemia. Helpful: discipline in dietary habits; foods such as cucumber to soothe the system, asparagus as a cleanser and spices such as sage, cloves and nutmeg. Herbs such as chicory address liver impurities; dandelion is an aid to the liver and a general tonic; red clover is a good blood purifier; and thyme and rosemary are tonic for the liver.

CAPRICORN

The last of the three earth signs, Capricorn, is represented by the goat at the knees. This is a sign that strengthens as it ages. Capricorn rules the skin, knees, joints, hair, teeth and nails. Capricorn does best in a warm environment as getting chilled can lead to illness. Capricorn needs sufficient calcium to maintain bones and teeth. Problems: falls, bruises, colds and chills, weak knees, skin disorders, dental problems and stiff joints. Helpful Herbs: bay for skin trouble, camphor rub for chills, chamomile and cloves for toothache, rose hips to retain flexibility of cartilage and slippery elm to strengthen the skeletal system. A dogmatic sign, Capricorn needs to loosen up by swimming, stretching, deep breathing exercises or massage.

AQUARIUS

The last of the air signs, Aquarius, a sign of oxygenation, is represented by the water bearer at the shins. Aquarius can become high strung and restless due to an abundance of nervous energy. Aquarius rules the electrolytes of the body, the lower legs and ankles, the valves of the heart and the retina of the eyes. Problems: circulatory complaints, leg complaints, varicose veins, nervous disorders, hormonal imbalance, sprained or broken ankle and impurities of the bloodstream. Helpful: exercises such as bicycling, yoga and deep breathing, and a good night's sleep to recharge the nervous system. Herbs such as bergamot aid relaxation, borage cleanses the bloodstream and is helpful for sprains, rosemary stimulates circulation and valerian quiets the nerves. Aquarius would do well to avoid chemicals and processed foods.

PISCES

Pisces, the last of the water signs, is represented by the fish at the feet. Pisces can experience low energy and needs plenty of vitamins and minerals to build up the vital powers in the body. The ability to imagine and help others is an aid to good health in Pisces. This sign rules the lymphatic system of the body, the feet and the toes. Problems: a tendency toward bunions, gout, swelling of the feet, colds and infections, weak lungs, psychosomatic illnesses and alcoholism. Helpful: living near water, swimming, walking and meditation. Pisces may benefit from ginseng as a tonic, chicory to eliminate mucous and kelp as a source of iron. Foods high in iron such as liver, raisins or dried apricots, are beneficial to Pisces.

Recommended reading for further study:
- Cramer, Diane, M.S.: *Managing Your Health & Wellness*. Llewellyn Publications, Woodbury, MN, 2006
- Cramer, Diane, M.S.: *Medical Astrology: Let the Stars Guide You to Good Health*, Jove Press, New York, NY, 2010
- Geddes, Sheila: *Astrology and Health*, The Aquarian Press, Wellingborough, Northhamptonshire, 1984.
- Muir, Ada: *Healing Herbs*, Llewellyn Publication, St. Paul Minnesota, 1995.

Disclaimer: This material is for informational and entertainment purposes only and does not replace nor is it to be used for the purpose of medical diagnosis or treatment. For medical attention, see a licensed medical professional.

BEST AND WORST DAYS
FOR VARIOUS ACTIVITIES

"Best" and "worst" are relative terms. You might think of these dates as "better" or "worse" than the other days of the year specifically for the activities listed. Sometimes "best" is "as good as it gets" in light of other factors in place, and certainly not perfect. Every attempt was made to find at least one "best" and one "worst" for each month in each category.

To put a date into context or to select a particular part of a day, see the weekly Highlights, daily messages, 2015 On a Page and the Star Pages (including Mutual Receptions and planets Out of Bounds). As usual, take precautions when Mercury or Venus is Retrograde, especially for activities related to these planets. And of course you wouldn't undertake important action when the Moon is Void. Using This Planner (p. 2) explains Void Moons and what to consider if your birthday is on this list.

In many cases, only part of a day is better or worse for a type of activity. The parentheses after the date point you to morning (morn), afternoon (aft), evening (eve) or a combination, such as morning and afternoon (morn & aft). "Worst" days are warnings that these activities are likely to run into problems if undertaken then. These time frames apply to time zones in North America, from Atlantic (one hour earlier than Eastern) to Pacific, and they take Daylight Saving Time into account.

After the type of activity, the planets and signs associated with the arena are listed in brackets. If you know additional activities associated with these factors, these dates apply to them, as well. See the Keywords on pp. 98-99 and at Janet's Plan-its.com.

♈ ♂ [Aries, Mars]
PHYSICAL ACTIVITIES, SPORTS, COMPETITION, RISK-TAKING

BEST: 1/13 (eve), 2/3, 3/2, 3/12 (aft & eve), 3/25 (morn), 4/6 (morn), 4/10, 4/12, 4/22, 5/28, 6/10, 6/19 (morn), 6/26 (eve), 6/30 (morn), 7/7 (aft & eve), 7/26 (aft), 8/13 (morn), 9/10 (aft & eve), 9/20, 10/14, 10/19 (aft), 11/9 (eve), 11/15 (aft & eve), 12/5 (aft), 12/8 (aft & eve), 12/15 (eve)

WORST: 12/31/14 (eve), 1/1, 1/8, 1/9, 1/12, 1/25, 2/6, 2/21, 3/7, 3/11, 3/28, 4/5, 4/11 (eve), 5/5, 5/25, 5/29, 6/2, 6/27, 7/1 (morn & aft), 7/14, 7/15, 7/25, 7/29, 7/30, 8/29, 9/3, 9/25 (eve), 9/28, 10/1, 10/5, 10/7, 10/12, 10/16, 10/26, 10/30, 11/22, 11/28, 12/2, 12/6, 12/9 (aft & eve), 12/10, 12/16 (aft & eve), 12/20, 12/26

♉ ♀ [Taurus, Venus]
FINANCES, PURCHASES, INVESTMENTS

BEST: 1/14 (morn & aft), 1/17 (morn), 2/5 (eve), 3/2, 3/22 (aft & eve), 4/21 (aft & eve), 4/22, 5/16 (eve), 6/6, 6/10, 6/30 (morn), 7/9, 7/10, 7/13 (aft & eve), 8/14 (morn & aft), 9/20 (morn), 9/30 (morn), 10/3 (morn), 11/11 (aft & eve), 11/13 (morn), 11/24 (aft), 12/12, 12/17 (aft & eve)

WORST: 1/1 (morn), 1/2 (morn & aft), 1/18, 1/25, 1/26, 1/28, 2/1 (aft & eve), 2/9, 3/4, 3/11, 3/19, 3/26 (morn), 3/27, 4/5 (eve), 4/7, 4/14 (eve), 4/25, 4/29, 5/14, 5/25, 5/29, 6/12, 6/13, 6/16, 7/11, 7/15, 7/25, 8/1, 8/4, 8/7, 8/28, 8/31 (morn), 9/6, 9/29, 10/7, 10/10, 10/12, 10/16, 10/27, 11/20 (aft & eve), 11/22 (morn), 11/23, 11/28, 12/6, 12/31

♊ ☿ [Gemini, Mercury]
COMMUNICATIONS OF ANY SORT, LOCAL TRAVEL OR TRANSPORTATION, NEIGHBORS, SIBLINGS

BEST: 1/17 (morn), 1/29 (morn), 2/7 (aft), 2/25 (eve), 3/25 (morn), 4/6 (morn), 4/22 (morn & aft), 5/10, 5/28, 6/15 (aft & eve), 6/19 (morn), 7/9 (eve), 8/9 (morn), 9/30 (morn), 10/3 (morn), 10/21 (aft), 11/13 (morn), 11/16 (aft & eve), 11/21 (morn), 12/17 (morn), 12/19 (morn)

WORST: 12/29/14, 1/1, 1/10, 1/21, 2/6, 2/11, 3/13, 3/19, 3/24 (eve), 4/7, 4/11, 4/20 (eve), 4/27 (morn), 5/1, 5/2, 5/3, 5/5, 5/9 (morn), 5/18, 5/29, 6/11, 7/3 (morn & aft), 7/15, 7/20, 8/8, 8/12, 8/28, 9/4 (aft & eve), 9/7 (morn & aft), 9/11 (morn), 9/17, 9/22 (morn), 10/9, 10/22, 10/26 (morn), 10/28, 10/29, 11/2, 11/3, 12/3 (eve), 12/7, 12/26, 12/30 (aft)

♋ ☽ [Cancer, Moon]

REAL ESTATE, DOMESTIC/ FAMILY MATTERS

BEST: 1/13 (eve), 1/17 (morn), 2/19, 3/2, 3/12 (aft & eve), 3/22 (aft & eve), 4/26 (morn & aft), 4/30, 5/10 (morn & aft), 6/15 (eve), 6/26 (eve), 6/30 (morn), 7/13 (aft & eve), 8/26 (eve), 9/13, 9/18 (morn), 9/30 (morn), 10/4 (morn), 10/31, 11/16 (aft & eve), 11/24 (aft), 12/5 (morn & aft), 12/8 (aft & eve), 12/17

WORST: 1/1, 1/12 (morn & aft), 1/16, 1/19, 2/1 (aft & eve), 2/4, 2/6, 2/24, 2/28, 3/8, 3/11, 3/15, 3/27 (eve), 3/28 (eve), 4/14 (eve), 4/27, 5/20, 5/21, 5/22 (morn) 5/25, 6/2 (morn), 6/12, 6/16, 6/17 (eve), 7/5, 8/1, 8/7 (eve), 8/11 (morn & aft), 8/29, 8/31, 9/4 (aft & eve), 9/7 (morn & aft), 10/5, 10/12, 10/16, 10/20, 10/26, 10/27 (morn & aft), 11/1 (aft), 11/3 (morn & aft), 11/29, 12/9 (aft & eve), 12/11

♌ ☉ [Leo, Sun]

ART, CREATIVITY, ACTIVITIES FOR CHILDREN
(or your inner child)

BEST: 1/7 (eve), 1/17 (morn), 2/3, 3/2, 3/12 (eve), 3/25 (morn), 4/6 (morn), 4/26 (morn & aft), 5/28, 6/6, 6/26 (eve), 6/30 (morn), 7/21, 7/23, 7/26 (aft), 8/9 (morn), 8/13 (morn), 8/14, 9/10 (aft & eve), 9/18 (morn), 9/20 (morn), 9/30 (morn), 10/3 (morn), 10/31, 11/15 (aft & eve), 11/16 (aft & eve), 11/30 (morn), 12/5 (aft), 12/8 (aft & eve)

WORST: 1/1, 1/6, 1/8, 2/4, 2/6, 2/18, 3/19, 4/11 (eve), 4/25, 5/21, 5/25, 6/2 (morn), 6/12, 6/16, 6/27, 7/6, 7/12, 7/17, 7/29, 8/1, 8/4, 8/7 (eve), 8/21, 8/22 (morn & aft), 8/28, 8/31, 9/1 (aft & eve), 10/6, 10/12, 10/16, 10/22, 10/27, 10/30, 11/2 (morn & aft), 11/3 (morn & aft), 11/20 (aft & eve), 11/22 (morn), 11/29, 12/14, 12/18

♍ ☿ [Virgo, Mercury]

EMPLOYMENT, SERVICE/SERVERS, HEALTH

BEST: 1/17 (morn), 1/29 (morn), 2/7 (aft), 3/5 (morn), 4/6 (morn), 5/28, 6/22 (aft & eve), 7/9 (eve), 8/17 (morn), 9/13, 9/30 (morn), 10/11 (morn & aft), 10/14 (morn & aft), 10/19 (morn & aft), 10/21 (aft), 11/13 (morn), 11/16 (aft & eve), 11/21 (morn), 12/8 (eve), 12/17 (morn), 12/19 (morn)

WORST: 12/29/14, 1/10, 1/21, 2/6, 2/11, 3/4, 3/13, 3/19, 3/31 (aft & eve), 4/7, 4/11, 4/27, 4/29, 5/1, 5/2, 5/3, 5/5, 5/9 (morn), 5/18, 5/25, 5/29, 6/11, 7/3 (morn & aft), 7/15, 7/20, 8/12, 8/28, 8/31, 9/1, 9/7 (morn & aft), 9/11, 9/17, 9/22 (morn), 9/25, 10/9, 10/22, 10/24, 10/26 (morn), 10/27, 10/28, 10/30, 11/2, 11/3, 11/6, 12/2, 12/3, 12/7, 12/26, 12/30 (morn & aft)

♎ ♀ [Libra, Venus]

RELATIONSHIPS, PARTNERSHIP, ROMANCE

BEST: 1/14 (morn & aft), 1/17 (morn), 2/5 (eve), 2/7 (aft), 3/2, 3/22 (aft & eve), 4/22, 4/30, 5/16 (eve), 5/28 (morn & aft), 6/6, 6/10, 6/19 (morn), 6/30 (morn), 7/9 (morn), 7/13 (aft & eve), 7/21, 8/17 (aft & eve), 9/20 (morn), 9/23 (aft), 9/30 (morn), 10/3 (morn), 10/11 (morn & aft), 10/21 (aft), 11/7 (aft & eve), 11/11 (aft & eve), 11/13 (morn), 12/5 (morn & aft), 12/12, 12/17 (aft & eve)

WORST: 1/1 (morn), 1/2 (morn & aft), 1/12, 1/18, 1/25, 1/26, 1/28, 2/1 (aft & eve), 2/8, 2/9, 3/4, 3/7, 3/8, 3/11, 3/19, 3/26 (morn), 3/27, 4/3 (morn & aft), 4/4, 4/7, 4/14 (eve), 4/29, 5/14, 5/25, 5/29, 6/12, 6/13, 6/16, 6/24, 7/11, 7/15, 7/25, 8/1, 8/4, 8/7, 8/18, 8/28, 8/31 (morn), 9/6, 9/16, 9/29, 10/7, 10/10, 10/12, 10/16, 10/22, 10/27, 11/20 (aft & eve), 11/22 (morn), 11/23, 11/28, 12/6 (morn & aft), 12/31

MARRIAGE ♎ ♀ [Libra, Venus]

It's advisable to get both partners' birth time and work with an astrologer to find a suitable date and time. Sometimes a day that's not great on its own can bring out the best in a couple's charts. Even on recommended days, certain hours are better than others. You can get legally married at a good time and then re-enact vows and have your reception when you want.

BEST: 3/2, 3/24 (aft), 4/30, 7/21, 9/23 (aft)*, 11/11 (aft & eve), 11/12 (early eve). Of these, the very best is 3/24 (see the Star Pages). *Use this date only if both partners are born with Mercury Retrograde. **WORST**: See Worst Days for Relationships

♏ ♇ [Scorpio, Pluto]

BUSINESS, FINANCES, RENOVATION, PROCREATION
(also see CAREER, FINANCE and PARTNERSHIP, if applicable)

BEST: 1/13 (eve), 2/19 (aft), 3/5, 4/6 (eve), 4/19 (aft & eve), 4/21, 4/22, 5/26 (morn), 6/4 (eve), 6/22 (aft & eve), 6/26 (eve), 7/10, 8/25 (eve), 9/18 (morn), 9/30 (morn), 10/14, 10/19 (aft), 10/31, 11/13 (morn), 11/15 (aft & eve), 12/8 (aft & eve), 12/12, 12/17 (aft & eve)

WORST: 1/1 (morn), 1/12 (morn), 1/15 (eve), 2/15 (morn & aft), 3/11, 3/16, 3/27 (eve), 4/5, 4/7, 4/11, 4/16, 5/1, 5/5 (morn), 5/21, 6/17 (eve), 6/20, 6/21 (morn), 6/28, 7/11, 7/15, 7/29, 8/1, 8/4, 8/7, 8/21, 8/22 (morn & aft), 9/7 (morn & aft), 9/25, 9/28, 10/22, 11/19 (aft & eve), 11/20 (aft & eve), 12/9 (aft)

♐ ♃ [Sagittarius, Jupiter]

EDUCATION, PROMOTION, LONG DISTANCE TRAVEL, CONTACT AT A DISTANCE
(includes online), LEGAL MATTERS

BEST: 1/7 (eve), 1/17 (morn), 2/3 (eve), 3/2, 3/12 (aft & eve), 3/25 (morn), 4/2 (morn & aft), 4/26 (morn), 5/19 (morn), 6/15 (eve), 6/22 (aft & eve), 6/30 (morn), 7/13 (aft & eve), 7/26 (aft), 8/25 (morn), 9/30 (morn), 10/14, 10/19 (aft), 10/25 (morn), 11/13 (morn), 11/24 (aft), 12/5 (morn & aft), 12/8 (aft & eve)

WORST: 12/31/14 (eve), 1/1, 1/16, 2/14, 3/11 (eve), 3/19, 3/26 (morn), 4/8, 5/5, 6/27, 7/4 (eve), 8/1, 8/4, 9/1 (morn & aft), 9/2, 9/19, 10/16, 11/2 (morn & aft), 11/26, 11/28, 11/29, 12/2 (eve), 12/3 (eve), 12/11, 12/14

♑ ♄ [Capricorn, Saturn]

CAREER MATTERS, ORGANIZAING, PLANNING

BEST: 1/13 (eve), 2/2 (eve), 3/5, 4/10, 4/19 (aft & eve), 5/26 (morn), 6/6, 6/22 (aft & eve), 7/21, 8/17 (morn), 8/25 (aft), 8/26 (eve), 9/13, 9/18 (morn), 9/26 (aft & eve), 9/27 (aft), 10/11 (morn & aft), 10/19 (morn & aft), 11/7 (aft & eve), 11/13 (morn), 11/15 (aft & eve), 11/16 (eve), 12/5 (morn), 12/8 (aft & eve), 12/12, 12/17 (aft & eve)

WORST: 1/1 (morn & aft), 1/2 (morn & aft), 1/6 (aft & eve), 1/19, 1/28 (eve), 2/15 (morn & aft), 3/1, 3/8, 3/14, 3/15, 3/27 (eve), 4/9, 4/11, 4/14 (eve), 5/1, 5/2, 5/3, 5/4, 5/5, 6/17 (eve), 6/20, 6/21 (morn), 6/28, 7/11, 7/14, 7/15, 7/29, 8/1 (aft & eve), 8/2, 8/7 (eve), 8/21, 8/22 (morn & aft), 9/7 (morn & aft), 9/14, 9/21, 9/22, 9/25, 9/28, 10/1, 10/10, 10/22, 10/25, 11/1 (aft), 11/16 (morn), 11/19 (aft & eve), 11/25 (eve), 11/26, 11/28, 11/29, 12/2 (eve), 12/13 (eve), 12/23 (aft), 12/26

♒ ♅ [Aquarius, Uranus]

SOCIALIZING, MEETINGS, COOPERATION, FRIENDS

BEST: 1/14 (morn & aft), 2/3, 3/2, 3/25 (morn), 4/6 (morn), 4/26, 5/10, 6/7 (morn), 6/10, 6/21 (aft), 6/22 (aft & eve), 6/30 (morn), 7/8 (eve), 8/9 (morn), 9/20 (morn), 9/23 (aft & eve), 10/14, 10/21 (aft), 11/7 (aft), 11/11 (aft & eve), 11/15 (aft & eve), 11/17 (aft), 12/1, 12/5 (morn & aft), 12/8 (aft & eve), 12/15 (eve)

WORST: 1/1, 1/8, 1/9, 1/12 (morn), 2/12, 2/18, 3/11, 3/16, 3/27 (eve), 4/4 (morn), 5/1, 5/2, 5/3, 5/4, 5/5, 5/25, 6/3, 6/14 (eve), 7/5, 7/12, 7/26, 8/1, 8/28, 8/29, 9/2, 9/15, 10/1, 10/12, 10/22, 11/2 (morn & aft), 11/22, 11/23, 12/16 (aft), 12/25, 12/31, 1/2/16

NEW VENTURES, ACTIVITIES or PROJECTS

are best begun during a waxing moon and out of the way of Mercury and Venus Retrograde and their stations. In 2015, these favorable launch periods are 2/19-3/4, 3/21-4/3, 4/19-5/3, 6/16-7/1, 7/16-7/21, 10/13-10/26, 11/11-11/25 and 12/11-12/22. Within these time frames, look for days with good ratings or messages applicable to your needs. Some stellar days are: 3/25 (morn), 4/21 (aft), 7/21, 10/14 (morn & aft), 10/19 (aft) and 12/12.

♓ ♆ ⚷ [Pisces, Neptune, Chiron]

CHARITABLE, SPIRITUAL, HEALTH

BEST: 1/14 (morn), 1/31 (morn & aft), 2/19 (aft & eve), 3/22 (aft & eve), 4/15 (morn), 5/16 (eve), 6/4 (aft & eve), 7/1 (eve), 7/10, 7/13 (aft & eve), 8/25 (aft), 8/30, 9/26 aft & eve), 10/4 (morn), 10/31, 11/24 (aft), 12/8 (aft & eve), 12/12, 12/17

WORST: 12/29/14, 1/1 (eve), 1/2 (morn & aft), 1/12, 2/1 (aft & eve), 2/26, 3/13, 3/19, 3/28 (morn), 4/11 (eve), 4/14 (eve), 5/9 (morn), 5/29, 5/31 (morn), 6/2 (morn), 6/12, 6/24, 7/30, 8/12, 8/29, 8/31, 9/1, 9/8, 10/6, 10/16, 10/24, 11/1 (aft), 11/2 (morn & aft), 11/3, 11/18, 11/19 (aft & eve), 11/25 (eve), 11/26, 11/27, 11/28, 11/29, 12/2 (aft & eve), 12/20

JANET'S PLAN-ITS KEYWORDS FOR ASTROLOGICAL TERMS

HEAVENLY BODIES/PLANETS

⊙ **SUN** leadership, ego, will power, creativity, vitality, spirit, purpose, identity

☽ **MOON** responses, habit patterns, feelings, receptivity, sensitivity, nurturing

☿ **MERCURY** rational mind, thinking processes, all forms of communications, local travel/transportation matters

♀ **VENUS** affections, attraction, aesthetics, desire for beauty, balance, values, harmony

♂ **MARS** aggressiveness, assertiveness, initiative, independence, pioneering, competition

⚳ **CERES** harvest, fertility, abundance, nurturing

♃ **JUPITER** growth, philosophy, higher education, long distance travel or communication

♄ **SATURN** structure, definition, limits, restriction, responsibility, organization, authority, maturity

⚷ **CHIRON** (asteroid) "Wounded Healer," hurts, healing, innovation, teaching

♅ **URANUS** the unusual or unexpected, uniqueness, individuality, revolution, reform

♆ **NEPTUNE** imagination, psychic sensitivity, confusion, fears, spirituality, the arts

♇ **PLUTO** (plutoid) finances, shared resources, transformation, death, re-birth, afterlife, sex

⚸ **ERIS** (plutoid) chaos, discord, strife, rivalry

SIGNS [followed by their ruling planets]

♈ **ARIES** [ruler: Mars] enthusiastic, outgoing, self-centered, energetic, pioneering, assertive

♉ **TAURUS** [ruler: Venus] stable, steadfast, patient, practical, stubborn, jealous, artsy

♊ **GEMINI** [ruler: Mercury] communicative, inquisitive, adaptable, versatile

♋ **CANCER** [ruler: Moon] sensitive, nurturing, receptive, home/family-oriented, emotional

♌ **LEO** [ruler: Sun] generous, showy, dramatic, creative, a leader, egotistical, fun-loving

♍ **VIRGO** [ruler: Mercury] analytical, discriminating, critical, detail-oriented, service-minded, useful

♎ **LIBRA** [ruler: Venus] diplomatic, other-oriented, peace-loving, refined, flirty, indecisive

♏ **SCORPIO** [ruler: Pluto] magnetic, powerful, intense, persevering, passionate, extreme

♐ **SAGITTARIUS** [ruler: Jupiter] idealistic, optimistic, scattered, honest, exaggerative, restless

♑ **CAPRICORN** [ruler: Saturn] ambitious, responsible, economical, efficient, disciplined, insensitive

♒ **AQUARIUS** [ruler: Uranus] impersonal, detached, original, humanitarian, independent, rebellious

♓ **PISCES** [ruler: Neptune] sympathetic, sentimental, caring, responsive, psychic, spiritual, escapist

Please note: Planets and signs are related to many more matters than the most common associations listed here.

ASPECTS (Angular distance between planets, linking their influences; multiple aspects can form patterns)

☌ **CONJUNCTION (0°)** [Planet joins/passes another] powerful emphasis, strength in the sign

⚺ **SEMISEXTILE (30°)** [one-twelfth of the sky apart] like sextile but weaker, favorable combo

∠ **SEMISQUARE (45°)** [one-eighth of the sky apart] similar to Square, grating

✶ **SEXTILE (60°)** [one-sixth of the sky apart] ease, put in effort for best results

□ **SQUARE (90°)** [a quarter of the sky apart] conflicting desires, inner struggles lead to action

△ **TRINE (120°)** [a third of the sky apart] automatic benefits, harmony, ease

⚼ **SESQUIQUADRATE (135°)** [three-eighths of the sky apart] similar to Square, friction, tension

Q **QUINTILE (72°) and Q² BIQUINTILE (144°)** [one-fifth and two-fifths of the sky apart] a talent or a choice to make between planets' influences

⚻ **QUINCUNX (150°)** [five-twelfths of the sky apart] a disconnect, need adjustment or compromise

☍ **OPPOSITION (180°)** [half of the sky apart] conflict, difficulties from outside oneself or differences requiring resolution, brings awareness

Learn about HOUSES on page 5.

Signs are grouped according to three characteristics – **Modes, Elements** and **Polarity** – indicating shared traits.

MODES *(also called Qualities)*

CARDINAL *(beginning of each season)* *[Aries, Cancer, Libra, Capricorn]*
active, energetic, dynamic, initiating, thrives on crisis

FIXED *(middle of each season)* *[Taurus, Leo, Scorpio, Aquarius]*
stable, persistent, willful, stubborn, resistant to change

MUTABLE *(end of each season)* *[Gemini, Virgo, Sagittarius, Pisces]*
adaptable, variable, restless, easy-going, scattered

ELEMENTS

FIRE *[Aries, Leo, Sagittarius]* impulsive, inspirational,
enthusiastic, intuitive, energetic

EARTH *[Taurus, Virgo, Capricorn]* practical, materialistic,
dependable, utilitarian, conservative

AIR *[Gemini, Libra, Aquarius]* intellectual, communicative,
abstract, idealistic, cooperative

WATER *[Cancer, Scorpio, Pisces]* emotional, sensitive,
protective, responsive, nurturing, psychic

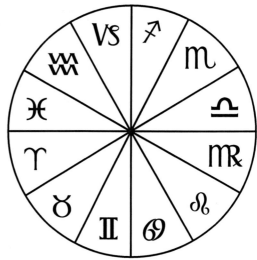

Look for squares and oppositions in the
same mode, trines in a shared element,
or sextiles and oppositions in a polarity.

POLARITY

YANG *[Fire and Air signs]* extroverted, out-going, assertive   **YIN** *[Earth and Water signs]* introverted, passive, receptive
Opposite signs share the same polarity. They often relate to a common theme, reflecting both ends of a spectrum.

RETROGRADE MOTION ℞

A planet's apparent backward motion. Shows a need to re-experience, review, or re-do according to sign and aspects.

LUNAR PHASES

● New Moon

◐ First Quarter Moon

○ Full Moon

◑ Third Quarter Moon

VOID OF COURSE MOON

A period of time when the Moon has finished
its aspects in its current sign. Until entering the
next sign, motivation is low and actions "run
out of steam." It's not a good time to make
major purchases or begin important activities.

ECLIPSES

☌ Solar Eclipse

☍ Lunar Eclipse

Read about lunar cycles
on page 90.

MOON'S NODES *(intersection of the Moon's orbit around the earth with the earth's orbit of the Sun)*

☊ **NORTH NODE** direction for progress, what is difficult to do but growth-producing, what one needs to develop
☋ **SOUTH NODE** path of least resistance, not growth-producing, traps from old habits

ASPECT PATTERNS

FINGER OF GOD (YOD): 2 planets sextile, both quincunx a third – strange twists of fate with a positive outcome

GRAND TRINE: 3 planets in an equilateral triangle, all trine one another *(usually with components in the same Element)*
          – *an easy flow of energy between planets, may yield luck in circumstances related to planets & signs involved*

GRAND CROSS (GRAND SQUARE): a cross or square box formed by 2 perpendicular oppositions, contains 4 squares
          (usually has components in same Mode) – *big difficulties for planets & signs involved*

KITE: Grand Trine with a planet opposite 1 point, sextile the other 2 – a challenge maximizes the Grand Trine

MYSTIC RECTANGLE: sextiles and trines on the sides, diagonal oppositions – cooperative and complementary energies mix

QUINTILE TRIANGLE ("QT"): a triangle comprised of quintiles and biquintiles – multiple talents or fortunate circumstances

STAR OF DAVID (Grand Sextile): 2 overlapping Grand Trines, with 6 sextiles *and* 3 oppositions (= 3 connected Kites)

T-SQUARE: 2 planets in opposition, both square a third – problems and dilemmas that force decisions or action

Contributors

to Janet's Plan-its Celestial Planner 2015 Astrology Calendar

Bryan R. Bonina, a visual artist and graphic designer for 28 years, has managed layout and design of the Celestial Planner since 2001. In addition to the calendar, he also produces Janet's collateral print material while providing her with marketing consulting services. Bryan's freelance business, Always Amazing Results ~ A Marketing & Communications Company, is based in Farmington, CT. Contact: bryan_r_bonina@sbcglobal.net.

Diane Cramer, MS, NCGR IV, wrote the companion article to the medieval illustration, Anatomical Man (p. 93), discussing astrological associations with the human body and health indications for the signs. A Consulting Astrologer certified by the National Council for Geocosmic Research (NCGR), she is a lecturer and teacher in all aspects of astrology, specializing in medical astrology and nutrition. Her four books – *Managing Your Health & Wellness, How to Give an Astrological Health Reading, Dictionary of Medical Astrology* and *Medical Astrology Let The Stars Guide You to Good Health* – are available at dianecramer.com. Her email is astroldiane@yahoo.com.

Sally Faubion, a professional numerologist from San Francisco, CA, offered insights into the year 2015 from a numerological standpoint for the Overview (p. 1). Her book, *Motivational Numerology And How Numbers Affect Your Life*, introduces her unique numerological technique, the Wizard's Star, a color-coded snapshot of a person's numbers. On her website, www.sfnumber.com, you can order her book, get your Wizard Star interpretation based on your name and birth data, or buy "CosmicMates," Sally's iApp that rates relationship potentials.

Dietrech Pessin, a professional astrologer in practice since 1974, is noted for her discovery of "moon families." *Lunar Shadows III The Predictive Power of Moon Phases and Eclipses* is a thorough study of this one-of-a-kind predictive tool, with tables covering 1927-2034. (See the excerpt for 2015 on p. 69.) At www.lunar-shadows.com, you can read and listen to her weekly astrology report, broadcast Saturday at 9:30 am Eastern on 90.3 FM WZBC in Newton, MA. Dietrech's book is available from her website or Amazon.com. She may be contacted at: dietrechpessin@lunar-shadows.com.

Ray Pioggia, a professional photographer, took Janet's portrait photos on the calendar back cover and on her website. The Blazing Sun art on her homepage is by his wife, artist Laurie Tavino. The creative couple owns and operates Lauray Studio & Gallery in Suffield, CT (lauraystudio@yahoo.com).

Maria Kay Simms (maria@astrocom.com), a professional astrologer and Wicca High Priestess, contributed the article about the eight phases of the Moon (p. 90), drawing from her book *Moon Tides, Soul Passages Your Astrological Cycles for Personal and Spiritual Development*. The book comes with software to calculate and print your astrological information to apply the book's interpretations. Maria was the first woman elected Chair of the National Council for Geocosmic Research (NCGR), serving from 1999 to 2004. She holds two professional certifications: NCGR Level IV and the American Federation of Astrologers' Professional Member status, PMAFA. Her companies, ACS Publications and Starcrafts, LLC, generously granted permission to reprint the 2015 ephemeris in Janet's Plan-its, excerpted from *The American Ephemeris for the 21st Century at Midnight*, by Neil F. Michelsen and Rique Pottenger, published by ACS Publications, an imprint of Starcrafts LLC (www.astrocom.com), also available in a noon version.

Ilene J. Wolf, MS, is a nationally recognized consultant in the field of emotional wellness and recovery. She founded the nonprofit Healing Emotionally Abused Lives (HEAL), emotionalheal.org, and contributes to various internet communities. Her personal coaching practice, Healing Wolf Tracks (healingwolf.net), is a resource for anyone in transition or transformation. In recent years, when not editing material for Janet's Plan-its, she's been producing videos on recovery and wellness.

Resources

For your further study and enjoyment, Janet recommends these resources. Many are in the Links section of the Information Booth at **AstrologyBooth.com**, home of **JanetsPlan-its.com**.

Looking for top-of-the-line monthly forecasts for the Sun signs? I highly recommend Susan Miller's **astrologyzone.com**. Sign up to receive your daily horoscope via email.

Gevera Bert Piedmont is an expert on the Mayan calendar and daycount. Jaguar Nights is the name of both her annual calendar and a companion book covering the existing base of knowledge thoroughly and adding significantly to it with her own insights and the unique techniques she's developed. She offers an individualized report (based on the date and year of birth) that outlines personal power days for setting intentions, receiving manifestation of those intentions, and letting off steam. Check out her website: **JaguarNights.info**.

To learn about a different way of seeing Venus and working with its influences, check out *Venus Star Rising: A New Cosmology for the 21st Century* by Arielle Guttman (**sophiavenus.com**), Sophia Venus Productions, Santa Fe, NM.

Dietrech Pessin has an outstanding weekly radio show—see the Contributors page.

Astronomy, mythology and history converge in the book *When the Dragon Wore the Crown*, a groundbreaking look at cultural trends across multiple millennia. In his column, Athena's Web (**athenasweb.com**), astro-historian Don Cerow has for decades explored (among other things) the astrological Great Ages. He graciously wrote an excellent article, *The Age of Aquarius*, specifically for the 2013 Janet's Plan-its.

Expand your study of astrology or network with other astrologers through membership in national or international astrology groups, such as:

- AFAN (the Association for Astrological Networking) - **AFAN.org**
- NCGR (National Council for Geocosmic Research) - **geocosmic.org**
- ISAR (International Society for Astrological Research) - **ISARastrology.com**

Read intriguing online articles at **mountainastrologer.com** (website of the excellent magazine, *The Mountain Astrologer*), where you can subscribe to the digital version. **StarIQ.com** also has wonderful articles. Current developments in the world of astrology are noted at **AstrologyNewsService.com**.

Astrology can be used to forecast the weather. See Carolyn Egan's fascinating site: **weathersage.com**.

Look up famous people's charts and read their biographies at **astro.com/astro-databank**.

Watch **LOOKING UP**, Janet's show on astrology on West Hartford Community Television. Episodes are archived at WHCTV.org.
Click on the Watch tab,
then Video on Demand
and
scroll down to Looking Up.
Or click the link on Janet's homepage, AstrologyBooth.com.

CPSIA information can be obtained at www.ICGtesting.com
Printed in the USA
BVOW01s2006121214

378906BV00002B/6/P